P9-CRJ-384

Haiti

WORLD BIBLIOGRAPHICAL SERIES

General Editors:
Robert G. Neville (Executive Editor)
John J. Horton

Robert A. Myers   Ian Wallace
Hans H. Wellisch   Ralph Lee Woodward, Jr.

John J. Horton is Deputy Librarian of the University of Bradford and currently Chairman of its Academic Board of Studies in Social Sciences. He has maintained a longstanding interest in the discipline of area studies and its associated bibliographical problems, with special reference to European Studies. In particular he has published in the field of Icelandic and of Yugoslav studies, including the two relevant volumes in the World Bibliographical Series.

Robert A. Myers is Associate Professor of Anthropology in the Division of Social Sciences and Director of Study Abroad Programs at Alfred University, Alfred, New York. He has studied post-colonial island nations of the Caribbean and has spent two years in Nigeria on a Fulbright Lectureship. His interests include international public health, historical anthropology and developing societies. In addition to *Amerindians of the Lesser Antilles: a bibliography* (1981), *A Resource Guide to Dominica, 1493-1986* (1987) and numerous articles, he has compiled the World Bibliographical Series volumes on *Dominica* (1987), *Nigeria* (1989) and *Ghana* (1991).

Ian Wallace is Professor of German at the University of Bath. A graduate of Oxford in French and German, he also studied in Tübingen, Heidelberg and Lausanne before taking teaching posts at universities in the USA, Scotland and England. He specializes in contemporary German affairs, especially literature and culture, on which he has published numerous articles and books. In 1979 he founded the journal *GDR Monitor*, which he continues to edit under its new title *German Monitor*.

Hans H. Wellisch is Professor emeritus at the College of Library and Information Services, University of Maryland. He was President of the American Society of Indexers and was a member of the International Federation for Documentation. He is the author of numerous articles and several books on indexing and abstracting, and has published *The Conversion of Scripts, Indexing and Abstracting: an International Bibliography* and *Indexing from A to Z*. He also contributes frequently to *Journal of the American Society for Information Science, The Indexer* and other professional journals.

Ralph Lee Woodward, Jr. is Professor of History at Tulane University, New Orleans. He is the author of *Central America, a Nation Divided*, 2nd ed. (1985), as well as several monographs and more than seventy scholarly articles on modern Latin America. He has also compiled volumes in the World Bibliographical Series on *Belize* (1980), *Nicaragua* (1983), *El Salvador* (1988) and *Guatemala (Rev. Ed.)* (1992). Dr. Woodward edited the Central American section of the *Research Guide to Central America and the Caribbean* (1985) and is currently associate editor of Scribner's *Encyclopedia of Latin American History*.

VOLUME 39

Haiti

Revised and expanded edition

Frances Chambers

Compiler

CLIO PRESS

OXFORD, ENGLAND · SANTA BARBARA, CALIFORNIA
DENVER, COLORADO

© Copyright 1994 by Clio Press Ltd.

All rights reserved. No part of this publication may be reproduced, stored in any retrieval system, or transmitted in any form or by any means, electronic, mechanical, photocopying or otherwise, without the prior permission in writing of the publishers.

British Library Cataloguing in Publication Data

Haiti – 2 Rev. ed. – (World
bibliographical series; vol. 39)
I. Chambers, Frances   II. Series
016.97294

ISBN 1–85109–215–3

Clio Press Ltd.,
Old Clarendon Ironworks,
35A Great Clarendon Street,
Oxford OX2 6AT, England.

ABC-CLIO,
130 Cremona Drive,
Santa Barbara,
CA 93116, USA.

Designed by Bernard Crossland.
Typeset by Columns Design and Production Services Ltd, Reading, England.
Printed and bound in Great Britain by
Bookcraft (Bath) Ltd., Midsomer Norton

3 1211 00525264 4

THE WORLD BIBLIOGRAPHICAL SERIES

This series, which is principally designed for the English speaker, will eventually cover every country (and many of the world's principal regions), each in a separate volume comprising annotated entries on works dealing with its history, geography, economy and politics; and with its people, their culture, customs, religion and social organization. Attention will also be paid to current living conditions – housing, education, newspapers, clothing, etc.– that are all too often ignored in standard bibliographies; and to those particular aspects relevant to individual countries. Each volume seeks to achieve, by use of careful selectivity and critical assessment of the literature, an expression of the country and an appreciation of its nature and national aspirations, to guide the reader towards an understanding of its importance. The keynote of the series is to provide, in a uniform format, an interpretation of each country that will express its culture, its place in the world, and the qualities and background that make it unique. The views expressed in individual volumes, however, are not necessarily those of the publisher.

VOLUMES IN THE SERIES

*For
Steve*

Contents

xi

Contents

Contents

Contents

Introduction

The republic of Haiti occupies the western third of the island of Hispaniola, bordered on the north by the Atlantic Ocean, on the west and south by the Caribbean Sea, and on the east by the Dominican Republic. The country covers an area of 27,700 kilometres that is largely mountainous, comprising five mountain ranges. The country's highest point is the 2,674 metre Pic la Selle in the southern Massif de la Selle. At one time the Haitian mountains were well-forested, but the exploitation of the land, which began in the seventeenth century and in which both demographic and political factors have played a role, resulted in rapid deforestation and concomitant catastrophic soil erosion. Haiti has no navigable rivers: its largest body of water is the Etang Saumâtre.

The island called 'Ayti' or 'Hayti' by its Amerindian inhabitants entered written history in 1492 when Columbus landed on its north coast and claimed the territory for Spain. Only a few decades later, the indigenous people decimated, the Spanish began importing Africans as slaves to labour in the fields of their colony of Santo Domingo. In 1697, Spain ceded the western part of the colony to France. As Saint-Domingue, the territory became known as 'The Pearl of the Antilles', France's richest colony, producing 60 per cent of the world's coffee and 40 per cent of its sugar. Its population increased throughout the eighteenth century, reaching an estimated 500,000 blacks and 60,000 whites and mulattoes by 1791.

Haiti's defining moment occurred at the end of the eighteenth century. Under the leadership of Toussaint Louverture, Jean-Jacques Dessalines, Alexandre Pétion, and Henry Christophe, the Haitians astonished the world by defeating the French in a war that established Haiti as an independent nation: the first black republic in the world; the second independent nation in the Western hemisphere; the first New World country to outlaw slavery and extend full citizenship to non-whites.

Introduction

Isolated as an anomaly in the nineteenth century, the black republic was drawn unhappily into great power relations in the twentieth. The country was occupied by the United States from 1915 to 1934, then ruled by a succession of dictatorial regimes, the longest-lasting that of the Duvaliers: François Duvalier, who ruled from 1957 until his death in 1971, and François's son, Jean-Claude Duvalier, who held power until he went into exile in 1986. The younger Duvalier's departure turned a page in Haitian history, but failed to end the political and economic turmoil that over the past decades has driven thousands of Haitians to flee their native land. The term of Jean-Bertrand Aristide, widely-heralded as a democratically-elected President, was truncated by a military coup in September 1991, which forced him into exile. At the present time, Aristide's return as Haiti's president has become the focus of the active involvement in Haiti of the United Nations and the United States.

Today, Haiti's population is estimated at over 6 million. The French colonial era in Haiti's history left the country with French as its official language and – after a long hiatus – Roman Catholicism as its recognized religion, but among the Haitian masses Haitian Creole rather than French was spoken and the Voodoo religion more widely practiced than Catholicism. In 1987 Haitian Creole was recognized as an official language of Haiti, sharing this status with French.

A large proportion of Haitians receive no education, and an estimated 70 per cent of the population are illiterate. Health care is inadequate, malnutrition widespread, and the AIDS epidemics of the 1980s added a new infectious disease to the list of those responsible for most adult deaths.

The *per capita* income of the average Haitian is the lowest in the Western hemisphere. More than one-half of the Haitian labour force is employed in agriculture, where production has been declining. The once-promising assembly manufacturing industry is at a standstill.

It is easy to quote depressing statistics about Haiti; it is much harder to communicate the positive factors that make Haiti a unique nation: the natural dignity of its people, its astonishing history, its vibrant art and literature. At the end of the eighteenth century the Haitians found the resources to amaze the world. Although at the end of the twentieth century Haiti appears to have reached an economic nadir, what the future holds for this remarkable country is impossible to predict.

About the bibliography
In the decade that has elapsed since the publication of the first edition of *Haiti*, much has been written about the nation, particularly in two categories. One of these categories – emigration – certainly

reflects the realities of the Haitian experience of the past decade. The other greatly expanded category – bibliography – signals the growing interest in Haiti of both the scholarly community and the general public. When the first edition of this book appeared in 1983, Max Bissainthe's *Dictionnaire de Bibliographie Haïtienne* stood virtually alone. Today, access to materials on Haitian subjects has been greatly facilitated by the appearance of two major bibliographical works: Michel Laguerre's *Complete Haitiana: a Bibliographic Guide to the Scholarly Literature, 1900-1980,* and Frantz Pratt's *Haiti: Guide to Periodical Literature in English, 1800-1990.* Another recent bibliographical compilation is Robert Lawless's *Haiti: a research guide to Haiti.*

Aimed at the English-speaking public, the second edition of *Haiti* is designed to provide guidance through the literature on Haiti to readers seeking information about the country. Like the first edition, this revised version takes a multidisciplinary approach. The 558 entries of the earlier work have been expanded to 913. New material has been added, but standard items and materials listed in the first edition that have not been superseded have been retained. Entries are followed by informative annotations. A chronology is included to aid the reader in dating the events of Haitian history. Entries in the main body of the book have been indexed by author, title and subject.

I would like to express my gratitude to all those who have helped me complete this bibliography, in particular my colleagues at the City College of the City University of New York. Most especially, my thanks go to Stephen Chambers for his reliable assistance and invaluable computer expertise.

Frances Chambers
New York City, 1993

Chronology

4000-400 BC	Migration of Amerindians (Casimiroid culture) from Middle America to the island of Hispaniola.
Ca. 400 BC	Migration of Amerindians of Arawak stock (Saladoid culture) from South America. Taino culture develops on Hispaniola.
Ca. 1000 BC	Migration of Caribs from South America.
5/6 December 1492	Columbus and his men land on 'Ayti', and are met by Taino Amerindians. Columbus claims the island for Spain, naming it Española (Hispaniola).
26 December 1492	La Navidad, first Spanish settlement in the New World, built.
1493	On his second voyage, Columbus returns to Hispaniola to find La Navidad burned and abandoned.
1503	Spanish settlement of Puerto Real founded on the north coast of Hispaniola.
1508	First census of Hispaniola.
1518-19	Smallpox epidemic.
1520s	African slaves first brought to Hispaniola.
1535	Santo Domingo incorporated into the Viceroyalty of New Spain (which includes Mexico and Central America).
1568	Census shows only thirteen Tainos still living on Hispaniola.
1578	Puerto Real ordered abandoned by the metropolitan Spanish government because of its participation in illegal trade.
1630	French buccaneers establish a base on the island of Tortuga (Île de la Tortue), off the north coast of Hispaniola.

Chronology

1650	Northern and western quarters of Hispaniola under de facto French control.
1659	The French establish the first permanent settlement on Tortuga (Île de la Tortue).
1664	French buccaneers move to mainland Hispaniola, which they call Saint-Domingue. French West India Company chartered.
1670	Cap Français (Cap Haïtien) founded.
1685	The *Code Noir*, Louis XIV's edict regulating treatment of black slaves in the West Indies, is issued.
1697	Spain cedes the western third of Hispaniola to France under the terms of the Treaty of Ryswick.
1749	Port-au-Prince founded as the capital of the French Windward Islands.
1751-57	Insurrection led by Macandal, maroon leader.
1758	Macandal executed.
1779	Black troops from Saint-Domingue at the Battle of Savannah.
1789	Revolution begins in France.
October 1790	Vincent Ogé and Jean-Baptiste Chavannes lead an unsuccessful mulatto uprising.
February 1791	Ogé and Chavannes executed.
22-23 August 1791	Slaves of the North province begin a general slave rebellion.
2 February 1793	The French Republic declares war on Great Britain. Toussaint Louverture joins the Spanish forces.
21 June 1793	Léger-Félicité Sonthonax and Etienne Polverel, commissioners appointed by the French Republic, issue a proclamation offering freedom to slaves willing to fight for France.
29 August 1793	Sonthonax proclaims general liberty and full French citizenship for slaves in the North province.
31 October 1793	Polverel emancipates remaining slaves in the South and West provinces.
1794	British forces land on Saint-Domingue.
1794	Toussaint Louverture deserts the Spanish army for the French.
4 February 1794 [16 Pluviose II]	The Convention outlaws slavery in France's colonies by the Decree of 16 Pluviose II.
June 1794	British forces capture Port-au-Prince.
22 July 1794	Peace agreement between France and Spain.

July 1795	Spain cedes the eastern part of Hispaniola to France by the terms of the Treaty of Bale.
March 1796	General Etienne-Maynard Laveaux appoints Toussaint Lieutenant Governor of Saint-Domingue.
1797	Sonthonax appoints Toussaint Commander-in-Chief of the French army.
September 1798	British forces expelled from Saint-Domingue.
November 1798	Toussaint writes to President John Adams asking for the resumption of trade between Haiti and the United States.
January 1801	Toussaint invades and annexes the Spanish part of Hispaniola. He establishes the island's autonomy under French suzerainty. Declares slavery abolished.
August 1801	Toussaint issues Haiti's first Constitution, which grants him power as governor general for life.
October 1801	France signs the preliminary Treaty of Amiens.
1802	War resumes between England and France.
January 1802	General Charles Victor Leclerc and an army of 16,000 to 20,000 men arrive in Haiti, sent by Napoleon to re-establish French rule and slavery.
5 May 1802	Toussaint surrenders to Leclerc.
June 1802	Leclerc arrests and deports Toussaint to France.
November 1802	Leclerc dies of yellow fever. General Donatien Rochambeau in command. Dessalines, Christophe, and Pétion lead Haitian War of Independence against the French.
7 April 1803	Toussaint Louverture dies in prison in France.
May 1803	Renewal of hostilities between France and Britain.
November 1803	Rochambeau flees Haiti for Jamaica, where he surrenders to the British.
1 January 1804	Dessalines proclaims Haitian independence.
1805	Constitution of Dessalines. Dessalines rules as Emperor.
1805	Dessalines's invasion of Santo Domingo fails.
1806	Henry Christophe becomes king of the northern Kingdom of Haiti.
1806	Alexandre Pétion becomes president of the southern Republic of Haiti.
1806-07	Civil war between Christophe's north and Pétion's south.
1809	Spain recovers the eastern part of Hispaniola.

Chronology

1811	Christophe crowns himself King Henry I of the northern Kingdom of Haiti.
1818	Pétion dies. Jean-Pierre Boyer becomes President of southern republic of Haiti.
1820	Christophe commits suicide: Boyer unites north and south in the Republic of Haiti.
1822	Haiti annexes Santo Domingo, incorporating it into Haiti as the Partie de l'Est.
1824	African Methodists and Baptists establish missions in Haiti.
1825	France concedes Haiti's independence in return for compensatory payments.
1838	France recognizes Haiti's complete independence.
1842	Cap Haïtien destroyed by an earthquake.
1843	Revolution of 1843. President Boyer resigns.
1843	English Wesleyans arrive in Haiti.
1844	Haitians withdraw from the eastern part of Hispaniola.
1860	Concordat signed with the Vatican restores Roman Catholicism in Haiti.
1861	First Episcopalians arrive in Haiti.
1862	The United States accords diplomatic recognition to Haiti.
1874	Revised Constitution of 1874 incorporates the principle of compulsory education.
1880	Banque Nationale d'Haïti established by a concession contract signed in Paris with a French bank, the Société Générale de Credit Industriel et Commercial.
1889-91	American negotiations to secure Môle St. Nicolas as a naval base come to nothing.
28 July 1915	Invasion and occupation of Haiti by US Marines.
1915	Cacos revolt. Haitians defeated.
1918-19	Cacos War. Haitians defeated.
1918	Adoption of American-sponsored Constitution, supposedly authored by Franklin Delano Roosevelt.
1928	Jean Price-Mars' *Ainsi parla l'oncle* published.
1934	US occupation of Haiti ends.
1937	Batista deports thousands of Haitian immigrants from Cuba and closes the country to them.
1937	Rafael Trujillo orders the massacre of Haitian workers in the Dominican Republic; at least 12,000 are slaughtered in three days.

1941	Jacques Roumain founds the Bureau of Ethnology of the Republic of Haiti.
1943	Public adult literacy programs established to teach reading and writing in Creole.
1945	Haiti becomes a charter member of the United Nations.
1946	Haitian Revolution of 1946. Estimé becomes President.
22 October 1957	François Duvalier elected President of Haiti.
1 April 1964	François Duvalier proclaims himself President for Life.
21 April 1971	François Duvalier dies; his son, Jean-Claude Duvalier, succeeds him as President for Life.
1978	Law passed making Creole the principal language of primary instruction; the orthography developed by the Institut Pédagogique National becomes standard for writing Creole.
7 February 1986	February Revolution. Jean-Claude Duvalier goes into exile abroad. Council of government formed under Lieut. Gen. Henry Namphy.
29 March 1987	New Constitution ratified by voters. Haitian Creole given equal status with French as an official language of Haiti.
29 November 1987	Election Day killings force cancellation of Presidential election.
17 January 1988	Leslie F. Manigat elected President.
19 June 1988	Manigat deposed by military coup; replaced by General Namphy.
17 September 1988	General Namphy ousted in coup. Lieutenant General Prosper Avril becomes President.
March 1990	General Avril flees Haiti; Judge Ertha Pascal-Trouillot becomes head of an interim civilian government.
16 December 1990	Jean-Bertrand Aristide elected President.
7 February 1991	Aristide takes office as Haiti's President.
29 September 1991	Aristide deposed by the army and exiled abroad. General Raoul Cedras assumes control of Haiti as head of a military junta. The United States does not accept the legitimacy of the Cedras government.
2 October 1991	The Organization of American States calls for a trade embargo against Haiti until Aristide is restored to office.

7/8 October 1991	Haiti's legislature declares presidency vacant; Supreme Court Justice Joseph Nerette is sworn in as provisional President.
19 June 1992	Marc Bazin appointed Prime Minister by provisional President Joseph Nerette.
9 June 1993	Prime Minister Marc Bazin resigns.
16 June 1993	The United Nations Security Council votes to impose a worldwide oil embargo on Haiti.
27 June 1993	United Nations mediators begin talks on Governors Island, New York City, with exiled President Jean-Bertrand Aristide and General Raoul Cedras.
3 July 1993	Governors Island Accord is signed; Cedras and Aristide agree that Aristide is to return to Haiti as President on October 30, 1993.
27 August 1993	UN Security Council suspends Haitian embargo.
30 August 1993	Robert Malval is appointed Prime Minister by Aristide.
18 October 1993	United Nations' oil and arms embargo is re-imposed on Haiti.
30 October 1993	General Cedras refuses to relinquish power.
30 November 1993	Prime Minister Robert Malval resigns.
6 May 1994	Near-total trade embargo imposed on Haiti by the United Nations.
May 1994	Emile Jonassaint installed by military junta as interim President of Haiti.

The Country and Its People

1 **Haiti: the breached citadel.**
Patrick Bellegarde-Smith. Boulder, Colorado: Westview Press, 1990.
217p. (Westview Profiles: Nations of Contemproary Latin America).
A country study of Haiti from its independence to 1988. Bellegarde-Smith analyses the nature of Haitian society, covering social structure, culture, economic development, and foreign policy, paying particular attention to the role and status of women and to Haitian history since the fall of the Duvalier régime. The volume also includes a bibliographical essay in which Bellegarde-Smith briefly comments on writings about Haiti.

2 **Haiti – against all odds.**
Charles E. Cobb, Jr. *National Geographic*, vol. 172, no. 5 (Nov. 1987),
p. 645-71. map.
Cobb describes Haiti in 1987 as its citizens prepared for the November presidential election. His outlook is optimistic as he visits both rural and urban areas, noting beauty in the midst of poverty, large problems but even greater hope. Photographs by James P. Blair complement the text.

3 **Caribbean pilgrims: the plight of the Haitian refugees.**
Daniel Dougé. Smithtown, New York: Exposition Press, 1982. 71p.
bibliog.
Despite its title, this volume does not focus on Haitian refugees in the United States; rather it examines the social, economic, environmental, and political pressures within Haiti that force its citizens to leave their country in search of a better life elsewhere. Chapters cover Haiti's social structure, racial and colour heriarchies, language and social mobility, foreign influences and the Haitian economy, as they were during the early 1980s.

4 Dominican Republic and Haiti: country studies.

Federal Research Division, Library of Congress. Edited by Richard A. Haggerty. Washington, DC: Headquarters, Department of the Army, for sale by Superintendant of Documents, G.P.O., 1991. 456p. maps. bibliog. (Area Handbook Series).

The Preface to this volume states that this work presents the various authors' own analysis and is not 'an expression of an official United States government position, policy, or decision'. The section on Haiti begins on page 194 and covers Haiti's history, society, economy, government and politics, and national security. Suggestions for further reading follow each chapter, and a lengthy bibliography is appended. The volume is based on research completed in December, 1989 and is a revised edition of two previously published United States government publications, *Area Handbook for the Dominican Republic* (1973), and *Area Handbook for Haiti* (1976).

5 Haiti – today and tomorrow: an interdisciplinary study.

Edited by Charles R. Foster, Albert Valdman. Lanham, Maryland: University Press of America, 1984. 389p. biblio.

Originally presented at the Wingspread Conference in Racine, Wisconsin, in September, 1982, these papers examine key aspects of Haitian life. The contributors appraise Haitian society as it was in the early 1980s, prior to the collapse of the Duvalier régime. The topics covered in this volume are culture, language and education, rural development, economics, politics, and migration.

6 Haunted Haiti.

Herbert Gold. *Holiday*, vol. 37, no. 3 (March 1965), p. 64-69.

An evocation of the unconquerability of the Haitian spirt amid the paradoxes of Haitian society. Gold illuminates the Haitian outlook by recounting anecdotes of the island's 'gods, werewolves, spooks and hobgoblins', whose reality is denied while their demands are appeased. The energy of the Haitian imagination is climactically expressed in the *déguisements* of Haiti's carnival during which Haitians exorcise their desperation. The article is illustrated with colourful drawings by André François.

7 Haiti.

Trudy J. Hanmer. New York: F. Watts, 1988. 96p. (A First Book).

Aimed at younger readers, this volume presents the story of Haiti: its history, economy, culture, arts, religion and people.

8 Haiti's bad press.

Robert Lawless. Rochester, Vermont: Schenkman Books, 1992. 261p. bibliog.

The author, an anthropologist, analyses the construction and perpetuation of a negative image of Haiti in the world's media. He examines and comments on the writings of journalists, historians, travellers, social scientists and writers of adventure stories in order to pinpoint the origins and trace the development of current biases about Haiti and its citizens. The narrative discussion is followed by a forty-three-page bibliography listing works on the country. Lawless's book complements J. Michael Dash's earlier work, *Haiti and the United States; national stereotypes and the literary imagination* (q.v.).

9 **Haiti: black peasants and Voodoo.**
Alfred Metraux, translated from the French by Peter Lengyel. New York: Universe Books, 1960. 109p. map.

This translation of Metraux's *La terre, les hommes et les dieux* is a general presentation of Haitian life and customs, written by an anthropologist who has acquired extensive professional experience in Haiti. The volume contains photographs taken by the author and by Pierre Verger.

10 **Haiti's future: views of twelve Haitian leaders.**
Edited by Richard M. Morse. Washington, DC: The Wilson Center Press, 1988. 129p. map.

Contains papers presented at the Conference on Democracy in Haiti, sponsored by the Latin American Program of the Woodrow Wilson International Center for Scholars, held 29-30 September, 1986. The contributors include: Richard M. Morse (history); Pierre-Raymond Dumas (politics); Jean Jacques Honorat (social structure); Jean Casimir (language and culture); Raymond Chassagne (democracy in Haiti); Odette Roy Fombrun (co-operative production); Germain Jean François (economics); Henricot Brutus (community development); Levadieu Dérané (agriculture and industry); René Laroche (culture and economics); Alain Rocourt (rural pesantry); Marie-Michèle Rey (women); and Ducheine Fortuné (US–Haitian relations).

11 **Haiti in Caribbean context: ethnicity, economy and revolt.**
David Nicholls. New York: Macmillan, 1985. 292p. map. bibliog. (St. Anthony/Macmillan Series).

Presents a collection of research essays by Nicholls – several of which have previously been published – in which he examines 'in historical perspective, connections between ethnic structures and the economy, showing how the phenomena of political domination and revolt are to be understood in the light of these connections'. A wide range of topics is covered, among them the ethnological movement of the early twentieth century, literature on the Haitian economy, Haitian entrepreneurial groups, Haitian women, the Voodoo religion and Haitian Creole, and recent migration from Haiti.

12 **Red, black, blond, and olive; studies in four civilizations: Zuni, Haiti, Soviet Russia, Israel.**
Edmund Wilson. New York: Oxford University Press, 1956. 500p.

In 'Haiti 1949' (p. 71-146), Wilson, a major American critic and literary stylist, combines his on-the-spot impressions of Haiti under the Estimé regime with later ruminations on the meaning of his travels. Wilson discusses the geographical features of the island, racial politics, literacy problems, the Creole language, Haitian literature, Voodoo, Catholic and Protestant missionary work, the theatre, the UNESCO Fundamental Education Pilot Project at Marbial and Maya Deren's account of Voodoo possession. He also draws an interesting parallel between the Haitian and Greek traditions of much-prized independence.

Geography

General

13 **The Caribbean islands.**
Helmut Blume, translated from the German by Johannes Maczewski,
Ann Norton.   London: Longman, 1976. 464p. maps. bibliog.

The volume provides a sound geographical study of the entire West Indian area,
covering physical, economic and social factors. The first part of the book is a general
survey of the region which examines: orography; topography; oceanography; climate;
land-forms; flora and fauna; the aboriginal inhabitants; the history of discovery and
development; population and social structure; agriculture; economy and international
trade; and contemporary problems. In this section, Haiti is referred to where relevant.
The second part of the book contains an island-by-island description, with Haiti
receiving detailed treatment in sections nineteen and twenty. An excellent bibliography, listing geographical materials about the Caribbean region to 1970 in English,
French, German and Spanish, complements the volume. This work was first published
in German as *Die Westindischen Inseln* in 1968; the English translation appeared in
1974.

14 **The Caribbean in the wider world, 1492-1992: a regional geography.**
Bonham C. Richardson.   Cambridge, England; New York: Cambridge
University Press, 1992. 236p. maps. bibliog. (Geography of the World
Economy).

Readers will find much about Haiti in this regional geography of the Caribbean.
Richardson views the area in a 'world-economy perspective' through which he attempts
'to show the ways in which external control of the Caribbean region has influenced
landscapes, ecological problems, settlement forms, demographic characteristics,
migration patterns, livelihood strategies, and other variables within the Caribbean'.
Chapters cover the early colonization of the island, plantations and their inhabitants to
1900, the extension of American control in the twentieth century, economic
dependency, migration, and political independence.

4

15   **Haiti, land of poverty.**
       Robert J. Tata.   Washington, DC: University Press of America, 1982.
       127p. maps. bibliog.

This modern regional geography views Haiti's contemporary problems against the background of its physical, social, cultural, economic and political systems. It is suitable either as a textbook or as a concise introduction to the country.

16   **Middle America: its land and peoples.**
       Robert C. West, John P. Augelli (et al.).   Englewood Cliffs, New
       Jersey: Prentice-Hall, 1989. 3rd ed. 494p. maps. bibliog.

This is the latest revision of the standard geography of the Central American and Caribbean region. Chapter six, 'The West Indies: the Hispanic territories and Haiti', has been updated by Thomas D. Boswell. Following a description of the physical environment of the island of Hispaniola, Boswell discusses social and economic factors in Haiti, and stresses the disequilibrium of people, land and resources which is prevalent in the country, and the retrogressive tendencies of its economy. Sections cover agriculture, land tenure, coffee and other export crops, peasant farming, and patterns of rural and urban settlement.

Special aspects

17   **Cultural dichotomy in the island of Hispaniola.**
       Raymond E. Crist.   *Economic Geography*, vol. 28, no. 2 (April 1952),
       p. 105-21. map.

'One of the most impressive natural features in the West Indies is the east-west [Great Fault Valley] which extends across southern Hispaniola from Port-au-Prince, Haiti, to Barajona, R. D. The physical traits of this semiarid corridor remain practically constant throughout its entire length, but it is cut in two by a definite political and cultural boundary line. [In this article], the cultural dichotomy of the valley [is] examined against the background of the physical conditions similar in both republics'. Crist notes great differences in the land use patterns of the two neighbouring countries of the island of Hispaniola. A small map and aerial photographs of the Great Fault Valley accompany the text.

18   **World climatic data: Latin America and the Caribbean.**
       Frederick L. Wernstedt.   Ann Arbor, Michigan: Edwards Brothers,
       1961. 87p. (World Climatic Data, no. 2).

Temperature and precipitation data for Haiti is found on pp. 48-49. The average temperature at Port-au-Prince is 52.92 degrees Farhrenheit.

19 **Northern Haiti: land, land use, and settlement; a geographical**
   investigation of the Département du Nord.
   Harold A. Wood.   Toronto: University of Toronto Press, 1963. 168p.
   maps, bibliog.

Investigates land use in 'the most densely populated department in the most densely populated country of Latin America', where 'it is possible to observe something very close to the maximum productivity possible, under primitive techniques, in a variety of types of land'. An introductory chapter deals with the facts of the Département du Nord: size and location; relief; climate; drainage; natural vegetation; soils; historical developemnt; administration; population; economy; farming techniques; intensity of land use; land tenure; living standards; transport; trade; and population mobility. The author then devotes separate chapters to the geology, and morphology of the region, its climate, soils, geographic regions, rural land utilization and settlement, towns, villages, and markets. The work is illustrated with maps and photographs. Appendices are included on bedrock characteristics, climatic statistics, analyses and potential yields of soils, productivity ratings for Haitian soils, and characteristics of the commonly cultivated plants of the region.

20 **Stream piracy in the Central Plateau of Hispaniola.**
   Harold A. Wood.   *Canadian Geographer*, no. 8 (1956), p. 46-54.

This geomorphological study 'deals with the incidence and effects of river capture . . . in the area known in Haiti as the Plateau Central'. This type of drainage diversion has a profound effect on man's use of land, and such surface modification in the Plateau Central has had overall an adverse effect on the economic potential of Haiti.

Toponymy

21 **Jewish toponymies in Haiti.**
   Zvi Loker.   *Jewish Social Studies*, vol. 40, nos. 3-4 (summer/fall 1978),
   p. 287-92.

A pioneer effort, written by Loker during the period he spent as the Israeli ambassador to Haiti. Loker examines and seeks a possible source for Jewish place-names in colonial Saint-Domingue (such as 'Anse-à-Juifs' and 'Pont-à-Juif') that associate a Jewish presence with certain geographical locations. Although documentary proof is lacking, Loker feels that such a presence was a possibility, given the scope of known Jewish commercial endeavour in the Caribbean during the colonial period. Jews in Haiti were probably of Portuguese-Sephardic extraction. Loker's article is almost equally divided between text and footnotes, and the discussion in the former is supplemented by much additional information in the latter.

22 **Noms de lieux d'epoque coloniale en Haiti: essai sur la toponymie du
    Nord à l'usage des étudiants.** (Place names of the colonial era in Haiti:
    an essay on the toponymy of the Nord for undergraduates.)
    Jean-Baptiste Romain.   Port-au-Prince: Imprimerie de l'État, 1960.
    205p. map. bibliog. (Revue de la Faculte d'éthnologie, no. 3).
A study of the origins of geographical names found in what was formerly Saint-
Domingue's province of the Nord.

Maps, Atlases and Gazetteers

23 **Caribbean history in maps.**
Peter Ashdown.   Port of Spain, Trinidad: Longman Caribbean;
London: Longman, 1979. 84p. maps.

A student's atlas of maps delineating the historical geography of the Caribbean area.
The volume also contains simplified biographical information on distinguished West
Indians.

24 **Atlas d'Haïti.** (Atlas of Haiti.)
Centre d'Etudes de Géographie tropicale et Université de Bordeaux 3.
Talence, France: Centre d'Études de géographie tropicale (C. N. R. S.)
et Université de Bordeaux 3, 1985. 84p. maps. 1:1,000,000.

This is a folio-sized atlas of coloured maps, prepared under the direction of Guy
Lasserre, Paul Moral and Pierre Usselmann. Maps delineate economic and social
conditions.

25 **Haiti: official standard names approved by the United States Board on
Geographic Names.**
Defense Mapping Agency Topographic Center.   Washington, DC: US
Government Printing Office, 1973. 2nd ed. 211p. map. (US Board on
Geographic Names. Gazetteer no. 28).

An expanded revision of the first edition issued in 1956, this is an authoritative
gazetteer prepared by an American governmental agency, the United States Board on
Geographic Names. For each geographical name listed, the following information is
given: approved and unapproved variants; type of place or feature; latitude and
longitude; Universal Transverse Mercator Grid Reference; and JOG Sheet number.

26 **Haiti: index annoté des travaux de photographie aérienne et des cartes topographiques et des ressources naturelles.** (Annotated index of aerial photographic coverage and mapping of topography and natural resources.)
Department of Economic Affairs, Pan American Union. Washington, DC: Pan American Union, 1964. 9p. maps.

This index atlas shows the map coverage available at various scales by aerial photographs and by topographical, geological, soil and land use, and vegetation maps.

27 **The atlas of Central America and the Caribbean.**
The Diagram Group. New York: Macmillan Publishing Co., 1985. 144p. maps. bibliog.

An atlas of regional maps showing political history, geology, climate, biology, and oceanography, accompanied by brief information. The 'Haiti' section (p. 98-101) provides a map, tables and a short summary of facts on the nation.

28 **Haiti: carte topographique.** (Haiti: topographical map.)
Port-au-Prince: Service de Géologie et de Cartographie, 1974- . Scale: 1:25,000.

An official topographical series in 270 sheets. The Service de Géologie et de Cartographie also produces two other series of topographical maps, a series in seventy-eight sheets on a scale of 1:50,000 and a series in twenty-eight sheets on a scale of 1:100,000.

29 **Maps and charts of North America and the West Indies 1750-1789: a guide to the collections in the Library of Congress.**
Compiled by John R. Sellers, Patricia Molen Van Ee. Washington, DC: Library of Congress, 1981. 495p. maps. bibliog.

Provides a meticulous list of the maps and charts of North America and the West Indies located in the Geography and Map Division of the Library of Congress. The 'Hispaniola' section of the volume on p. 396-409, lists French, English, Spanish and Dutch maps of both French and Spanish areas of the island during the colonial period. The entries are informatively annotated.

Geology

30 **The geology of Hispaniola.**
Carl O. Bowin. In: *The Ocean basins and margins, vol. 3: The Gulf of Mexico and the Caribbean.* Edited by Alan E. M. Nairn, Francis G. Stehl. New York: Plenum Press, 1975, p. 501-52. maps. bibliog.

Bowin summarizes the extent of geological knowledge of Hispaniola as of 1975 and describes and interprets the island's geography, general geology and structure, stratigraphy, igneous rocks, radiometric ages, gravity anomalies, seismicity and geological evolution. Maps, charts and tables clarify the information which has been presented in the text, and a bibliography lists scholarly articles.

31 **Plate tectonics in the Hispaniola area.**
Dewey R. Bracey, Peter R. Vogt. *Geological Society of America Bulletin*, vol. 81, no. 9 (Sept. 1970), p. 2, 855-60. maps. bibliog.

Claims that 'seismic and other geophysical and geological evidence suggest that the Caribbean plate, at eastern Hispaniola, is being underthrust by a relatively small slab of Americas plate'. A fold-out map shows earthquake epicentres on the island of Hispaniola.

32 **La géologie de la République d'Haiti et ses rapports avec celle des regions voisines.** (The geology of the Republic of Haiti and its relation to that of neigbouring regions.)
Jacques Butterlin. Paris: Imprimerie Jouve, 1954. 446p. maps. bibliog. (Memoires de l'Institut Français d'Haiti, no. 1).

This volume is a revised version of Woodring, Brown, and Burbank's survey, *Geology of the Republic of Haiti* (q.v.), corrected in the light of additional field observations and topographical information. The work contains a geological map of Haiti on a scale of 1:250,000.

33 **Géologie générale et régionale de la République d'Haïti.** (General and
regional geology of the Republic of Haiti.)
Jacques Butterlin.   Paris: Institut des Hautes Etudes de l'Amérique
latine, 1960. 194p. maps. bibliog. (Travaux et mémoires de l'Institut des
Hautes Etudes de l'Amérique latine, no. 6).
This authoritative examination of Haiti's geology has remained in print since its
publication in 1960.

34 **Haiti.**
Jacques Butterlin.   In: *The encyclopedia of world regional geology, part
1: Western hemisphere (including Antarctica and Australia).* Edited by
Rhodes Fairbridge.   Stroudsburg, Pennsylvania: Dowden, Hutchinson
& Ross, 1975, p. 326-27. bibliog. (Encyclopedia of Earth Sciences,
vol. 8).
Butterlin, one of the leading authorities on the geology of Haiti, presents basic facts on
the geology of the country in an easy-to-read format.

35 **Petrology of the Terre-Neuve igneous province, northern Haiti.**
Stephen E. Kesler.   In: *Caribbean geophysical, tectonic, and petrologic
studies.* Edited by Thomas W. Donnelly.   Boulder, Colorado:
Geological Society of America, 1971, p. 119-37. bibliog. (Memoirs of the
Geological Society of America, no. 130).
Relates igneous rock formation in northern Haiti to regional geology and suggests a
possible origin for igneous rocks in the Greater Antilles.

36 **Antillean tectonics.**
Howard A. Meyerhoff.   *Transactions of the New York Academy of
Sciences*, Series 2, vol. 16, no. 3 (Jan. 1954), p. 149-55. map.
Presents information on the causes of the earth structure patterns of the Caribbean
region, including the island of Hispaniola.

37 **Neogene of central Haiti.**
W. A. van den Bold.   *American Association of Petroleum Geologists
Bulletin*, vol. 58, no. 3 (March 1974), p. 533-39. maps. bibliog.
The 'study of maps and samples, compiled and collected by geologists of the Atlantic
Refining Co. during their survey of Haiti about 1940, permits new interpretations of
age and facies relations of previously established formations, generally resulting in
younger age determinations'. Formations covered include: the Madame Joie
Formation; the 'Arc' Formation; the Thomonde Formation; and the Las Cahobas
Formation.

38 **Geology of the Republic of Haiti.**
Wendell P. Woodring, John S. Brown, Wilbur S. Burbank. Port-au-Prince: Service Géologique; Baltimore, Maryland: Lord Baltimore Press, 1924. 631p. maps. bibliog. Reprinted, New York: Gordon Press, 1972.

Geologically, Haiti was *terra incognita* until Woodring, Brown and Burbank undertook this study in 1920-21 under the auspices of the United States Geological Survey. The work was issued simultaneously in a French edition. This reconnaissance survey of Haiti is still the basic geological account in English, although it has been superseded by Jacques Butterlin's revision of the work in French (q.v.).

Travel Guides

39 **1994 Cribbean islands handbook.**
Edited by Sarah Cameron, Ben Box.   Bath, England: Trade and Travel
Publications; New York: Prentice-Hall General Reference, 1993. 5th ed.
816p. maps. (Travelers' World Guides).
By far the most useful guidebook to the Caribbean region. Revised annually since its
first publication in 1989, this handbook is both convenient and reliable.

40 **Shopping and traveling the exotic Caribbean.**
John W. Edmiston, Nancy B. Edmiston, Bruce Bennett.   Manassas
Park, Virginia: Impact Publications, 1991. 304p. (Impact Guides).
This book offers travellers guidance in finding quality arts and crafts at reasonable
prices on the islands of the Caribbean, including Haiti. Features provide tips on
culturally appropriate shopping strategies, advice on bargains, and recommendations
on specific shops. The guide also includes information on accommodation, sightseeing
and restaurants.

41 **Haiti: the black republic; the complete story and guide.**
Selden Rodman.   Old Greenwich, Connecticut: Devin-Adair
Publishing, 1984. 6th rev. ed. 217p. maps. bibliog.
This mini-encyclopedia-cum-guidebook has been revised many times by its author since
it was first published in 1954. In this latest edition, Rodman sets Haiti of the early
1980s in its historical context and then describes the country's religion, art and culture.
In chapter six, he recommends sightseeing and recreational activities in Port-au-Prince
and in other parts of Haiti.

42 **Fielding's Caribbean 1993.**
Margaret Zellers.   New York: Fielding's Travel Books/Morrow, 1993.
15th ed. 928p. maps.
The section on 'Haiti' (p. 417-44) provides standard information for the tourist.
Accommodation and sights are listed for Port-au-Prince, Cap Haïtien and Jacmel.

Travellers' Accounts

43 Haiti, highroad to adventure.
Hugh B. Cave. New York: Holt, 1952. 306p. map.

A cheerfully written volume, describing the travels of Cave, his wife and his two sons through Haiti in the early 1950s. The work is illustrated with photographs by the author.

44 Black Bagdad.
John H. Craige. New York: Minton, Balch, 1933. 276p.

Presents the personal reminiscences of a captain in the US Marine Corps who served in Haiti during the American occupation, first as an officer with the Gendarmerie d'Haiti and later as the Chief of Police of Port-au-Prince. Craige's work provides many details on the social life and folk customs of the period, but his observations are marred by his racist viewpoint. Craige wrote another book on Haiti in very much the same vein, *Cannibal cousins* (New York: Minton, Balch, 1934).

45 Island possessed.
Katherine Dunham. Garden City, New York: Doubleday, 1969. 280p.

A personal, but perceptive view of Haiti by an American black dancer and anthropologist who was also an initiate in the Voodoo cult. Dunham maintained a long relationship with Haiti, beginning with her early experiences there as a research fellow in anthropology. Her book recounts her Haitian years from 1935 onwards.

46 Roaming through the West Indies.
Harry A. Franck. New York: Blue Ribbon Books, 1920. 486p.

Presents entertaining observations by an experienced traveller. In a section entitled 'The American West Indies' (p. 106-88), Franck depicts Haiti in three chapters: 'Under the palm-tree of Haiti'; 'The death of Charlemagne'; and 'Hither and yon in the Haitian bush'. Emphasizing the sensational, Franck freely mixes fiction with his facts.

47 **Best nightmare on earth: a life in Haiti.**
Herbert Gold, introduction by Jan Morris. New York: Prentice-Hall, 1991. 1st ed. 303p. maps.

Haiti first cast its spell over Herbert Gold when, anticipating only a short stay, he travelled to the island as a young writer in the early 1950s. In this autobiographical account, Gold details his personal involvement in the country over nearly four decades.

48 **A continent of islands; searching for the Caribbean destiny.**
Mark Kurlansky. Reading, Massachusetts: Addison-Wesley Publishing Co., 1992. 324p. map. bibliog.

Provides an account of an American journalist's travels in the Caribbean area. By using the index, the reader can find Kurlansky's trenchant remarks on Haiti's contemporary problems: the AIDS epidemic; deforestation and environmental destruction; the drug trade; malnutrition; prostitution; and emigration.

49 **Haiti: its dawn of progress after years in a night of revolution.**
John Dryden Kuser. Boston, Massachusetts: R. G. Badger, 1921. 108p. Reprinted, Westport, Connecticut: Negro Universities Press, 1970; New York: Gordon Press, 1976.

A racist-capitalist tract, written by an American who visited Haiti in 1920. Kuser expresses enthusiastic support for a continued US presence in the country: 'We have a bright future for Haiti, if the United States remains'.

50 **The traveller's tree: a journey through the Caribbean Islands.**
Patrick Leigh Fermor. London: Penguin; New York: Viking Penguin, 1984. 365p. map.

This book, first published in 1950, has become a travel classic. It describes the author's journey through the Caribbean in the late 1940s, and while Leigh Fermor's attitudes do not transcend his time, his account of the Haitian Voodoo ceremonies that he attended is noted for its descriptive power.

51 **Voodoo fire in Haiti.**
Richard A. Loederer, translated from the German by Desmond Ivo Vesey. Garden City, New York: Doubleday, Doran, 1935. 274p. maps.

This work was written and illustrated by a Viennese artist who spent several months in Haiti. Reviewers at the time of publication criticized this study for its distorted image of Haiti, based on errors and misinformation.

52 **Black Haiti: a biography of Africa's eldest daughter.**
Blair Niles, photographs by Robert Niles, Jr. New York: Putnam's, 1926. 325p. bibliog.

Provides a skillfully written account of the author's travels in Haiti in the 1920s, where her experiences inspired her to narrate tales of the nation's past.

53 **Where black rules white: a journey across and about Hayti.**
Hesketh Prichard.   London: Constable, 1900. 288p. Reprinted,
Freeport, New York: Books for Libraries, 1971. (Black Heritage Library
Collection).

Prichard describes his journey through Haiti in 1899. His racist and imperialist
comments on the nation and its citizens are almost entirely negative.

54 **Hayti or the Black republic.**
Sir Spenser Buckingham St. John.   London: Smith, Elder, 1889.
2nd ed. 389p. map. Reprinted, London: Cass, 1971. (Source Books on
Haiti, no. 9).

Sir Spenser Buckingham St. John began his career as an associate of Sir James Brooke,
the white rajah of Sarawak. In 1863 he became the British chargé d'affaires in Haiti
and was appointed Minister Resident and Consul-General in 1872. His *Hayti, or the
Black republic*, first published in 1884, begins an era in the bibliography of the nation –
the lurid portrayal of Voodoo as a religion of cannibalism and human sacrifice. The
reprinted edition contains a new preface by Robert I. Rotberg.

55 **The magic island.**
William Buehler Seabrook, drawings by Alexander King.   New York:
Harcourt, Brace, 1929. 336p. Reprinted, New York: Paragon House,
1989. (The Armchair Traveller Series).

Seabrook's sensationalized presentation of Voodoo in this narrative of his adventures
in Haiti brought strong objections from many Haitians. The book contains the author's
photographs and an appendix, 'From the author's notebook'.

56 **A puritan in Voodooland.**
Edna Taft.   Philadelphia: Penn, 1938. 407p. maps. bibliog. Reprinted,
Detroit, Michigan: Tower Books, 1971.

A young lady from New England provides a somewhat breathless description of her
social whirl among the Haitian *haute monde* in the 1930s.

57 **Bonjour Blanc! A journey through Haiti.**
Ian Thomson.   London: Hutchinson, 1992. 352p. map.

Thomson proves an intrepid and determined traveller as he travels through Haiti to
collect a mixed bag of observations on a floundering country.

58 **Hot countries.**
Alec Waugh, woodcuts by Lynd Ward.   New York: Farrar & Rinehart,
1930. 304p. Reprinted, New York: Paragon House, 1989.

This book was also published under the title *The Coloured countries* (London:
Chapman & Hall, 1930). A section 'The Black Republic' gives an Englishman's
impressions of Haiti in the 1920s. Waugh is also the author of a historical novel, *No
quarter* (London: Cassell, 1932), set in colonial Saint-Domingue.

59 **The rainy season: Haiti since Duvalier.**
Amy Wilentz. New York: Simon & Schuster, 1989. 427p. bibliog.

A journalist's account of Haiti since 1986. Wilentz conveys her shrewd personal observations on Haitian life and politics, based on her interaction with Haiti's complex culture.

Flora and Fauna

General

60 Caribbean treasure.
Ivan T. Sanderson.   London: Hamish Hamilton, 1940; New York:
Viking Press, 1939. 292p. map.

Sanderson, a British zoologist, recounts his expeditions to Trinidad, Surinam and Haiti
to collect specimens. The book contains thirty-two illustrations by the author.

61 The cruise of the *Esperanza* to Haiti.
Alexander Wetmore, Watson M. Perrygo.   In: *Explorations and field-
work of the Smithsonian Institution in 1930.*   Washington, DC:
Smithsonian Institution, 1931. p. 59-66.

The members of the Parish-Smithsonian expedition sailed to Haiti in 1930 on the yacht
Esperanza to collect zoological material from the islands lying off the Haitian coast. 'In
its objective of collecting specimens on remote islands little known zoologically the
expedition was singularly successful, the many specimens obtained, particularly of
birds and reptiles, forming a valuable addition to the Haitian collection of the United
States National Museum'.

62 Zoological exploration in Hispaniola.
Alexander Wetmore.   In: *Explorations and field-work of the
Smithsonian Institution in 1927.*   Washington, DC: Smithsonian
Institution, 1928, p. 33-40.

Describes zoological explorations in Haiti by Wetmore, between 27 March and 3 June
1927, conducted in an attempt to supplement the specimen collections previously made
for the US National Museum by W. L. Abbott.

Flora

63 **Flore d'Haïti, clé et description des ordres-familles et genres des
spermatophytes d'Haïti avec la liste de la plupart des espèces.** (Flora of
Haiti, key and description of the families and genera of the
spermatophytes of Haiti with a list of most of the species.)
Henry D. Baker, William S. Dardeau.   Port-au-Prince: Service
Technique du Département de l'Agriculture et de l'Enseignement
Professionnel, 1930. 456p. bibliog. (Haiti. Republic. Département de
l'Agriculture et de l'Enseignement Professionnel. Service Technique.
Ensemble des Ouvrages Universitaires, no. 7).
The basic work on Haiti's seed plants.

64 **Plant resources of Hispaniola.**
H. D. Barker.   In: *Plants and plant science in Latin America*. Edited by
Frans Verdoom.   Waltham, Massachusetts: Chronica Botanica Co.,
1945, p. 78-81. map. (New Series of Plant Science Books, no. 16).
Barker lists and comments on fifty-one families of plants cultivated on Hispaniola. A
small map of land use, reprinted from Preston E. James' *Latin America* (New York,
1942), indicates the regions where coffee, cacao, tobacco, henequen, sugar, cotton and
other crops are grown.

65 **Neoabbottia, a new cactus genus from Hispaniola, with four plates.**
N. L. Britton, J. N. Rose.   Washington, DC: Smithsonian Institution,
1921. 6p. (Smithsonian Miscellaneous Collections, vol. 72, no. 9).
Describes a new genus of cactus identified by W. L. Abbott and E. C. Leonard in the
Cul-de-sac region, northeast of Port-au-Prince in 1920. The new genus was named in
honour of Abbott.

66 **Botanizing in Haiti.**
Erik L. Ekman.   *United States Naval Medical Bulletin*, vol. 24, no. 1
(1926), p. 483-97.
Ekman was an eminent Swedish botanist who, during the 1920s, documented the
diverse plant life of Haiti's rain forest jungle. See also his account of botanical field
work in the Massif de la Hotte region in 'A botanical excursion in La Hotte, Haiti', in
Svensk Botanisk Tidskrift, vol. 22, nos. 1-2 (1928), p. 200-29.

67   **Phytogeographic survey of North America: a consideration of the
     phytogeography of the North American continent, including Mexico,
     Central America, and the West Indies, together with the evolution of
     North American plant distribution.**
     John W. Harshberger, German extract by O. Drude.   Leipzig: W.
     Engelmann; New York: G. E. Stechert, 1911. 790p. maps. bibliog. (Die
     Vegetation der Erde . . . 13). Reprinted, Weinheim, Bergstr., Germany:
     H. R. Engelmann; New York: Hafner Pub. Co., 1958. 2nd (reprint) ed.
     Although it has been superseded in many respects, this older work continues to be of
     use, especially for its extensive bibliographical coverage. The section 'West Indian
     islands' (p. 87-92) lists all titles concerned with the botany of the Caribbean region
     from the sixteenth to the early twentieth century. The plant life of Haiti is studied in
     the chapter 'The Santo Domingan district of the Antillean region' (p. 680-83).

68   **A brief sketch of the flora of Hispaniola.**   ·
     L. R. Holdridge.   In: *Plants and plant science in Latin America.*
     Edited by Frans Verdoom.   Waltham, Massachusetts: Chronica
     Botanica Co., 1945, p. 23-37. map. (New Series of Plant Science Books,
     no. 16).
     An early, but still useful, discussion by a forestry expert of the forest types and timber
     species found on the island of Hispaniola. An original map of the main forest types is
     included.

69   **Floristic study of La Visite and Macaya National Parks, Haiti.**
     Walter S. Judd.   Gainesville, Florida: US Agency for International
     Development/Haiti, 1986. 98p. bibliog.
     Analyses the vascular plants and classifies the botany of Haiti's two national parks.

70   **Phytothérapie haïtienne: nos simples.** (Haitian plant therapy: our
     simples.)
     Rulx Leon.   Port-au-Prince: Imprimerie de l'Etat, 1959. 79p.
     Discusses the medicinal use of plants and herbs in Haiti.

71   **Botanical exploration of northwestern Haiti.**
     E. C. Leonard.   In: *Explorations and field-work of the Smithsonian
     Institution in 1929.*   Washington, DC: Smithsonian Institution, 1930.
     p. 129-36.
     Presents an anecdotal account of an adventurous trip in 1928-29 through Haiti to
     collect botanical specimens. Leonard was able to return to the United States with
     approximately 15,000 plant specimens for the Haitian collection in the US National
     Herbarium.

**Floristic inventory of tropical countries: the status of plant systematics,
collections, and vegetation, plus recommendations for the future.**
See item no. 98.

Recent vegetation changes in southern Haiti.
See item no. 102.

Stewardship plan for the national parks of Haiti.
See item no. 104.

Mammals

72 **Wildlife in danger.**
James Fisher, Noel Simon, Jack Vincent and members and
correspondents of the Survival Service Commission of the International
Union for Conservation of Nature and Natural Resources, foreword by
Harold J. Coolidge and Peter Scott, preface by Joseph Wood Krutch.
New York: Viking Press, 1969. 368p. maps. (A Studio Book).
A selective version of the IUCN's Red Data Book which has been specially prepared
and illustrated for the layman. The work includes an article on *Plagiodontia aedium*,
the Haitian hutia or Cuvier's hutia, describing the animal, its habitat and behaviour
(p. 59).

73 **The mammals of Parc National La Visite and Parc National Pic Macaya,
Haiti.**
Charles A. Woods.   Gainesville, Florida: US Agency for International
Development/Haiti, 1986. 80p.
Of the twenty-eight species of terrestrial mammals endemic to Haiti, only two have
survived: the Haitian hutia (*Plagiodontia aedium*) and the solenodon (*Solenodon
paradoxus*). Haiti's recently created national parks are the last refuges of these
threatened rodents.

74 *Solenodon paradoxus* **in southern Haiti.**
Charles A. Woods.   *Journal of Mammalogy*, vol. 57, no. 3
(Aug. 1976), p. 591-92. bibliog.
Woods reports his discovery of two solenodon (zagouti) carcasses in Haiti's southern
peninsula, indicating that a small population of the rare mammals may survive there.

Birds

75 **The birds of Haiti and San Domingo.**
Charles B. Cory.   Boston, Massachusetts: Estes & Lauriat, 1885. 198p.
map.
Charles B. Cory, indefatigable ornithologist and sharpshooter, made two bird-collecting expeditions to Hispaniola, the first between January and March 1881, and the second between 1882 and 1883. In this publication he describes 111 species of birds found on the island. Colour illustrations are also included.

76 **Zouazo Ayiti yo.** (The birds of Haiti.)
Roger Nelson.   Port-au-Prince: Boukan, 1979. 103p.
Illustrated with colour plates of Haiti's birds, Nelson's text is in Haitian Creole, with nomenclature indexed in Latin, English and French.

77 **Birds collected in Cuba and Haiti by the Parish-Smithsonian expedition of 1930.**
Alexander Wetmore.   US National Museum. Proceedings, vol. 81,
art. 2 (1932), p. 1-40.
Presents the results of the scientific expedition of the yacht *Esperanza*, undertaken in order to collect zoological specimens from the islands off the coast of Haiti. An annotated list of those birds which were found on the islands is included.

78 **The birds of Haiti and the Dominican Republic.**
Alexander Wetmore, Bradshaw H. Swales.   Washington, DC: US
Government Printing Office, 1931. 483p. map. bibliog. (Smithsonian
Institution. US National Museum Bulletin 155).
This comprehensive work on the avifauna of the island of Hispaniola contains lists of and annotations on all species of birds, either native or migrant to Hispaniola and its minor surrounding islands. It is a superior scientific accomplishment, the result of exhaustive field-work carried out in Haiti and the Dominican Republic by W. L. Abbott and the zoologists, biologists and ornithologists of the Smithsonian Institution. Much of the information about Haiti and the Dominican Republic found in the introduction to this work will prove of interest to historians as well as to scientists for it includes a chronological account of all ornithological investigations conducted on the island, and a survey of the research carried out by naturalists between the sixteenth and the twentieth centuries. The bibliography lists all known publications on Hispaniolan birds, as well as citations of other zoological materials. The book is illustrated with black-and-white photographs and drawings.

79 **Additonal notes on the birds of Haiti and the Dominican Republic.**
Alexander Wetmore, Frederick C. Lincoln.   *US National Museum.
Proceedings*, vol. 82, art. 25 (1933), p. 1-68.
Supplements Wetmore's and Swales's *Birds of Haiti and the Dominican Republic* (q.v.). It is based on additional field-work on Hispaniola.

80 **The birds of Parc National La Visite and Parc National Pic Macaya,
Haiti.**
Charles A. Woods, Jose A. Ottenwalder.   Gainesville, Florida: US
Agency for International Development/Haiti, 1986. 238p. maps. bibliog.
A survey of the birds whose natural habitat is in the montane forest areas which are
located almost exclusively within Haiti's two national parks. Most of Haiti's endemic
avifauna can now be found only in the most remote areas of Haiti's highest mountain
range.

Reptiles and amphibians

81 **The herpetology of Hispaniola.**
Doris M. Cochran.   Washington, DC: US Government Printing Office,
1941. 398p. bibliog. (Smithsonian Institution. US National Museum.
Bulletin 177).
This is a fundamental work on the amphibians and reptiles of Haiti and the Dominican
Republic, prepared under the auspices of the Smithsonian Institution, Washington,
DC. All species known to exist on the island at the time of compilation are described.
The bibliography lists all previous scientific publications on the herpetology of
Hispaniola.

Fishes

82 **Beneath tropic seas: a record of diving among the coral reefs of Haiti.**
William Beebe.   New York, London: Putnam's, 1928. 234p. map.
Beebe combines personal adventure with scientific observation in this engaging account
of the five months which he spent exploring Haitian waters off Port-au-Prince as
Director of the Tenth Expedition of the Department of Tropical Research of the New
York Zoological Society. The volume is heavily illustrated with photographs of marine
fauna; it has often been reprinted and was translated into French as *Sous la mer
tropicale* (Paris: Stock, 1931). Several appendices follow the main text, among them:
'The Haitian expedition January 1-May 23, 1927 – a report on its objects and results';
'List of Haitian birds observed' and 'Families and number of species of Haitian fish
collected during the expedition'.

83 **The fishes of Port-au-Prince Bay, Haiti: with a summary of the known species of marine fish of the island of Haiti and Santo Domingo.**
William Beebe, John Tee-Van. *Zoological Scientific Contributions of the New York Zoological Society*, vol. 10, no. 1 (Dec. 1928), p. 1-279.

The main body of this report, the 'Annotated list of fish of Port-au-Prince Bay, Haiti', is the fundamental work on Haiti's marine fish. Until its publication, no adequate catalogue of this subject had existed. The specimens upon which this report is based were collected by the Tenth Expedition of the Department of Tropical Research of the New York Zoological Society, under the direction of William Beebe. The work was carried out from the schooner, *The Lieutenant*, which was anchored off Port-au-Prince between February and May 1927. From Haitian waters, the expedition collected 6,122 specimens of 270 species of fish, comprising eighty-four families. Each species is examined and illustrated. (See also item no. 82).

84 **Cichlid fishes in the West Indies with especial reference to Haiti, including the description of a new species of Cichlasoma.**
John Tee-Van. *Zoologica: Scientific Contributions of the New York Zoological Society*, vol. 10, no. 2 (Nov. 1935), p. 281-300. bibliog.

This article covers the mainly freshwater family *Cichlidae*, which were omitted from the main account. A list of references is also included. (See also item no. 82).

85 **An annotated list of the cyprinodont fishes of Hispaniola, with descriptions of two new species.**
George S. Myers. *Zoologica: Scientific Contributions of the New York Zoological Society*, vol. 10, no. 3 (Nov. 1935), p. 301-16. bibliog.

Studies cyprinodont fish specimens obtained in Haiti by Beebe and Tee-Van during the 1927 expedition of the Department of Tropical Research of the New York Zoological Society. The article lists and describes the known species of cyprinodonts and provides a bibliography of recent literature on the group.

86 **Additions to the fish fauna of Haiti and Santo Domingo.**
William Beebe, John Tee-Van. *Zoologica: Scientific Contributions of the New York Zoological Society*, vol. 10, no. 4 (Nov. 1935), p. 317-19.

Presents the fourth and final publication of the results of the 1927 expedition to Haiti of the Department of Tropical Research of the New York Zoological Society. This paper completes the reports of those species which were investigated by the expedition.

87 **Zoogeography of the Antillean freshwater fish fauna.**
George H. Burgess, Richard Franz. In: *Biogeography of the West Indies: past, present, and future.* Edited by Charles A. Woods. Gainesville, Florida: Sandhill Crane Press, 1989, p. 263-304. maps. bibliog.

Seventy-one freshwater fish species are found in the Antilles, thirty-five in Hispaniola. The authors of this study state that 'based on the most recent geological literature and modern fish distributions, we propose a zoogeographic model that merges elements of dispersal and vicariance to explain Antillean [freshwater] fish distribution'. Following an introduction to the region's fish fauna, Burgess and Franz discuss separate geographical areas. Hispaniola is covered on p. 267-70. The article ends with a presentation of the authors' explanatory zoogeographical model.

Butterflies

88   **The butterflies (Lepidoptera: Rhopalocera) of Morne la Visite and Pic Macaya, Haiti.**
Frank Gali, Albert Schwartz.   Gainesville, Florida: US Agency for International Development/Haiti, 1986. 16p.
This is a biogeophysical survey of the butterflies of Haiti's two national parks.

89   **The butterflies of Hispaniola.**
Albert Schwartz.   Gainesville, Florida: University of Florida Press, 1989. 580p. maps. bibliog.
Provides authoritative scholarship on the nearly 200 species of butterflies that live on the island of Hispaniola. This is the first major study of Haiti's (and the Dominican Republic's) diverse Lepidoptera, which includes sixty endemic species. Information on the natural history, ecology, taxonomy, elevational distribution, feeding habits, and seasonal occurrence of Hispaniola's butterflies is accompanied by distribution maps for each species and a descriptive key in Spanish and English.

Fossils

90   **Remains of mammals from caves in the Republic of Haiti.**
Gerrit S. Miller, Jr.   Washington, DC: Smithsonian Institution, 1922. 8p. (Smithsonian Miscellaneous Collections, vol. 74, no. 3).
In 1921 members of the US Geological Survey uncovered fossils in two caves at St. Michel and l'Atalaye in northwest Haiti. In this paper – the first scientific report on the discovery – Gerrit S. Miller, Jr., Curator of Mammals at the US National Museum, identifies a number of the bones as faunal remains.

91   **Remains of birds from caves in the Republic of Haiti.**
Alexander Wetmore.   Washington, DC: Smithsonian Institution, 1922. 4p. (Smithsonian Miscellaneous Collections, vol. 74, no. 4).
Wetmore identifies fossil remains of birds removed from caves at St. Michel and l'Atalaye in 1921.

25

Flora and Fauna. Fossils

92 **Explorations of Haitian caves.**
Gerrit S. Miller, Jr. Washington, DC: Smithsonian Institution, 1926.
(Smithsonian Miscellaneous Collections, vol. 78, no. 1).
Provides a general account of field-work undertaken by Miller in the caves at St.
Michel and l'Atalaye in 1925. Interest in the exploration of these sites was initiated by
the fossils unearthed in 1921.

93 **A second collection of mammals from caves near St. Michel, Haiti (with
ten plates).**
Gerrit S. Miller, Jr. Washington, DC: Smithsonian Institution, 1929.
30p. (Smithsonian Miscellaneous Collections, vol. 81, no. 9).
The second scientific description by Miller of faunal remains from the caves at St.
Michel and l'Atalaye. The bones were collected by Miller during his expedition to the
caves in 1925 and were the second group of fossils removed from the site.

94 **Further exploration of Haitian caves.**
Arthur J. Poole. In: *Explorations and field-work of the Smithsonian
Institution in 1928.* Washington, DC: Smithsonian Institution, 1929,
p. 55-62.
Presents an account of an expedition by Arthur J. Poole of the Division of Mammals of
the US National Museum to the caves near St. Michel where, in 1921, members of the
US Geological Survey had discovered deposits of bones of extinct mammals. These
deposits were examined by Gerrit S. Miller, Jr., at the cave sites in 1925, and were
found to be of such importance that this second expedition to the cave was organized.
The article reports on several other caves besides those at St. Michel and l'Atalaye and
also on the collection of biological specimens.

95 **Explorations in Haitian caves.**
Arthur J. Poole. In: *Explorations and field-work of the Smithsonian
Institution in 1929.* Washington, DC: Smithsonian Institution, 1930,
p. 63-76.
In 1928-29 Poole made his second foray into Haitian caves in search of the bones of
extinct birds and mammals, visiting unexplored caves in the St. Michel and l'Atalaye
districts as well as caves at San Rafael, Don Don and Cerca La Source. This article
also includes some interesting observations on Haitian life and customs.

96 **Three small collections of mammals from Hispaniola (with two plates).**
Gerrit S. Miller, Jr. Washington, DC: Smithsonian Institution, 1930.
10p. (Smithsonian Miscellanous Collections, vol. 82, no. 15).
Describes three groups of Hispaniolan fossils: the first found on the Massif de la Selle;
the second on the Ile de la Gonâve; and the third in the Dominican Republic.

97   **Vertebrate fauna from Locus 39, Puerto Real, Haiti.**
    Elizabeth J. Reitz.   *Journal of Field Archaeology*, vol. 13 (1986),
    p. 317-28. maps.
Reitz's paper is a professional study of cattle bones excavated in 1981 from one section
of Puerto Real, a Spanish colonial town founded between 1502 and 1504 on Haiti's
north coast.

Environment and Conservation

98 **Floristic inventory of tropical countries: the status of plant systematics, collections, and vegetation, plus recommendations for the future.**
Edited by David G. Campbell, H. David Hammond. Bronx, New York: New York Botanical Garden, 1989. 545p.

More than sixty scientists contributed to this major phytogeographical reference work which surveys and evaluates the status of plant inventory and collections of rain forest vegetation in tropical countries, and pays special attention to endangered habitats and species and zones of endemism. The condition of Haiti's threatened vegetation and of its rapidly vanishing ecosystem is included in the regional report from the Caribbean.

99 **Environmental degradation in Haiti: an analysis of aerial photography.**
W. B. Cohen. Gainesville, Florida: US Agency for International Development/Haiti, 1984. 35p.

Quantifies the extensive loss of forest cover and habitat in Haiti by means of an analysis of aerial photographs taken in 1956, 1978 and 1984. Forest cover in Haiti in 1989 was less than 1.5 per cent: total deforestation is possible by the year 2000.

100 **Haiti, country environmental profile: a field study.**
Marko Ehrlich (et al.). Washington, DC: Agency for International Development, 1985. 120p. maps. bibliog.

Prepared under the auspices of the United States government, this study examines Haiti's natural resources and threatened environment. Readers will find the volume's bibliography of especial use for its listing of environmental research reports.

101 **Desert in the making.**
James Ferguson. *New Scientist*, vol. 118, no. 1613 (May 19 1988), p. 68.

Briefly assesses the damage caused by cutting trees for charcoal, the only fuel of the poor in Haiti. Ferguson describes the Agroforestry Outreach Project of USAID that provides free seedlings to Haitian peasants in an attempt to establish reforestation.

102 **Recent vegetation changes in southern Haiti.**
Antonia Higuera-Gundy.   In: *Biogeography of the West Indies: past,*
present, and future. Edited by Charles A. Woods.   Gainesville,
Florida: Sandhill Crane Press, 1989, p. 191-200. maps. bibliog.

Reports on the historical ecology of Haiti, based on data derived from a stratigraphic
study of the physical, chemical and biological characteristics of sediment cores bored in
the floor of Lake Miragoane, a deep, freshwater lake on Haiti's southern peninsula.
Higuera-Gundy's investigation of the vegetation history of the area reveals that the
human impact on the environment which began 500 years ago has resulted in 'acute
local deforestation and consequent soil erosion'.

103 **Conservation strategies and the preservation of biological diversity in**
Haiti.
Paul Paryski, Charles A. Woods, Florence Sergile.   In: *Biogeography*
of the West Indies: past, present, and future. Edited by Charles A.
Woods.   Gainesville, Florida: Sandhill Crane Press, 1989, p. 855-78.
maps. bibliog.

Haiti is uniquely endowed with endemic plants and animals. However, the country is
now experiencing an environmental disaster, and it may soon be no longer possible to
preserve the remnants of Haiti's mountain cloud forests, the habitat for Haiti's natural
heritage. This article provides an excellent summary of Haiti's physiogeography, forest
cover, flora and what little remains of its native fauna. The major part of the article
describes two national parks created by Presidential decress in 1983, the Parc National
la Visite at Morne la Visite and Parc National Pic Macaya at Pic Macaya. The authors
discuss the serious problems facing these parks and propose specific conservation
measures.

104 **Stewardship plan for the national parks of Haiti.**
Charles A. Woods, Lawrence Harris.   Gainesville, Florida: US
Agency for International Development, 1986. 263p. maps. bibliog.

A USAID-funded study that suggests positive steps to protect the Massif de la Hotte
watershed and the newly created national park areas where the remaining specimens of
Haiti's rare endemic plants and animals can still be found. Includes tables of the fungi,
macrolichens and endemic seed plants occurring in Parc National La Visite and Parc
National Pic Macaya.

Prehistory and Archaeology

Pre-Colombian inhabitants

105 **Langue et littérature des aborigènes d'Ayti.** (Language and literature of
the original inhabitants of Haiti.)
Jean Fourchard. Port-au-Prince: Editions Henri Deschamps, 1988.
122p.

Gathers together historical and archaeological information from published sources in
an attempt to summarize what is presently known about the language and oral
literature of the Amerindian tribes that inhabited Haiti at the time of Columbus's
discovery of the island during his first voyage.

106 **Aborigines of the ancient island of Hispaniola.**
Herbert W. Krieger. In: *Annual Report of the Smithsonian Institution,
1929.* Washington, DC: Smithsonian Inbstitution, 1929, p. 473-506.
map. bibliog.

This informative article describes the Arawak culture which existed on Hispaniola at
the time of the Spanish arrival in the New World in 1492 and which had been
destroyed by 1550. Those topics covered are: travel and trade routes; cultural
diffusion; population distribution; habitations; weapons; food resources; agriculture;
hunting and fishing; implements and decorative objects; religious objects; clothes;
metals; and pottery. A detailed bibliographical note annotating the primary literature
of exploration pertaining to Hispaniola, black-and-white illustrations of the artifacts
discussed and a reproduction of Charlevoix's 1730 map of the aboriginal provinces of
the island are included in the areticle.

107 **Origins of the Tainan culture, West Inbdies.**
Sven Loven. Gothenburg, Sweden: Elanders Boktryckeri Aktiebolag,
1935. 696p. bibliog. Reprinted, New York: AMS Press, 1979.

This revised second edition of Loven's earlier *Uber die Wurzeln de Tainischen Kultur*
(1924) is an early anthropological treatise on the Taino, the Arawak tribe inhabiting
Hispaniola at the time of Columbus.

108 **Arte Taino.** (Taino art.)
Frank Moya Pons, photographs by Onorio Montas, Pedro Jose
Borrell. Santo Domingo: Banco Central de la Republica Dominicana,
1985. 2nd ed. 231p. bibliog.

Presents the art of the Taino Indians of Hispaniola. The volume consists largely of
illustrations which are accompanied by a Spanish text.

109 **The Tainos of Hispaniola: the island's first inhabitants.**
Frank Moya Pons, translated from the Spanish by Judith C. Faerron.
Caribbean Review, vol. 13, no. 4 (fall 1984), p. 20-23 ff.

Provides a translated excerpt from the author's *Arte Taino* (Santo Domingo,
Dominican Republic: Banco Central de la Republica dominicana, 1982). The Tainos
achieved the highest level of cultural development of any pre-Columbian Hispaniolian
Amerindian tribe. Moya Pons describes their lifestyle, family and social structure,
political organization, and myth and religious expression. This is a good general article
with some interesting illustrations of Taino artifacts.

110 **Hisoire des Caciques d'Haïti.** (History of the Caciques of Haiti.)
Emile Nau. Paris: Guerin & Cie., 1894. 2nd ed. 365p. map. bibliog.
Reprinted, Port-au-Prince: Editions Panorama, 1963. 2 vols.

A nineteenth-century work on the aboriginal inhabitants of what is now Haiti. Three
appendices are included: 'Géographie primitive d'Haïti' ('Primitive geography of
Haiti'); 'De la langue et de la littérature des aborigènes d'Haïti' ('The language and
literature of the aborigines of Haiti'); and 'Flora indienne d'Haïti' ('Indian flora of
Haiti').

111 **The entry of man into the West Indies.**
Irving Rouse. In: *Papers in Caribbean anthropology*. Edited by
Sidney W. Mintz. New Haven, Connecticut: Yale University,
Department of Anthropology, 1960, p. 3-26. map. bibliog. (Yale
University Publications in Anthropology, nos. 57-64). (Reprinted, New
Haven, Connecticut: HRAF Press, 1970).

In publication no. 61 in this collection, Rouse uses the results of his extensive
archaeological research in Haiti in his examination of three hypotheses concerning the
migration of the Meso-Indians to the islands of the Caribbean.

112 **Origin and development of the indians discovered by Columbus.**
Irving Rouse.   In: *Columbus and his world; proceedings of the First San Salvador Conference held October 30-November 3, 1986, at the College Center of the Finger Lakes, Bahamian Field Station, San Salvador Island, Bahamas.* Compiled by Donald T. Gerace.   Fort Lauderdale, Florida: The Station, 1987, p. 293-312. maps. bibliog.

A short paper, adapted from Rouse's *Migrations in prehistory: inferring population movement from cultural remains* (New Haven, Connecticut: Yale University Press, 1986, p. 106-56). Rouse discusses the ethnohistorical, linguistic and archaeological research that indicates that 'the ancestors of the Taino Indians, whom Columbus met during his first voyage, came from South America and advanced into the West Indies at the expense of the ancestors of the Guanahatabey Indians, whom the Admiral encountered during his second voyage'.

113 **The Tainos: rise and decline of the people who greeted Columbus.**
Irving Rouse.   New Haven, Connecticut: Yale University Press, 1992. 232p.

This significant work is the first substantial revision of the archaeology of the Caribbean region since 1935. Rouse summarizes the findings of his years of study of the archaeology and anthropology of the Caribbean region in this presentation of the Taino culture of Hispaniola. He reconstructs Taino culture as it was in 1492, then retraces the Tainos' ancestral roots in the successive migrations to the West Indies of Amerindians from the South American continent. Although the Tainos did not long survive their contact with the Europeans, Rouse believes that their contribution to Caribbean culture was not negligible.

114 **The West Indies.**
Irving Rouse, Pedro Garcia Valdes.   In: *The handbook of the South American Indians, vol. 4: The circum-Caribbean tribes.* Edited by Julian H. Steward.   Washington, DC: Bureau of American Ethnology, Smithsonian Institution, 1945. bibliog. (Bulletin, 143).
(Reprinted, New York: Cooper Square Publishers, 1963, p. 495-539).

Provides a basic source for the ethnography of the Ciboney and the Arawak. The authors summarize what was known about the aboriginal inhabitants of Hispaniola as of 1945. Later archaeological research has, of course, augmented and modified the information given in this article.

115 **The cave of the Jagua: the mythological world of the Tainos.**
Antonio M. Stevens-Arroyo.   Albuquerque, New Mexico: University of New Mexico Press, 1988. 282p. bibliog.

An important study of the mythology and religion of the Taino Indians, the pre-Columbian inhabitants of the island which is currently shared by Haiti and the Dominican Republic. Stevens-Arroyo concentrates on the Taino myths of the Creation and the Hero which he considers to be central to an understanding of the Taino cosmos.

116 **A Taino tale: a mythological statement of social order.**
Antonio M. Stevens-Arroyo. *Caribbean Review*, vol. 13, no. 4
(fall 1984), p. 24-26.
Stevens-Arroyo interprets the Taino myth of the Creation as 'a symbolic tale of the
formation of the [Taino] people in terms of a discovery of group leadership'.

117 **Hispaniola: Caribbean chiefdoms in the age of Columbus.**
Samuel M. Wilson. Tuscaloosa, Alabama: University of Alabama
Press, 1990. 170p. maps. bibliog.
Descriptively reconstructs the culture of the Taino as it existed during the contact
period, 1492-1520, when Europeans first arrived on the island of Hispaniola. Covering
the whole island at the time of this encounter, Wilson emphasizes the complex socio-
political organization which existed on Hispaniola when Columbus landed on its north
coast near Guarico, the village of the Taino chieftain Guacanagari. Wilson's work
provides a valuable perspective on a rich Caribbean culture, doomed by the arrival of
the Europeans.

Essays in population history: Mexico and the Caribbean.
See item no. 319.

On the contact population of Hispaniola: history as higher mathematics.
See item no. 321.

The population of Hispaniola at the time of Columbus.
See item no. 325.

Aboriginal sites

118 **A distinctive artifact common to Haiti and Central America.**
William R. Coe, II. *American Antiquity*, vol. 22, no. 2 (Jan 1957),
p. 280-82. bibliog.
Records the presence, both in Middle America and the Greater Antilles, of a flint
implement – 'a tanged, elongated triangular blade, triangular to trapezoidal in section
and of variable length – the form and technique of which seem relevant to the problem
of areal relationships, pointing to interactions between the mainland and the islands'.
An illustration of the implement accompanies the article.

119 **Culture sequence in Haiti.**
Herbert W. Krieger. In: *Explorations and field-work of the
Smithsonian Institution in 1931.* Washington, DC: Smithsonian
Institution, 1932, p. 113-24.
Krieger carried out archaeological excavations in Haiti from January to May 1931,
trenching many Arawak sites in order to obtain samples of aboriginal pottery and other
midden debris. This article forms a brief report of the results of his investigations and
presents a few suggestions for further research.

120 **Excavations in the Ft. Liberté region, Haiti [and] Culture of the Ft. Liberté region, Haiti.**
Froelich G. Rainey, Irving Rouse. New Haven, Connecticut: Yale University Press; London: H. Milford, Oxford University Press, 1941. 48p., 196p. maps. bibliogs. (Yale University Publications in Anthropology, nos. 23 and 24). Reprinted, New York: AMS Press, [n.d.].

This double publication presents two articles, each based on data drawn from archaeological investigations undertaken in Haiti. Rainey's report provides a thorough and highly specialized record of artifacts excavated in the Fort Liberté Bay area and several other parts of Haiti in 1934 and 1935. Rouse's contribution is 'the first detailed archaeological study of the culture of Haiti's pre-Columbian inhabitants', describing and classifying the culture of the Fort Liberté Bay region using as data the materials presented in Rainey's paper. The book was published for the Department of Anthropology, Yale University.

121 **A new prehistoric culture in Haiti.**
Froelich G. Rainey. *Proceedings of the National Academy of Sciences of the United States*, vol. 22, no. 1 (Jan. 1936), p. 4-8.

Reports on archaeological investigations undertaken in the region of Fort Liberté Bay, northern Haiti, in the spring of 1935. The unearthing of flint implements without accompanying ceramic deposits is evidence, according to the author, of 'a distinct prehistoric culture which preceded the pottery-making culture that extended over the West Indies [in 1492]'. Pottery-making sites without flint implements were also excavated. Rainey concludes that these sites represent 'a later culture which correlates with the Shell Culture pattern (probably Arawak) that has been found distributed over the Greater Antilles and the Virgin Islands'.

122 **Prehistory in Haiti: a study in method.**
Irving Rouse. New Haven, Connecticut: Yale University Press, 1939. 202p. maps. bibliog. (Yale University Publications in Anthropology, no. 21). (Reprinted, New Haven, Connecticut: HRAF Press, 1964).

A highly technical study of pottery, flint, and stone artifacts from archaeological sites in Haiti. 'This paper reports a study made in the Laboratory for Prehistoric Archaeology of the Peabody Museum, Yale University, of some twelve thousand specimens from the region around Fort Liberté Bay, Haiti. The specimens were obtained by F. G. Rainey, assisted by [Rouse] during the course of three months' excavation in eleven sites near Fort Liberté Bay in 1935'.

Historic sites

La Navidad

123 **Initial encounters: Arawak responses to European contact at the En Bas Saline site, Haiti.**
Kathleen Deagan. In: *Columbus and his world; proceedings of the First San Salvador Conference, held October 30-November 3, 1986, at the College Center of the Finger Lakes, Bahamian Field Station, San Salvador Island, Bahamas.* Compiled by Donald T. Gerace. Fort Lauderdale, Florida: The Station, 1987, p. 341-54, map. bibliog.
Summarizes the results of three years of archaeological research at the site where, it is believed, Columbus established the tiny fortress-colony of La Navidad in the town of Guacanacaric, the Arawak chieftain who assisted the Admiral and his men following the wreck of the *Santa Maria* in December 1492. Guacanacaric and his people were thus the first native Americans to encounter European settlers in the Caribbean. Much information about the Arawaks has been culled from the site. Deagan describes the history of the site itself, and the archaeological evidence that points to it as the location of La Navidad.

124 **Searching for Columbus's lost colony.**
Kathleen A. Deagan. *National Geographic*, vol. 172, no. 5 (Nov. 1987), p. 672-75.
The wreck of the *Santa Maria* on a coral reef off the north coast of Haiti (near the present town of Bord de Mer de Limonade) led to the establishment of the settlement/ fort of La Navidad on December 26 1492. The crewmen left there by Columbus thus became the first Spanish settlers in the New World. When Columbus returned eleven months later, La Navidad had been razed to the ground and the Spaniards had vanished. This article reports on the discovery of archaeological evidence that is believed to indicate the site of La Navidad.

125 **The route of Columbus along the north coast of Haiti and the site of Navidad.**
Samuel E. Morison. *Transactions of the American Philosophical Society*, n.s., vol. 31, pt. 4 (Dec. 1940), p. 239-85. maps.
Presents an engrossing account of a scholarly adventure. 'During the month of January, 1939, [Morison] made a personal reconnaissance of the north coast of Haiti, in order to ascertain the exact course of Christopher Columbus on his First Voyage and to identify, if possible, the site of Navidad, the first settlement attempted by Europeans in the New World. . . . These investigations accompanied by an intensive study of the relevant documents and ancient maps enabled [Morison] to arrive at a fairly definitve conclusion as to the reef where the *Santa Maria* was wrecked and the site of Navidad'.

Puerto Real

126 **From Spaniard to Creole: the archaeology of cultural formation at
Puerto Real, Haiti.**
Charles R. Ewen. Tuscaloosa, Alabama: The University of Alabama
Press, 1991. 155p. maps. bibliog.
Offers a fresh perspective on new archaeological evidence in this study of culture
contact and cultural change. Based on investigations on the site of Puerto Real, a
Spanish settlement founded on the north coast of Haiti in 1503, abandoned in 1578,
and rediscovered in 1974, Ewen is able to depict the life led by Hispaniola's first
European settlers as they interacted with their new environment. He states that
'through the combination and exchange of Old World and New World cultural and
physical elements, the colonists created an adaptive tradition that characterized the
pioneer Spanish settlements and represented the earliest expression of Hispanic-
American culture'.

127 **The short, unhappy life of a maverick Caribbean colony.**
Charles R. Ewen. *Archaeology*, vol. 41, no. 4 (July/August 1988),
p. 41-46. map.
A popular presentation of life in the Spanish town of Puerto Real on Haiti's north
coast, as revealed by the University of Florida's archaeological excavation of the site.
Interpretation of data derived from the site shows that although life in the colonial city
was outwardly Spanish, in private the colonists blended Hispanic with native traditions.
Puerto Real flourished between 1503 and 1578, when the Spanish metropolitan
government ordered that it it be abandoned because of its participation in illegal trade
with the French, English and Portuguese. Excellent colour photographs of artifacts
recovered from the site enhance the text.

128 **Sub-surface patterning at Puerto Real: a 16th century town on Haiti's
north coast.**
Maurice W. Williams. *Journal of Field Archaeology*, vol. 13 (1986),
p. 281-96. maps.
Reproduces results of a sub-surface testing and contour mapping project carried out in
1982 on the site of Puerto Real in preparation for future archaeological investigations.
This is a professional study, but some details of life in a sixteenth-century Spanish
colonial town which may be of interest to the layman can be gleaned from this article.

History

General

129 Etudes sur l'histoire d'Haïti suivies de la vie du général J.-M. Borgella.
(Studies on the history of Haiti, followed by the life of General J.-M. Borgella.)
Beaubrun Ardouin. Edited by Francois Dalencour. Port-au-Prince: F. Dalencour, 1958, 2. ed. conforme au texte original, annotée et precedée d'une notice biographique sur B. Ardouin par Francois Dalencour. 11 vols in 1.

Beaubrun Ardouin (1796-1865) was a Haitian statesman and diplomat who, while in exile in France during the Soulouque régime, expanded Thomas Madiou's *Histoire d'Haiti* (q.v.) through research in French archives. His work was originally published in Paris, 1853-60.

130 Histoire du peuple haïtien, 1492-1952. (History of the Haitian people, 1492-1952.)
Dantès Bellegarde. Port-au-Prince: 1953. 365p. (Collection du tricinquantenaire de l'independance d'Haïti).

This work is generally considered to be a balanced history of Haiti. The Constitution of 1950 is appended.

131 Port-au-Prince au cours des ans. (Port-au-Prince through the years.)
George Corvington, Jr. Port-au-Prince: Impr. H. Deschamps, 1972. 2. ed. 7 vols.

A historical survey of the growth and development of Haiti's capital. The volumes are: vol. 1: *La ville coloniale, 1743-1789*; vol. 2: *Sous les assauts de la Révolution, 1789-1804*; vol. 3: *La métropole haitienne du XIXe siècle, 1804-1888*; vol. 4: *La métropole haitienne du XIXe siècle, 1888-1915*; vol. 5: *La capitale d'Haïti sous l'occupation, 1915-1922*; vol. 6: *La capitale d'Haïti sous l'occupation, 1922-1934*; and vol. 7: *La ville moderne, 1915-1950.*

132   **Black democracy: the story of Haiti.**
      H. P. Davis, preface by Alec Waugh.   New York: Dodge, 1936.
      rev. ed. 360p. maps. bibliog. (Reprinted, New York: Biblio & Tannen,
      1967).
Readers of Haitian history will often see *Black democracy* listed as a source. Its author, H. P. Davis, was an American whose business interests took him to Haiti during the US military occupation. In his book, first published in 1928 and revised in 1931 and 1936, Davis attempts an impartial history of Haiti. Haitians who have commented on the work remark on Davis's sympathy for their country, but criticize several of his views.

133   **Haiti and its institutions from colonial times to 1957.**
      Max H. Dorsinville.   In: *The Haitian potential; research and resources of Haiti.* Edited by Vera Rubin, Richard P. Schaedel.   New York: Teachers College Press, 1975, p. 183-220. (Publications of the Center for Education in Latin America).
A compact and lucid historical survey.

134   **Cuba, Haiti and the Dominican Republic.**
      James E. Fagg.   Englewood Cliffs, New Jersey: Prentice-Hall, 1965.
      181p. map. bibliog. (Modern Nations in Historical Perspective).
Contains an undergraduate-level political history of these three countries. The main part of the book narrates the history of Cuba. The section on Haiti (p. 113-39) summarizes the main points of the nation's history from colonial times to 1961. A critical bibliography refers the student to further reading.

135   **Guide des sources de l'histoire de l'Amérique latine et des Antilles dans les archives françaises.** (Guide to sources for the history of Latin America and the Antilles in French archives.)
      France. Archives nationales.   Paris: Archives Nationales, 1984. 711p. bibliog.
Several centuries of historical documentation on Latin America and the West Indies await researchers in the archives of France; those interested in Haitian history will find this volume an invaluable aid. Designed as a 'fil d'Ariane' to lead the seeker through the labyrinth of French depositories, it is not an inventory of holdings but a guide, providing the researcher with the contents of important collections. Descriptions are provided for the National Archives, and for the archives of departments, communes, the French National Assembly and Senate and government ministries. Published archives, private papers and missionary archives are also described. The book includes two useful lists of those interested in the history of Haiti: 'Gouverneurs de Saint-Domingue, 1641-1802'; and 'French representatives to Haiti, 24 août 1825 to 17 octobre 1952'.

136   **Santo Domingo, past and present: with a glance at Hayti.**
Samuel Hazard.   London: S. Low, Marston, Low & Searle; New
York: Harper & Brothers, 1873. 511p. map. bibliog. (Reprinted, Santo
Domingo, Dominican Republic: Editora de Santo Domingo, S.A.,
1974; New York: Gordon Press, 1976).

A combined history and travelogue that begins with Columbus's discovery of
Hispaniola in 1492 and ends with an account of the author's visit to the island in 1871.
Hazard, who was an artist as well as a writer, provides a fresh and sympathetic view of
Haiti, which is enhanced with charming illustrations.

137   **Written in blood: the story of the Haitian people, 1492-1971.**
Robert D. Heinl, Jr., Nancy Gordon Heinl.   Boston, Massachusetts:
Houghton Mifflin, 1978. 785p. maps. bibliog.

Presents a massive journalistic history of Haiti, from the arrival of Columbus in 1492 to
the death of François Duvalier in 1971. The authors do not hesitate to recount the
horrors of Haitian history, including several shocking episodes that took place during
Duvalier's administration.

138   **Haiti: her history and her detractors.**
Jacques Nicolas Leger.   New York; Washington, DC: Neale, 1907.
372p. Reprinted, Westport, Connecticut: Negro Universities Press,
1970; New York: Gordon Press, 1976.

The author, a former Haitian minister to the United States, defends his country in this
general narrative of Haiti from its discovery by Columbus to the presidency of Nord
Alexis.

139   **Guide des sources de l'histoire d'Amérique latine conservées en
Belgique.** (Guide to sources for the history of Latin America preserved
in Belgium.)
Leone Liagre, Jean Baerten.   Brussells: Archives Générales du
Royaume, 1967. 132p. bibliog. (Guide des Sources de l'Hiostoire des
Nations, A.: Amérique Latine, fasc. 3, 1).

This is a guide to documents held in Belgian libraries and archives. Haitian material
can be found through the index.

140   **Haiti and the Dominican Republic.**
Rayford W. Logan.   New York; London: Oxford University Press for
the Royal Institute of International Affairs, 1968. 220p. map. bibliog.

This succinct, clearly written book is, according to its author, the first comparative
history of Haiti and the Dominican Republic from their colonial origins to the 1960s.
The work is divided into three sections: the first covers physical geography and
population; the second, history and contemporary politics; the third, social and
economic conditions. In his last chapter, 'The two countries compared', Logan
summarizes the basic differences between the two nations.

History. General

141 **Documentos para la historia de Haiti en el Archivo Nacional [de Cuba].**
(Documents for the history of Haiti in the National Archives [of
Cuba].)
Edited by Jose Luciano Franco. Havana: Archivo Nacional de Cuba,
1954. 259p. (Publicaciones del Archivo Nacional de Cuba, 37).
Provides a source for those materials pertaining to Haitian history which can be found
in Cuba's National Archives.

142 **Histoire d'Haïti.** (History of Haiti.)
Thomas Madiou. Port-au-prince: Editions Henri Deschamps, 1989-
1991. 8 vols.
Madiou was a nineteenth-century scholar who also played a role in Haiti's government
and foreign relations. This new volume, containing his important historical work
combines a reissue of earlier work with the first publication of material that had been
left in manuscript form at his death. Pradel Pompilus explains in his introduction to
Volume 4 of this set that Madiou published the first, second and third volumes of his
work in 1847 and 1848 and that the Madiou family issued out a fourth volume in 1904.
The manuscript parts of Madiou's history were inherited by his descendants. This vast
work, which consists of more than 4,000 pages, traces Haitian history from 1492 to
1846. Volume 8 includes a 'Postface' by Michèle Oriol in which she writes on Madiou
as a historian. The scholarly value of the work is enhanced by an index of personal
names and places, texts of documents included in appendices to the volumes and well-
selected illustrations.

143 **Historical dictionary of Haiti.**
Roland I. Perusse. Metuchen, New Jersey: Scarecrow Press, 1977.
124p. maps. bibliog. (Latin American Historical Dictionaries, no. 15).
A useful reference aid. Short definitions of terms pertaining to Haitian biography,
geography, history, sociology, diplomacy, politics, and culture are arranged alphabetically, from Acaau to Zombi. A chronology to 1974, a list of Haitian chiefs of state,
1804-1971, a seven-page bibliographical essay, and 'a highly selective list of one
hundred of the most useful titles with respect to Haiti and Haitian life' are also
included.

144 **Haiti: monuments historiques et archéologiques.** (Haiti: historical and
archaeological monuments.)
Catts Pressoir. Mexico City: Instituto Panamericano de Geografía e
Historia, 1952. 32p. map. (Instituto Panamericano de Geografía e
Historia, 143; Comision de Historia, 41; Monumentos Historicos y
arqueologícos, 5).
A helpful pamphlet also contains a detailed map of those sites of archaeological and
historical interest in Haiti.

145 **Historiographie d'Haïti.** (Historiography of Haiti.)
Catts Pressoir, Ernst Trouillot, Henock Trouillot. Mexico City:
Editorial Fournier, 1953. 298p. bibliog. (Instituto Panamericano de
Geografía e Historia. Comision de Historia, Publ. 66; Historiografias,
Vol. 1; Instituto Panamericano de Geografía e Historia, Publ. 168).
Evaluates historical writing on Haiti and supplies biographical information on Haitian
historians. The majority of the works discussed are in French or Spanish, and deal with
pre-twentieth-century Haiti, although some books in English are included.

146 **The Alfred Nemours collection of Haitian history: a catalogue.**
Edited by Jane Toth, William A. Trembley. *Caribbean Studies*,
vol. 2, no. 3 (Oct. 1962), p. 61-70.
In 1962 General Alfred Nemours, an expert on Toussaint Louverture and his family,
donated his collection of materials – books, pamphlets, documents, paintings and
prints – pertaining to the history of Haiti to the University of Puerto Rico. Nemours
was greatly interested in the 1791-1806 period, and his collection reflects this. The
authors of this article have compiled an unannotated list of these pieces.

Colonial Hispaniola (Española) and Saint-Domingue 1492-1791

147 **The origins of abolition in Santo Domingo.**
George W. Brown. *The Journal of Negro History*, vol. 7, no. 4
(Oct. 1922), p. 365-76.
This narrative account, which is drawn from printed sources, outlines the context
within which slave emancipation took place in France's West Indian colony of Saint-
Domingue. Although somewhat imprecise when citing dates, this article forms a useful
summary of the background and process that led to the abolition of slavery in the
colony.

148 **Histoire de l'Île Espagnole ou Saint-Dominique, écrite particulièrement
sur les mémoires manuscrits du P. Jean-Baptiste Lepers, Jésuite
Missionaire à Saint-Dominique, et sur les pièces originales qui se
conservent au Dépôt de la Marine.** (History of the island of Hispaniola
or Saint-Domingue, based on the manuscript memoirs of Father Jean-
Baptiste Lepers, Jesuit missonary at Saint-Domingue, and on original
documents preserved at the Dépôt de la Marine.)
Pierre Francois Xavier de Charlevoix. Paris: Guerin, 1730-31. 2 vols.
The standard work on early Saint-Domingue, written by a Jesuit priest.

149 **French pioneers in the West Indies, 1624-1664.**
Nellis M. Crouse.   New York: Columbia University Press, 1940. 294p.
maps. bibliog. (Reprinted, New York: Octagon, 1972).

Presents a reliable account of the first phase of French penetration into the West Indies. A chapter on Tortuga (Île de la Tortue) discusses its role as headquarters for French buccaneers. These adventurers brought a French presence to the Spanish Main, and their island camp served as the site from which the French were to challenge Spanish domination of Hispaniola. Students of the period will also find Crouse's book useful for its critically annotated bibliography of the printed sources upon which it is based.

150 **The French struggle for the West Indies, 1665-1713.**
Nellis M. Crouse.   New York: Columbia University Press, 1943. 324p.
bibliog. (Reprinted, New York: Octagon, 1966).

A sequel to the author's *French pioneers in the West Indies, 1624-1664* (q.v.). Saint-Domingue is discussed in context and a specific chapter entitled 'Haitian interlude' is also included.

151 **The Declaration of the Rights of Man in Saint-Domingue, 1788-1791.**
Philip D. Curtin.   *The Hispanic American Historical Review*, vol. 30, no. 2 (May 1950), p. 157-75.

Discusses how each segment of society in the French colony Saint-Domingue – white colonists, *gens de couleur* and black slaves – interpreted the Declaration of the Rights of Man, 'the epitome of revolutionary ideas', when it was proclaimed in the mother country.

152 **Le Maniel: further notes.**
Yvan Debbasch.   In: *Maroon societies: rebel slave communities in the Americas.* Edited by Richard Price.   Baltimore, Maryland: Johns Hopkins University Press, 1979, 2d ed., p. 143-48.

An abbreviated English translation of Debbasch's 'Le marronage: essai sur la désertion de l'esclave antillais' ('The maroons: an essay on Antillean slave desertion') *L'Année sociologique*, (1961), p. 1-112; (1962), p. 117-95. Debbasch discusses Le Maniel, a settlement founded by runaway slaves in southern Saint-Domingue.

153 **Les engagés pour les Antilles (1634-1715).** (Indentured emigration to the Antilles [1634-1715].)
Gabriel Debien.   Paris: Société de l'histoire des colonies françaises, 1952. 277p. (Bibliothèque d'histoire coloniale, nouv. sér.).

One of the few studies to examine this aspect of the method by which the French colonies in the West Indies – including Saint-Domingue – were populated. The author concludes that it was mainly as a result of migration by French men and women as indentured servants to the islands in the seventeenth and early eighteenth centuries.

154 **Les esclaves aux Antilles françaises, XVIIe-XVIIIe siècles.** (Slaves in the
French Antilles, 17th and 18th centuries.)
Gabriel Debien. Basse-Terre: Société de'Histoire de la Guadeloupe;
Fort-de-France: Société d'Histoire de la Martinique, 1974. 529p. map.
bibliog.
This is Debien's most comprehensive work on the conditions under which the slaves
lived and worked in France's West Indian colonies. Drawing on many earlier studies,
Debien assembles detailed information on the slaves' diet, health, work, housing,
religion, ethnicity and resistance to slavery.

155 **Études antillaises: XVIIIe siècle.** (Antillean studies: 18th century.)
Gabriel Debien. Paris: Colin, 1956. 186p. map. (Cahiers des Annales,
11).
This volume brings together two of Debien's many studies on the social and economic
life of colonial Saint-Domingue: 'Dans un quartier neuf de Saint-Domingue: un colon,
une caféière (1743-1799)' ('In a new section of Saint-Domingue: a settler, a coffee
plantation (1743-1799)'), and 'Les débuts de la Révolution à Saint-Domingue, vus des
plantations Bréda' ('The beginnings of the Saint-Domingue revolution, as seen from
the Breda plantations').

156 **Marronage in the French Caribbean.**
Gabriel Debien. In: *Maroon societies: rebel slave communities in the
Americas.* Edited by Richard Price. Baltimore, Maryland: Johns
Hopkins University Press, 1979, 2d ed., p. 107-34. bibliog.
An edited translation of Debien's essay 'Le marronage aux Antilles Françaises au
XVIIIe siècle', *Caribbean Studies*, vol. 6, no. 3 (Oct. 1966), p. 3-44. Debien describes
the activities of bands of fugitive slaves in Saint-Domingue as well as in other islands of
the Caribbean, mentioning the decrees issued against marronage, punishments meted
out to runaways and attempts to control the slaves and prevent desertion.

157 **Une plantation de Saint-Domingue: la sucrerie Galbaud de Fort
(1690-1802).** (A Saint-Domingue plantation: the Galbaud du Fort sugar
estate [1690-1802].)
Gabriel Debien. Cairo: Presses de l'Institut Français d'Archéologie
du Caire, 1941. 136p. maps. bibliog.
Debien makes brilliant use of manuscript sources in this study of the Galbaud-Dufort
family's sugar plantation in Saint-Domingue. He is also the author of a number of
other studies of individual colonial estates, among them *Plantations et esclaves à Saint-
Domingue: sucrerie Cottineau* (Dakar, 1962), a study of the Cottineau plantation, 1750-
1777 and *Plantations et esclaves à Saint-Domingue: sucrerie Foache* (Dakar, 1962), a
study of the estate of Stanislas Foache at Jean-Rabel. For Debien's extensive writings
on colonial plantation life, see the listings in Laguerre's *Complete Haitiana* (q.v.),
vol. 1, p. 205-14.

158 **The free people of color in Louisiana and St. Domingue: a comparative portrait of two three-caste slave societies.**
Laura Foner. *Journal of Social History*, vol. 3, no. 4 (summer 1970), p. 406-30.

Foner compares and contrasts the racial patterns that marked the treatment and social position of the ex-slave in slave societies, as exemplified by colonial Louisiana and Saint-Domingue. She discusses the creation of a free coloured population – a third caste between whites and blacks – through interracial sexual relations between master and slave and subsequent manumission, and finds that both demographical and cultural factors controlled social attitudes toward the ex-slave. Although the colour line in a three-caste society was flexible, it remained a source of tension. The contrast made in this article between the social position of the free people of colour in Louisiana and those in Saint-Domingue is instructive, although in both cases the free-coloured caste was used by the whites as a buffer group between themselves and the black slaves.

159 **The Haitian maroons: liberty or death.**
Jean Fouchard, translated from the French by A. Faulkner Watts, with a preface by C. L. R. James. New York: Edward W. Blyden Press, 1981. 386p. map.

This comprehensive work on the runaway slaves or maroons is based on research in the newspapers of colonial Saint-Domingue and makes a major contribution to the knowledge of this phase in Haitian history. Fouchard covers the conditions of slavery, characterizes the maroons and provides an analysis of marronage. C. L. R. James writes in his preface that 'Fouchard establishes that the Haitian nation, the result of the only successful slave revolt in history, was formed, organized, and maintained by the maroons, the slaves who had run away from the slave society organized by the Metropolitan forces and made a place for themselves in the inaccessible hills'.

160 **The major port towns of Saint Domingue in the late eighteenth century.**
David Geggus. In: *Atlantic port cities: economy, culture, and society in the Atlantic world, 1650-1850*. Edited by Franklin W. Knight, Peggy K. Liss. Knoxville, Tennessee: University of Tennessee Press, 1991, p. 87-116.

A heavily-documented study of Port-au-Prince and Cap Français, colonial Saint-Domingue's largest commercial and trading centres. Geggus concentrates on the period between the American and French revolutions, and, making use of all available data, details the trade and commerce, defence, administration and population of the two cities.

161 **On the eve of the Haitian revolution: slave runaways in Saint Domingue in the year 1790.**
David Geggus. In: *Out of the house of bondage: runaways, resistance and marronage in Africa and the New World*. Edited by Gad Heuman. London: Cass, 1986, p. 112-28.

The fugitive slave occupies a controversial position in Haitian history. Historians are divided over whether the *marrons* played a central or a peripheral role during the colonial period and the Haitian Revolution. In this essay, Geggus selects data from the main colonial newspaper, the *Affiches Américaines*, in order to determine the number of fugitive slaves in Saint-Domingue in 1790. According to the newspaper's reports, 2020 runaways were jailed and 632 were advertised as missing. By analysing these fugitives by sex, ethnicity, age and occupation, Geggus makes a valuable contribution to the small amount of material available on slave runaways in Saint-Domingue.

162 **L'esclavage aux Antilles françaises (17e-19e siècle): contribution au problème de l'esclavage.** (Slavery in the French Antilles [17th-19th century]: a contribution to the problem of slavery.)
Antoine Gisler. Fribourg, Switzerland: Editions Universitaires, 1965. 213p. bibliog. (Studia Friburgensia. Nouv. Ser. 42). (Reprinted, Paris: Karthala, 1981).
Examines the experience of slavery in the French colonies within the larger context of the question of the legitimization of the social institution of slavery itself. Gisler provides a detailed analysis of the sixty articles of the 1685 *Edit du roi concernant la discipline de l'église et l'état et la qualité des nègres esclaves aux Îles de l'Amérique* (the *Code Noir*), showing how this law was applied in practice. Several chapters discuss the Roman Catholic clergy in relation to slavery. The book is well-documented and is based on both archival and printed materials.

163 **The West Indian slave-laws of the eighteenth century.**
Elsa V. Goveia. *Revista de Ciencias Sociales*, vol. 4, no. 1 (March 1960), p. 75-105.
An accessible study for those English-language readers who are interested in learning about the slave law enforced by the French in Saint-Domingue. The author examines the *Code Noir* on pages 92-103, summarizing its most important clauses and contrasting it with British and Spanish slave laws. This article was reissued in a separate publication by the Caribbean Universities Press in 1970 (*The West Indian slave laws of the 18th century*, by Elsa V. Goveia [and] *A new balance of power: the 19th century*, by C. J. Barlett).

164 **Saint-Domingue.**
Gwendolyn Midlo Hall. In: *Neither slave nor free: the freedman of African descent in the slave societies of the New World.* Edited with an introduction by David W. Cohen, Jack P. Grene. Baltimore, Maryland: Johns Hopkins University Press, 1972, p. 172-92.
Discusses the social position of free coloured subjects in Saint-Domingue. Hall notes that it was not racial attitudes, but rather fundamental military, economic, social and political concerns which were crucial in determining the policy followed in regard to slave affranchisement in the French colony. Her valuable contribution to the subject covers illegal forms of emancipation, slave control of the market, racism as an instrument of social and political domination, the origin of the colonial élite, social conflict between coloured and white élites, and the manipulation of racial conflict in the face of the threat of independence.

165   **Social control in slave plantation societies: a comparison of St. Domingue and Cuba.**
Gertrude Midlo Hall.   Baltimore, Maryland: Johns Hopkins Press, 1971. 166p. bibliog. (Johns Hopkins Studies in Historical and Political Science, series 89, no. 1).

A comparative history of two colonial slave systems – eighteenth-century Saint-Domingue and nineteenth-century Cuba – which were established under European governments. Hall highlights the problem of the slave control as being of paramount importance to these systems. The metropolitan governments supported 'humane' modifications to slavery that would stabilize the systems, and thus came into conflict with the planters, anxious to exploit all opportunities for gain. Chapters are entitled: 'The problem of survival of the slave population'; 'Magic, witchcraft, and religion'; 'Black resistance and white repression'; 'Protective aspects of slave law'; 'Emancipation and the status of the free'; and 'Racism as an instrument of social and political domination'.

166   **The buccaneers in the West Indies in the XVII century.**
C. H. Haring.   New York: Dutton, 1910. 298p. maps, bibliog.
Reprinted, Hamden, Connecticut: Archon Books, 1966.

This well-researched study, presented as the author's thesis in Modern History at Oxford University in 1909, remains a good English-language source of information on Hispaniola in the 17th century.

167   **The memoirs of Père Labat, 1693-1705.**
Jean-Baptiste Labat, translated from the French and abridged by John Eaden, with an introduction by Philip Gosse.   London: Constable, 1931. 262p. Reprinted, London: Cass, 1970. (Cass Library of West Indian Studies, no. 8).

Le Père Labat travelled to the West Indies as a missionary. Most of his career was spent in Guadeloupe and Martinique, but he visited Saint-Domingue in 1700, arriving at Cap François and visiting several towns on the island. His eight-volume chronicle of his adventures in the West Indies, *Nouveau Voyage aux Îles de l'Amérique*, first published in 1722, is considered to be of value for its detailed descriptions of the social and economic life of the Caribbean, as well as for Labat's candid observations. In this abridged version, the section on Haiti begins on p. 143. The complete work is not available in English.

168   **The relationship between marronage and slave revolts and revolution in Saint-Domingue-Haiti.**
Leslie F. Manigat.   In: *Comparative perspectives on slavery in New World plantation societies*. Edited by Vera Rubin, Arthur Tuden.
New York: New York Academy of Sciences, 1977, p. 420-38. (Annals of the New York Academy of Sciences, vol. 292).

Manigat states that 'the starting point for this study must be an attempt to define marronage in St. Domingue and to review the perception of marronage held by observers and students who have tried to assess it'. This chapter provides a lucid examination of marronage and the maroons, as well as of the ideological viewpoints and motivations of scholars and historians who have debated the subject.

169 The early years of the French Revolution in San Domingue.
Herbert E. Mills. Poughkeepsie, New York: A. V. Haight, 1892. 98p.

Presented as the author's thesis at Cornell University in 1889, Mills' study remains the most detailed account of the failed mulatto insurrection in Saint-Domingue led by Vincent Ogé in 1790. The part played by the mulattoes in unrest in Saint-Domingue is also treated in Chapter 4 of Shelby T. McCloy's *Negro in the French West Indies* (Lexington, Kentucky: University of Kentucky Press, 1966).

170 The border maroons of Saint-Domingue: Le Maniel.
Médéric-Louis-Elie Moreau de Saint-Méry. In: *Maroon societies: rebel slave communities in the Americas*. Edited by Richard Price. Baltimore, Maryland: Johns Hopkins University Prss, 1979, 2d ed., p. 135-42.

An English translation of Moreau de Saint-Méry's account of eighteenth-century military expeditions undertaken by colonists against maroon settlements in southern Saint-Domingue. The account is taken from the first edition of Moreau's *Description topographique, physique, civile, politique et historique de la partie française de l'isle Saint-Domingue* (Philadelphia: published by the author, 1797-98), vol. 2, p. 497-503.

171 A civilization that perished: the last years of white colonial rule in Haiti: a topographical, physical, civil, political and historical description of the French part of the island of Santo Domingo with general observations on its population, on the character and customs of its diverse inhabitants, on climate, culture, production, administration, etc.
Médéric-Louis-Elie Moreau de Saint-Méry, translated from the French and abridged and edited by Ivor D. Spencer. Lanham, Maryland: University Press of America, 1985. 295p. bibliog.

A drastically abridged version of Moreau de Saint-Méry's two-volume *Description topographique, physique, civile, politique et historique de la partie française de l'isle Saint-Domingue* (q.v.), published between 1797 and 1798. This is the first appearance of the work in English, and although it is not a scholarly edition and translates only one-seventh of the French text, it will be of interest to students of Haitian history. Spencer provides an introduction to the volume in which he discusses Moreau and his book.

172 Description topographique, physique, civile, politique et historique de la partie française de l'isle Saint-Domingue. (Topographical, physical, civil, and historical descriptions of the French part of the island of Saint-Domingue.)
Médéric-Louis-Elie Moreau de Saint-Méry. Edited by Blanche Mauriel, Etienne Taillemite. Paris: Société de l'Histoire des Colonies Françaises, 1958, Nouv. éd. entièrement rev. et completé sur le manuscrit. 3 vols. maps. bibliog. (Bibliothèque d'Histoire Coloniale, Nouv. Sér.). Reprinted, Paris: Société Française d'Histoire d'Outre-mer, 1984. (Bibliothèque d'Histoire d'Outre-mer).

Moreau de Saint-Méry's detailed, descriptive masterpiece is the major primary printed source for the social and economic life of the French colony of Saint-Domingue. This is a modern text of the work that, based on a re-examination of Moreau's manuscripts preserved in France's National Archives, restores suppressed passages; it is not, however, a reprint of the edition which was published by Moreau in Philadelphia in 1797. The editors provide a biography of Moreau and a list of the manuscript and printed sources which have been used in this edition.

173 **The Caribbean as Columbus saw it.**
Samuel Eliot Morison, Mauricio Obregon.   Boston, Massachusetts: Little, Brown, 1964. 252p. maps.
The fifth chapter of this work, entitled 'Hispaniola', is a readable summary of Columbus's voyages around, and sojourns in, what is now Haiti.

174 **L'esclavage aux Antilles françaises avant 1789.** (Slavery in the French Antilles before 1789.)
Lucien Peytraud.   Paris: Hachette, 1897. 472p. bibliog.
Peytraud's book remains an excellent account of slavery in the French colonies before the French Revolution. The volume also contains the complete French text of Louis XIV's 1685 edict regulating the treatment of slaves in the colonies that became known as the *Code Noir*.

175 **La Révolution française et l'abolition de l'esclavage.** (The French Revolution and the abolition of slavery.)
Paris: Editions d'Histoire Sociale, 1968. 12 vols.
A fascimile collection of eighty-nine anti-slavery texts in French – pamphlets, speeches, laws, and decrees – which were printed between 1770 and 1798. Materials in the first five volumes deplore the treatment of slaves and the institution of slavery in France's colonies. Volumes six to nine contain the publications of the abolitionist organization, La Société des Amis des Noirs. Volumes ten and eleven document the revolt of the slaves in the West Indies, and volumes eleven and twelve reprint the nine laws and decrees of the National Assembly and of the National Convention relating to the abolition of slavery. Toussaint Louverture's 'Constitution de la colonie française de Saint-Domingue, du 17 août 1801 (29 thermidor an 9)' is included in volume eleven.

176 **The French in the West Indies.**
W. Adolphe Roberts.   Indianapolis, Indiana: Bobbs-Merrill, 1942. 335p. bibliog. Reprinted, New York: Cooper Square, 1971.
Presents a narrative history of the French colonies in the Caribbean from the 1500s to 1942. Saint-Domingue receives two chapters: 'Opulent Saint-Domingue', and 'The French Revolution in Saint-Domingue and the Leclerc debacle'.

177 **A Creole succession: the Saint-Domingue properties of the Comtesse d'Ampus and the Marechale de Levis, 1678-1803.**
Elizabeth L. Saxe.   In: *Working papers in Haitian society and culture.* Edited by Sidney W. Mintz.   New Haven, Connecticut: Yale University, Antilles Research Program, 1975, p. 1-33. (Occasional Papers, no. 4).
Provides a substantial study of plantation life in colonial Saint-Domingue.

178 **Bibliography of Saint-Domingue: especially for the period of 1700-1804.**
Magdaline W. Shannon. *Revue de la Société Haitienne d'Histoire,
Géographie et Géologie*, vol. 37, no. 125 (Dec. 1979), p. 5-55.
A guide to literature on the history of the French colony and on the Haitian War of
Independence.

179 **The abolition of slavery in the North, West, and South of Saint
Domingue.**
Robert Stein. *The Americas*, vol. 41, no. 3 (Jan. 1985), p. 47-55.
Attempts to provide an exact chronology of the events pertaining to the emancipation
of the slaves in Saint-Domingue's three provinces – a subject about which much
confusion exists – and 'to show that [abolition] was due primarily to the efforts of one
man, Léger Félicité Sonthonax, aided somewhat reluctantly by Etienne Polverel'.
Stein's conclusions are based on careful study of documents in the French National
Archives.

180 **Léger Félicité Sonthonax: the lost sentinel of the Republic.**
Robert Louis Stein. Rutherford, New Jersey: Fairleigh Dickinson
University Press, 1985. 234p. bibliog.
Supplies a biography of Sonthonax, appointed Civil Commissioner in Saint-Domingue
by the Terror régime, who abolished slavery in the North province of the colony on
August 29, 1793. Stein uses primary sources to re-evaluate Sonthonax's contribution to
this period of Haitian history.

181 **Saint-Domingue; la société et la vie créoles sous l'ancien régime (1629-
1789).** (Saint-Domingue; Creole life and society under the monarchy
[1629-1789].)
Pierre de Vaissière. Paris: Perrin et Cie., 1909. 384p. map.
This excellent, modern, scholarly monograph details the social organization of Saint-
Domingue during the colonial era.

182 **Saint-Domingue à la veille de la révolution: souvenirs du Baron de
Wimpffen: annotés d'après les documents d'archives et les mémoires
[avec] illustrations documentaires.** (Saint-Domingue on the eve of the
revolution: souvenirs of Baron de Wimpffen: annotated according to
archival materials and memoirs [with] documentary illustrations.)
François Alexandre Stanislas, Baron de Wimpffen, edited by Albert
Savine. Paris: La Michaud, 1911. 190p. map. (Collection historique
illustrée).
The Baron de Wimpffen was a German aristocrat of French upbringing who travelled
to Saint-Domingue shortly before the French Revolution. In his memoirs he relates his
observations of Saint-Dominguan society during the last years of the colonial era.

183 **A voyage to Saint Domingo in the years 1788, 1789 and 1790.**
François Alexandre Stanislas, Baron de Wimpffen, translated from the original French manuscript by J. Wright. London: Cadell & Davies, 1799. 371p. map.
A valuable contemporary account translated from an unpublished manuscript.

Haitian Revolution 1791-1804

184 **Black liberator: the life of Toussaint Louverture.**
Stéphen Alexis, translated from the French by William Stirling. New York: Macmillan, 1949. 227p. map. bibliog. Reprinted, 1970.
This biography of Toussaint Louverture was the first written by a Haitian to appear in English. Alexis's undocumented account of Haiti's national hero is both sympathetic and objective.

185 **History of the island of St. Domingo, from its first discovery by Columbus to the present period.**
Sir James Barskett, with a new preface to the reprint by Robert I. Rotberg. London: Constable, 1818. 446p. Reprinted, London: F. Cass, 1972. (Source Books on Haiti, no. 1).
Covers the Spanish period; early French and British struggles for control of the island (with the French succeeding in taking possession); the revolution and wars that began in 1789; and the independent reigns of Henry Christophe and Alexandre Pétion. The work is particularly informative when describing the British involvement in Saint-Domingue, since its author was the commander of a British naval vessel. A reprint of the first edition, published anonymously in London in 1818. Rodberg states in his preface that 'Admiral Sir James Barskett has long been assumed to be [the book's] author'.

186 **The life of Toussaint L'Ouverture, the Negro patriot of Hayti: comprising an account of the struggle for liberty in the island, and a sketch of its history to the present period.**
John Relly Beard. London: Ingram, Cooke & Co., 1853. 335p. map. (Reprinted, Westport, Connecticut: Negro Universities Press, 1970).
An unabridged reprint of Rev. John R. Beard's biography of Toussaint Louverture.

187 **Toussaint L'Ouverture: a biography and autobiography.**
John Relly Beard, edited by James Redpath. Boston, Massachusetts:
Redpath, 1863. 366p. Reprinted, Freeport, New York: Books for
Libraries, 1971. (Black Heritage Library Collections.) Reprinted,
Salem, New Hampshire: Ayer Company, 1991.
James Redpath omitted sections of Beard's *Life of Toussaint L'Ouverture, the Negro
patriot of Hayti* (q.v.) in this reprint, but did append 'Memoirs of Toussaint
L'Ouverture', taken from Saint-Remy's *Memories du général Toussaint-Louverture,
ecrits par lui-meme* (Paris, 1853) and 'Notes and testimonies'.

188 **The black rebellion in Haiti: the experience of one who was present
during four years of tumult and massacre.**
**Pierre Etienne Chazotte, edited by Charles Platt. Philadelphia:
Privately printed, 1927. 122p.**
Chazotte's graphic eyewitness account of Dessalines' extermination of the French in
1804 was originally published in New York in 1840 as *Historical sketches of the
revolutions, and the foreign and civil wars in the island of St. Domingo, with a narrative
of the entire massacre of the white population of the island.* Both the 1840 and 1927
editions of the book are now rare items.

189 **My odyssey: experiences of a young refugee from two revolutions.**
A Creole of Saint-Domingue, translated from the French and edited by
Althea de Puech Parham, introduction by Selden Rodman. Baton
Rouge, Louisiana: Louisiana State University Press, 1959. 205p. map.
A first-hand account of the early days of the Haitian Revolution written by a
participant who fought on the side of the white planters. The anonymous author, 'P',
an ancestor of the editor-translator, was a white West Indian living in France who fled
the country upon outbreak of the French Revolution, returning to Saint-Domingue just
as the slave revolt erupted in 1791. He emigrated to the United States in 1793,
returned to Saint-Domingue in 1794, and left again for New York in 1798.

190 **Voyage d'un naturaliste en Haiti, 1799-1803.** (The voyage of a naturalist
in Haiti.)
Michel Etienne Descourtilz. Edited by Jacques Boulenger. Paris:
Plon, 1935. 232p. map.
A separate publication of material pertaining to Haiti which has been taken from
Descourtilz's 1809 three-volume *Voyages d'un naturaliste, et ses observations faites sur
les trois règnes de la nature, dans plusieurs ports de mer français, en Espagne, au
continent de l'Amérique septentrionale, à Saint-Yago de Cuba, et à Saint-Domingue, où
l'auteur devenu le prisonnier de 40,000 noirs révoltés, et par suite mis en liberté par une
colonne de l'armée française, donne des détails circonstanciés sur l'expédition du général
Leclerc.* (*Voyages of a naturalist, and his observations on the three kingdoms of nature
in several ports of the French sea, in Spain, in the continent of North America, at Saint-
Yago de Cuba, and in Saint-Domingue, where the author became the prisoner of 40,000
black revolutionaries and was eventually freed by a column of the French army, giving
exact details on the expedition of General Leclerc.*).

191 **Jean-Jacques Dessalines and Charles Belair.**
Maurice de Young. *Journal of Inter-American Studies*, vol. 2, no. 4
(Oct. 1960), p. 449-56.
De Young has used fresh documentary evidence in the Collection Rochambeau at the
University of Florida Library in order to clarify Jean-Jacques Dessalines' role in the
capture of Toussaint Louverture's nephew, Charles Belair. Newly discovered letters
indicate that Dessalines did not betray Belair to the French, and thus there is no
inconsistency in Dessalines' being offered leadership of the revolutionary forces shortly
after the execution of Belair.

192 **La vie de J.-J. Dessalines, chef des noirs révoltés de Saint-Domingue,
avec des notes très détaillées sur l'origine, le caractère, la vie et les
atrocités des principaux chefs des noirs, depuis l'insurrection de 1791.**
(The life of J.-J. Dessalines, leader of the rebel blacks of Saint-
Domingue, with detailed notes on the origin, the character, the life,
and the atrocities of the principal leaders of the blacks since the 1791
insurrection.)
Louis Dubroca. Paris: Dubroca, 1804, 142p.
Represents one of the few attempts to record the life of Jean-Jacques Dessalines.

193 **The history, civil and commercial of the British West Indies: with a
continuation to the present time.**
Bryan Edwards. London: Whittaker, 1819. 5th ed. 5 vols. [and] atlas.
Reprinted, New York: AMS Press, 1966. 5 vols.
The third volume of this set includes Edward's *Historical survey of the French colony in
the island of St. Domingo: comprehending an account of the revolt of the Negroes in the
year 1791, and a detail of the military transactions of the British army in that island in
the years 1793 & 1794.* This is a corrected version of a separate work which was
originally published in 1796. The work provides firsthand observations on the black
revolt and on the turmoil of the early 1790s. On pages 408-409 of the same volume,
Edwards adds a 'Postscript to the historical survey of Saint Domingo; containing a
brief review of the transactions and condition of the British Army there during the
years 1795, 6, 7, and 8, until the final evacuation of the country'. On pages 112-92 in
the fifth volume of the set, the editors add a supplement to Edwards' work, 'History of
St. Domingo; from the retreat of the British troops in 1798 to the present time [i.e.
1818]' and a 'Letter concerning Haiti', dated September 1, 1818.

194 **The making of Haiti: the Saint-Domingue revolution from below.**
Carolyn E. Fick. Knoxville, Tennessee: University of Tennessee
Press, 1990. 355p. maps. bibliog.
Forms an important contribution to the study of the Haitian Revolution. The author
views the revolution from a new perspective, and, drawing data from primary sources,
interprets the Haitian revolution as a mass movement 'from below', focusing on 'the
independent activities of the black masses and the various forms of rebellion used to
resist and finally to overthrow the rule of the white masters, to destroy slavery itself,
and to achieve independence.' In the first two sections of the book, she provides a
background for the situation and traces slave resistance in Saint-Domingue throughout
the eighteenth century, discussing revolts in all three of the country's provinces, the

North, West and South. The third part of the book concentrates on popular movements in the South province.

195 **Historia de la Revolucion de Haiti.** (History of the Haitian Revolution). José L. Franco. Havana, Cuba: Instituto de Historia, Academia de Ciencias, 1966. 306p. bibliog. (La Batalla por el Dominio del Caraibe y el Golfo de Mexico, 3).
Although this study of the Haitian Revolution is based largely on printed sources, Franco also cites, and includes excerpts from, Spanish documents held in the national archives of Cuba and the Dominican Republic.

196 **Marronage, Voodoo, and the Saint-Domingue slave revolt of 1791.** David Geggus. In: *Proceedings of the fifteenth meeting of the French colonial historical society Martinique and Guadeloupe, May 1989; Actes du quinzieme colloque de la Société d'histoire coloniale française Martinique et Guadeloupe mai 1989.* Edited by Patricia Galloway, Philip P. Boucher. Lanham, Massachusetts: University Press of America, 1992, p. 22-35.
Geggus analyses primary sources in order to critically assess 'the evidence concerning two elements often said to be involved in the August (1791) uprising in Saint-Domingue's northern plain'. Firstly, he examines the role of marronage in the event: 'whether the revolt grew out of a rising tide of marronage that had built up through the colonial period, and whether more specifically the revolt was organized by maroons'. Secondly, he studies the connection of Voodoo to the slave revolt, particularly in regard to the Bois Caiman ceremony that preceded the uprising; with regard to the latter point, he concludes that 'whether voodoo played a critical role . . . in the 1791 uprising itself remains to be proven'.

197 **Slavery, war, and revolution: the British occupation of Saint Domingue, 1793-1798.** David Patrick Geggus. Oxford: Clarendon Press; New York: Oxford University Press, 1982. 492p. maps. bibliog.
An exhaustive examination of the British occupation of Haiti during the Haitian Revolution, a subject that has received scant attention from the historians. Through detailed study of primary sources, Geggus seeks to bring factual accuracy to what has, historically, been a clouded issue. Following background chapters which analyse Saint-Domingue's social structure as it was in the late 1780s, all aspects of British intervention, occupation and eventual disengagement are considered.

198 **Unexploited sources for the history of the Haitian revolution.** David P. Geggus. *Latin American Research Review*, vol. 18, no. 1 (1983), p. 95-103.
Indicates materials that have been largely neglected by students of the Haitian Revolution. The author provides details of documents in Spain (holdings in Spanish archives contain important material on marronage and the revolution); in the Caribbean area (Dominican Republic, Jamaica); in Great Britain (papers concerning British attempts to conquer Saint-Domingue); in France (plantation records, the

papers of colonial notaries; unpublished manuscripts); and in the United States (the Rochambeau papers and the Jérémie papers at the University of Florida, and Lieutenant Howard's Journal at the Boston Public Library).

199 **Yellow fever in the 1790s: the British army in occupied Saint Domingue.**
David Geggus. *Medical History*, vol. 23, no. 1 (Jan. 1979), p. 38-58.
A well-researched essay on how the pandemic of yellow fever in Saint-Domingue during 1793-98, affected British troops which had been sent there to extend Great Britain's influence to the island. Geggus eradicates any misconceptions regarding the reasons for the spread of the pestilence among the British and the number of soldiers stricken with the illness. This article should remain the definitive examination of the subject for some time to come.

200 **Secret history: or, the horrors of St. Domingo, in a series of letters written by a lady at Cape François, to Colonel Burr, late vice-president of the United States, principally during the command of General Rochambeau.**
Mary Hassal.   Philadelphia: Bradford & Inskeep, 1801. 225p.
Reprinted, Freeport, New York: Books for Libraries Press, 1971.
(Black Heritage Library Collection).
An anecdotal account of events in Haiti, from June 1801, to November 1803 following Toussaint Louventure's capture and during the abortive attempt at the reoccupation of the Island by the French.

201 **The Haitian journal of Lieutenant Howard, York Hussars, 1796-1798.**
Thomas Phipps Howards.   Edited, with an introduction by Roger Norman Buckley.   Knoxville, Tennessee: University of Tennessee Press, 1985. 194p.
Edited from a manuscript in the Boston Public Library, this recent publication is a primary source for the study of the British attempt to control Saint-Domingue during the Haitian Revolution. Lieutenant Thomas Howard and his regiment were part of Sir Ralph Abercromby's expeditionary force which sailed to the Caribbean in 1796. Howard's journal is a vivid personal narrative of the final two years of the British occupation of Saint-Domingue, and a testimony to the effectiveness of Toussaint Louverture's army. The journal covers the period from February 8 1796 to February 8 1798.

202 **The black Jacobins: Toussaint L'Ouverture and the San Domingo revolution.**
C. L. R. James.   New York: Dial Press, 1938. 328p. bibliog.
2nd rev. ed., New York: Vintage Books, 1963, reprinted 1989. 426p. map. bibliog.
Written by a Trinidadian Marxist, this is an indispensable aid to the study of the Haitian Revolution. The work focuses on Toussaint Louverture and is well documented with an excellent annotated bibliography. James has made few alterations to his 1938 text in the revised edition (1963), but he has added a 17-page appendix on the political history of the Caribbean region: 'From Toussaint L'Ouverture to Fidel Castro'.

203   **Letters of Toussaint Louverture and of Edward Stevens, 1798-1800.**
[Edited by J. Franklin Jameson.]   *The American Historial Review*,
vol. 16, no. 1, (Oct. 1910), p. 64-101.

Presents primary material on Toussaint Louverture, reprinted, with editor's notes, from the consular files of the US State Department. Edward Stevens was a native West Indian sent as Consul-General to Haiti in 1799 to deal with problems of trade and commerce. The editor states that 'of the letters printed, the first eight (two of Toussaint, six of Stevens) are in 'Consular Letters, Cape Haytian, vol. I, the remaining eleven (of Stevens) in vol. II. of the same'. The first letter, dated 'le 16 Brumaire An 7' [i.e. November 6, 1798] is from Toussaint to President John Adams, requesting the resumption of trade between Haiti and the United States This correspondance provides an extremely interesting picture of the diplomatic side to Toussaint's career. Stevens' letters present an astute assessment of Haitian revolutionary politics at this time, based on his first-hand experiences of the tension and hostilities between Toussaint and Rigaud.

204   **Citizen Toussaint.**
Ralph Korngold.   Boston, Massachusetts: Little, Brown, 1944. 351p.
map. bibliog. Reprinted, Westport, Connecticut: Greenwood Press,
1979.

A satisfactory biography of Toussaint Louverture has not yet been written; however, Korngold's work is regarded as the most adequate and accurate English-language introduction to this remarkable man.

205   **Une correspondance familiale au temps des troubles de Saint-Domingue:
lettres du marquis et la marquise de Rouvray à leur fille, Saint-
Domingue – Etats-Unis, 1791-1796.** (A family correspondence at the
time of the troubles in Saint-Domingue: letters from the Marquis and
the Marquise de Rouvray to their daughter, Saint-Domingue – United
States, 1791-1796.)
Edited by M. E. McIntosh, B. C. Weber.   Paris Société de l'Histoire
des Colonies françaises, 1959. 179p. (Bibliothèque d'Histoire
Coloniale. Nouvelle série).

Laurent François Le Noir, Marquis de Rouvray, was a Saint-Domingue planter and an officer in the royal army. By publishing these letters, written by the Marquis and his wife to their daugher, the comtesse Lostanges, the editors make available a contemporary source of the early history of the Haitian Revolution.

206   **A calendar of Rochambeau papers at the University of Florida Libraries.**
Compiled by Laura V. Monti.   Florida: University of Florida
Libraries, 1972. 329p. bibliog.

Donatien Marie Joseph de Vimeur, vicomte de Rochambeau, sailed to Saint-Domingue as part of General Leclerc's expedition to regain the island for the French, and became capitaine-général of the colony upon the death of his superior officer. The collection of his papers, housed at the University of Florida, provides an inexhaustible source for information on the history of Saint-Domingue, especially for the last years of the Haitian Revolution. Monti's calendar dates the documents in the collection between 1744 and 1805.

207 **Black triumvirate: a study of Louverture, Dessalines, Christophe – the men who made Haiti.**
Charles Moran. New York: Exposition Press, 1951. 160p. bibliog.

Supplies an account of three heroes of Haiti's revolutionary era: Toussaint Louverture, Jean-Jacques Dessalines, and Henry Christophe. In his essay 'Makers of a nation' in *Americas*, vol. 5 no. 11 (Nov. 1953), p.8ff., Haitian poet Leon Laleau adds Alexandre Pétion to the list of those who created Haiti.

208 **Histoire militaire de la Guerre d'Indépendance de Saint-Domingue.**
(Military history of Saint-Domingue's War of Independence).
Alfred Nemours. Paris: Berger-Levrault, 1925-1929. 2 vols. bibliog.

Although now outdated, this work by General Nemours, a Haitian, remains the standard military history of the War of Independence.

209 **The Haitian Revolution, 1789-1804.**
Thomas O. Ott. Knoxville, Tennessee: University of Tennessee Press, 1973. 232p. maps. bibliog.

Attempts to provide an objective presentation of the beginning, events and conclusion of the Haitian Revolution. The bibliography lists manuscript collections, newspapers containing sailors' accounts, ships' logs, public documents, journals, memoirs, diaries and secondary sources, and includes a brief bibliographic essay evaluating previous publications on the period.

210 **Poland's Caribbean tragedy: a study of Polish legions in the Haitian War of Independence 1802-1803.**
Jan Pachoński, Reuel K. Wilson. Boulder, Colorado: East European Monographs, 1986. 378p. maps. bibliog. (East European Monographs no. CXCIX).

The first monograph in English on the involvement of Polish units in the Haitian War of Independence, a subject about which little has been written, in any language. Pawns in Napoleon's political game, the Poles served in the Emperor's legions in the hope of obtaining French support for a restored Poland. Pachoński conducted lengthy and detailed research as part of his effort to recreate the history of the two Polish demi-brigades who fought in Haiti – both their service in Haiti (of the 5,000 Polish soldiers who arrived on the Island, 4,000 died of yellow fever or were killed in combat), and what happened to them after the French defeat. This work provides a fascinating insight into a little-known aspect of the Haitian War of Independence.

211 **'This gilded African' Toussaint L'Ouverture.**
Wanda Parkinson. London; Melbourne, New York: Quartet Books, 1978. 212p. map. bibliog.

A highly readable account of the life of Toussaint Louverture and of his leadership of the Haitian Revolution. The text is undocumented but is drawn largely from French sources which are listed in the bibliography.

212 **Histoire de Toussaint-Louverture.** (The history of Toussaint Louverture.)
Horace Pauleus Sannon.   Port-au-Prince: A. A. Heraux, 1920-1933.
3 vols.

This biography, along with Victor Schoelcher's *Vie de Toussaint-Louverture* (q.v.), is commonly accepted as being one of the classic stories of the life of Haiti's revolutionary hero.

213 **Sketches of St. Domingo from January, 1785, to December, 1794, written by a resident merchant at the request of a friend, 1835.**
Samuel G. Perkins, communicated, with notes, by Charles C.
Perkins. *Proceedings of the Massachusetts Historical Society*, 2nd ser., vol. 2, (April 1886), p. 305-90.

Contains a transcript of the memoirs of Samuel G. Perkins, a Boston merchant, written in December 1835, in which he recounts his experiences from 1785 to 1784 at Cap Français, where he was engaged in commercial activity. He describes the slave uprising, the emanicipation of the slaves of Saint-Domingue, and the destruction of Cap Français and the massacre of its inhabitants. Perkins was not sympathetic to the slaves, and blames the insurrection in Haiti on the nefarious ideas propagated by the French Revolution. The manuscript was presented at a meeting of the Massachusetts Historical Society by Perkin's great-nephew, Charles C. Perkins. In addition to its inclusion in the Society's proceedings, it was also published separately as *Reminiscences of the Insurrection in Santo Domingo* (Cambridge, Massachusetts: J. Wilson & Son, University Press, 1886).

214 **Histoire militaire de la révolution de Saint-Domingue.** (Military history of the Saint-Domingue revolution).
Henry de Poyen-Bellisle.   Paris: Imprimerie Nationale, 1899. 555p.
maps.

Provides a French perspective on the military campaigns of the Haitian Revolution.

215 **An historical account of the black empire of Hayti: comprehending a view of the principal transactions in the revolution of Saint Domingo, with its ancient and modern state.**
Marcus Rainsford.   London: J. Cundee, 1805. 467p. map. Reprinted, London: Frank Cass, 1972. (Source Books on Haiti, no. 6).

Written by a commissioned officer in the British army, this work offers a first-hand account of the Haitian Revolution. Captain Rainsford visited Saint-Domingue in 1799, where he met Toussaint Louverture and was also arrested and sentenced to death as a spy. Subsequently reprieved, he described his adventures in this book and in an earlier pamphlet entitled *A memoir of transactions that took place in St. Domingo, in the spring of 1799; affording an idea of the present state of that country, the real character of its black governor, Toussaint L'Ouverture, and the safety of our West-India islands from attack or revolt; including the rescue of a British officer under sentence of death* (London: R. B. Scott, 1802).

216 **Memoires du général Toussaint-L'Ouverture écrits par lui-meme, pouvant servir à l'histoire de sa vie; orné d'une beau portrait gravé par Choubard: précedés d'une étude historique et critique, suivis de notes et renseignements, avec un appendice contentant les opinions de l'empereur Napoleon ler sur les événements de Saint-Domingue, par Saint-Rémy.** (Memoirs of General Toussaint-L'Ouverture written by himself, constituting a history of his life, ornamented with an engraved portrait by Choubard: preceded by a historical and critical study, followed by notes and information, with an appendix containing the opinions of the emperor Napoleon I on the events of Saint-Domingue, by Saint-Remy.) Joseph Saint-Rémy. Port-au-Prince: Editions Fardin, 1982. 159p.

A facsimile reprint of the first edition which was published in Paris by Pagnerre in 1853.

217 **Vie de Toussaint Louverture.** (The life of Toussaint Louverture.) Victor Schoelcher. Paris: Ollendorf, 1889. 455p. Reprinted, Paris: Karthala, 1982. map.

A classic biography of Toussaint, written by a French abolitionist (slavery was not abolished in all France's colonies until 1848). Interwoven in the narrative are many documents and letters pertaining to Toussaint and the Haitian Revolution. The reprinted edition includes a modern introduction by Jacques Adelaide-Merlande.

218 **The crisis of the sugar colonies: or, an enquiry into the objects and probable effects of the French expedition to the West Indies, and their connection with the colonial interests of the British Empire, to which are subjoined sketches of a plan for settling the vacant lands of Trinidada. In four letters to the Right Hon. Henry Addington, Chancellor of the Exchequer.** James Stephen. London: Hatchard, 1802. 222p. Reprinted, New York: Negro Universities Press, 1969; Reprinted, Westport, Connecticut: Greenwood Press, 1970.

James Stephen was a British barrister who practised in the West Indies between 1783 and 1794. He was also the brother-in-law of the British abolitionist William Wilberforce. His writings consider the implications for Great Britain's Caribbean possessions of the slave revolution in Saint-Domingue and the Leclerc expedition to retake the island for France. The first section of the book presents a chilling description of the practice of 'driving' slave gangs with a cart whip.

219 **The Haitian Revolution, 1791 to 1804, or sidelights on the French Revolution.** T. G. Steward. New York: Crowell, 1914. 292p. map. bibliog. Reprinted, New York: Russell & Russell, 1971.

Despite being old-fashioned in its approach, this detailed narrative, which is interspersed with letters and documents pertaining to the events of the Haitian Revolution, should still prove useful to students. The author's sympathies lie with the Haitians, but he manages to remain objective in his outlook.

220 **The French Revolution in San Domingo.**
T. Lothrop Stoddard.   New York: Houghton Mifflin, 1914. 410p.
maps. bibliog. (Reprinted, Westport, Connecticut: Negro Universities
Press, 1970).

This is the first scholarly history of the Haitian Revolution, based on research in
primary materials in French archives. The author has been criticized for his racist
viewpoint and for his denial of the effectiveness of Toussaint's black troops. A recent
critique of Stoddard's views can be found in the 'Postscript', (p. 134-37), to Roger
Norman Buckley's edition of *The Haitian journal of Lieutenant Howard, York Hussars,
1796-1798* (q.v.).

221 **Toussaint L'Ouverture.**
Edited by George F. Tyson, Jr.   Englewood Cliffs, New Jersey:
Prentice-Hall, 1973.

Presents selected texts by and about Toussaint Louverture. A bibliographical note
(p. 178-82), evaluates the literature pertaining to this hero of Haitian independence.

222 **An essay on the causes of the revolution and civil wars of Haiti, being a
sequel to the political remarks upon certain French publications and
journals concerning Hayti.**
Pompée Valentin de Vastey, translated from the French by
W. H. M. B.   Exeter, England: Printed at the Western Luminary
Office, 1823. 249p. (Reprinted, New York: Negro Universities Press,
1969).

The Baron de Vastey has a place in both Haitian history and literature. While
employed as private secretary to King Henry Christophe (and as tutor to the King's
children), Vastey wrote a series of essays arguing Haiti's case. He favoured a British
connection for Haiti, to counteract the perceived threat of French or American
control.

223 **The black consul.**
Anatolii Vinogradov, translated from the Russian by Emile Burns.
New York: Viking Press, 1935. 438p. bibliog.

This novelized account of Toussaint Louverture and revolutionary events in France
and Haiti is a good example of popular history, but it is closer to fiction that it is to
fact.

Independent Haiti 1804-1915

224 **L'empereur Souoloque et son empire.** (Emperor Souloque and his
empire.)
Gustave d'Alaux. Paris: Michel Lévy Frères, 1856. 286p. (Reprinted,
Port-au-Prince: Editions Fardin, 1988).

Provides a substantial, if unflattering, presentation of the Souloque régime. 'Gustave
d'Alaux' was said to be the pseudonym of Maxime Raybaud, France's diplomatic
representative in Haiti from 1846 to 1852. *L'empereur Souloque et son empire* was
first published between December 1850 and February 1851, as a series of articles in the
Revue des Deux Mondes. An English version of the book was issued in Richmond,
Virginia in 1861 (*Souloque and his empire*, translated and edited by John H.
Parkhill).

225 **The presidency of Nicolas Geffrard.**
John Edward Baur. *The Americas: a Quarterly Review of
Inter-American Cultural History*, vol. 10 (April 1954), p. 425-61.

General Fabre Nicolas Geffrard overthrew the Souloque régime in 1859 and was
subsequently head of the Haitian government unitl 1867. Geffrard's presidency was
significant for its achievements in ending Haiti's isolation from the rest of the world: a
Concordat was signed with the Vatican restoring relations with the Holy See in 1860,
and the United States accorded diplomatic recognition to Haiti in 1862. Baur's article
is one of the few discussions of Geffrard's administration available in English.

226 **Mulatto Machiavelli: Jean-Pierre Boyer and the Haiti of his day.**
John Edward Baur. *Journal of Negro History*, vol. 32, no. 3 (July
1947), p. 307-53.

This lengthy contribution is one of the few articles in English to discuss the 1818-1843
presidency of Jean-Pierre Boyer. Baur characterizes the politically astute Boyer as
being a 'colored Machiavelli,' but then praises his achievement of Haitian unity and his
success in guiding Haiti through a critical period in its history.

227 **Santo Domingo's struggle for independence from Haiti.**
Ian Bell. *History Today*, vol. 31 (April 1981), p. 42-7. maps. bibliog.

Haiti annexed Santo Domingo in February 1822, designating it a province of Haiti,
called the Partie de l'Est, and imposing the French language and Haitian law and
customs on the Dominicans. This article describes the Dominicans' struggles between
1843 and 1844 to liberate their territory from Haitian control – but with the aim of
establishing a French protectorate rather than an independent state. Bell has written a
lucid and factual article on a subject little about which is available in English. He
emphasizes the Dominican aspect of the issue, but he also briefly quotes from the
dispatches of Thomas N. Ussher, the British Consul at Port-au-Prince during these
years.

228   **Alexandre Pétion: the founder of rural democracy in Haiti.**
Dantes Bellegarde.   *Caribbean Quarterly*, vol. 3, no. 3 (Dec. 1953),
p. 167-73.

Alexandre Pétion is the least-known of the founders of Haiti, although he played a key
role in Latin American history. In this article, Bellegarde supplies a readable
biography of Pétion. Elected President of the southern Republic of Haiti in March,
1807, Pétion divided the land of former colonial plantations among the rural
population, instituted free elementary education, and aided Simon Bolívar with
money, arms and a printing press.

229   **The black man: or, Haitian independence.**
Mark Baker Bird.   New York: The author, 1869. 461p. (Reprinted,
Freeport, New York: Books for Libraries, 1971) (Black Heritage
Library Collection).

Describes the Boyer and Soulouque régimes as witnessed by the Englishman who
established and directed the Methodist Church in Haiti for forty years. Other books by
nineteenth-century missionaries who were fairly sympathetic to the Haitians are John
Candler's *Brief notices of Hayti: with its conditions, resources, and prospects* (London:
Ward, 1842; reprinted, London: Cass, 1972), and S. W. Hanna's *Notes of a visit to
some parts of Haiti, Jan.-Feb., 1835* (London: Seeley, Burnside & Seely, 1936).

230   **The history and present condition of St. Domingo.**
Jonathan Brown.   Philadelphia: Marshall, 1837. 2 vols. (Reprinted,
London; Cass, 1972). (Source Books on Haiti, no. 8).

This work is considered to be a reliable source for the history of colonial Saint-
Domingue, the reign of Henry Christophe and the first eighteen years of the Boyer
administration.

231   **Christophe: King of Haiti.**
Hubert Cole.   London: Eyre & Spottiswoode: New York: Viking
Press, 1967. 307p. maps. bibliog.

Well-documented, with information from both primary and secondary sources, this
detailed work is generally considered to be the best summary available of the life and
reign of Henry Christophe. A table of events, several photographs and maps are also
included.

232   **La independencia de Haiti y su influencia en Hispanoamerica.** (Haitian
independence and its influence in Latin America.)
Eleazar Cordova-Bello.   Caracas, Venezuela: Instituto Panamericano
de Geografia e Historia, 1967. 376p. (Instituto Panamericano de
Geografia Comision de Historia. Comite de Origenes de la
Emanicipation. Publicacion no. 13).

This is the only full-length study of the impact of the Haitian Revolution and its
aftermath on the struggle for independence in the countries of Latin America, 1806-
1830.

233 **The present state of Hayti (Santo Domingo) with remarks on its agriculture, commerce, laws, religion, finances, and populations, etc. etc.**
James Franklin, preface to the reprint by Robert I. Rotberg. London: Murray, 1828. 411p. (Reprinted, London: Cass, 1971). (Source Books on Haiti, no. 4).
Following a historical section, Franklin describes Haiti during the early years of Boyer's presidency.

234 **Haiti's contribution to the independence of Spanish America: a forgotten chapter.**
Piero Gieijeses. *Revista/Review Interamericana*, vol. 9, no. 4 (winter 1979-80), p. 511-28.
An interesting re-evaluation that gives more weight to the importance of Haitian aid to Bolívar in the struggle for the independence of Spanish America. Few biographers, notes the author, devote more than three or four pages to Bolívar's stay in Haiti, 'Yet Haiti's aid to Bolívar was crucial, for it was given when the struggle for independence in Spanish America was at its lowest point. Moreover, it was unique: the Republic of Haiti was the only state in the world to provide direct assistance to the Spanish-American insurgents'.

235 **Henry Christophe & Thomas Clarkson: a correspondence.**
Edited by Earl Leslie Griggs, Clifford H. Prator. Berkeley, California: University of California Press, 1952. 287p. maps. bibliog. (Reprinted, New York: Greenwood Press, 1968).
Presents sixty letters exchanged from 1813 to 1824 between Thomas Clarkson, the British abolitionist, and Henry Christophe, King of Haiti, forms a measurable contribution to an unprejudiced evaluation of the black monarch's reign. As the editors state in their eighty-page introduction to the volume: 'This material forms a valuable commentary upon the obscure history of Haiti, and it tends to modify the interpretation which legend and fiction have woven around the personality and activities of Christophe. Instead of the spectacular and savage despot so often found in books dealing with him, Christophe becomes a wise and farsighted monarch dedicated to the welfare of his people'.

236 **Henry Christophe, king of Haiti.**
C. E. Hamshere. *History Today*, vol. 17, no. 3 (March 1967), p. 181-88. map.
Hamshere presents a positive assessment of the policies and reforms introduced in northern Haiti during the reign of Henry Christophe, crowned King Henry I in 1811. Unfortunately, he fails to avoid several racist generalizations in what is an otherwise informative article.

237 **Sketches of Hayti: from the explusion of the French to the death of Christophe.**
William Woodis Harvey, preface to the reprint by Robert I. Rotbert.
London: Seeley, 1827. 416p. (Reprinted, London, Cass, 1971).
(Source Books on Haiti, No. 5).

Harvey visited Christophe's Haiti and based his work on his own observations of the island and on printed sources, among them the *History of the island of St. Domingo, from its first discovery by Columbus to the present period*, attributed to Sir James Barskett (q.v.). In his urban eighteenth-century style, Harvey firstly reviews the circumstances of the emancipation of the Haitians and the reign of Dessalines, then devotes the larger part of his volume to Henry Christophe's rise, reign and fall. His assessment of the situation in Christophe's kingdom is optimistic and generally favourable to the Haitians.

238 **L'indemnité coloniale de Saint-Domingue et la question des rapatriés.**
(Colonial reparations from Saint-Domingue and the refugee issue).
Benoit Joachim. *Revue Historique*, vol. 246, no. 2 (Oct.-Dec. 1971), p. 359-76.

The French government under Charles X conceded Haitian independence in 1825 with the stipulation that Haiti pay former French colonists compensation amounting to 150 million francs over a fifty-year period. This imposed a heavy burden on the Haitians, but was accepted as the price for normalizing their international relations. The result of the agreement was that Franco-Haitian relations centred around this monetary obligation for half a century. Joachim relates the history of this debt in France: how it became a part of French politics and who profited from the compensatory payments.

239 **The first land reform in Latin America: the reforms of Alexander Pétion, 1809-1814.**
Robert K. Lacerte. *Inter-American Economic Affairs*, vol. 28, no. 4 (spring 1975), p. 77-85.

During his term as president of the southern Republic of Haiti (1806-1818), Alexandre Pétion initiated and implemented the first land reform in Latin America, distributing land abandoned by, or confiscated from, European planters to veterans of the Haitian Revolution. This article, one of the few studies ever made of Pétion's programme, describes his land distribution scheme and notes its effects, including its possible influence on Simon Bolívar.

240 **Xenophobia and economic decline: the Haitian case, 1820-1843.**
Robert K. Lacerte. *The Americas*, vol. 37, no. 4 (April 1981), p. 499-515.

Discusses the interrelated factors which brought about Haiti's economic decline during the presidency of Jean-Pierre Boyer: Haitian fear of military or economic domination; Boyer's Rural Code, promulgated to increase agricultural production; the non-investment of capital; anti-foreigner regulations which discouraged foreign merchants; and the burden of the French indemnity. The administration that succeeded the deposed Boyer sought to implement a more liberal policy with regard to foreign ties, but Haiti's continued economic decline caused the country to retreat into isolation once more. Lacerte comments that Haiti's problem was unique: how to define a place for itself as a black society in a white world, and how to establish the role of whites in Haiti. The article is based largely on research in British Foreign Office papers, and is of particular interesting for its assessment of Great Britain's failure to integrate Haiti into its economic sphere.

241 **Notes on Hayti, made during a residence in that Republic.**
Charles MacKenzie, preface to the reprint by Robert I. Rotberg.
London: Colburn & Bentley, 1830. 2 vols. map. (Reprinted, London: Cass, 1972). (Source Books on Haiti, no. 6).
MacKenzie was the British consul-general in Haiti. His book draws on his experiences in the country between 1826 and 1828.

242 **The Soulouque regime in Haiti, 1847-1859: a re-evaluation.**
Murdo J. MacLeod. *Caribbean Studies*, vol. 10, no. 3 (Oct. 1970), p. 35-48.
The praetorian, Napoleonic figure that recurs in Haitian history is usually viewed by political historians as an aberration. The accepted analysis of Faustin Soulouque's twelve years as Haiti's president, then emperor, follows this line and, in consequence, Soulouque is invariably depicted as a dullard and megalomaniac. In this highly interesting article, MacLeod criticizes the inconsistencies in this portrait of Soulouque and provides a reinterpretation of his régime. He stresses that while Soulouque is not an attractive political figure, he was by no means lacking a shrewd grasp of the political realities of his time. His legacy to Haiti can be detected in parallels that can be drawn between the use of Voodoo, nationalism and terror under his rule and similar practices during the more recent administration of François Duvalier.

243 **La politique agraire du gouvernment d'Alexandre Pétion (1807-1818): programme des classes terminales de l'enseignement secondaire.** (The agrarian policy of the government of Alexandre Pétion (1807-1818): a course for the higher classes of secondary schools.)
Leslie F. Manigat. Port-au-Prince: Impr. La Phalange, 1962. 74p.
(Collection pédagogique 'Le Livre du Maître, Guide de L'élève').
A textbook presentation of Pétion's land tenure reforms.

244 **A guide to Haiti.**
Edited by James Redpath. Boston, Massachusetts: Haitian Bureau of Emigration, 1861. 180p. map. (Reprinted, Westport, Connecticut: Negro Universities Press, 1970).
The author, who was committed to the cause of black emancipation, compiled this description of mid-nineteenth-century Haiti in an attempt to encourage black Americans to emigrate to the island.

245 **Haytian papers: a collection of the very interesting proclamations, and other official documents; together with some account of the rise, progress and present state of the Kingdom of Haiti.**
Edited with a preface by Prince Sanders. London, 1816. 288p.
Reprinted, Westport, Connecticut: Negro Universities Press, 1969.

Contains the English translations of a rather miscellaneous collection of documents brought together by Prince Sanders (also spelt 'Saunders') with the intention of enlightening the British public on Christophe's Haiti. The contents include: Code Henri; extracts from the registers of the deliberations of the consuls of the Republic; narrative of the accession of their royal majesties to the throne of Haiti; state of Hayti: proclamation by Henri Christophe; Constitutional law (of the Council of State establishing royalty in Haiti); Manifesto of the King (Henry Christophe); reflections of the editor (Sanders); Royal Gazette of Hayti of 4 January 1816; Proclamations (of Henry Christophe); reflections on the slave trade.

246 **France and Latin American independence.**
William Spence Robertson. Baltimore, Maryland: Johns Hopkins Press, 1939. 626p. maps. bibliog. (Reprinted, New York: Octagon Books, 1967).

Chapter twelve, entitled 'French acknowledgement of Haitian independence', is a competent account of the negotiations that led to France's recognition of the independence of its former colony in 1825.

247 **Invasiones Haitianas de 1801, 1805 y 1822.** (The Haitian invasions of 1801, 1805 and 1822.)
Emilio Rodríguez Demorizi. Ciudad Trujillo: Ed. del Caribe, 1955, 371p. (Publicaciones de la Academia Dominicana de la Historia, vol. 1).

Discusses three attempts by the Haitian military to conquer Santo Domingo, the Spanish-governed eastern portion of the island of Hispaniola: by Toussaint Louverture in 1801; by Jean-Jacques Dessaline in 1805; and by Jean-Pierre Boyer in 1822.

248 **The West Indies: their social and religious condition.**
Edward Bean Underhill. London: Jackson, Walford & Hodder, 1862. 493p. (Reprinted, Westport, Connecticut: Negro Universities Press, 1970).

Underhill's lengthy chapter on 'Hayti', p. 95-176, contains some interesting anecdotes on mid-nineteenth-century Haitian history, including an account of General Nicolas Geffrard's bloodless coup against the Emperor Faustin Soulouque and Gerard Prophète's failed conspiracy to overthrow Geffrard.

249 **Black majesty: the life of Christophe, King of Haiti.**
John W. Vandercook, with drawings by Mahlon Blaine. New York: Harper, 1928. 207p. bibliog.

A fictionalized, but not sensationalized, biography of Henry Christophe.

250 **The great Haitian epic.**
Guillermo de Zéndegui. *Americas*, vol. 22, no. 6 (June 1970),
p. 2-11.
Examines the reign of King Henry Christophe. This article is of most interest for its
photographs of the ruins of the impressive monuments which symbolized his rule, the
fortress of the Citadel and the palace of Sans Souci.

20th-century Haiti

American occupation 1915-1934

251 **Beyond nationalism: the social thought of Emily Greene Balch.**
Emily Greene Balch, edited by Mercedes M. Randall.   New York:
Twayne Publishers, 1972. 260p.
Contains Balch's 'Memorandum on Haiti' as well as her articles 'Social values in Haiti'
(1926) and 'Economic imperialism with special reference to the United States' (1926).

252 **Occupied Haiti: being a report of a committee of six disinterested
Americans representing organizations exclusively American who, having
personally studied conditions in Haiti in 1926, favor the restoration of
the independence of the Negro Republic.**
Edited by Emily Greene Balch, with an introduction to the reprint by
Mercedes M. Randall.   New York: Writers Publishing Co., 1927.
186p. (Reprinted, New York; London: Garland, 1972). (The Garland
Library of War and Peace).
Provides a personal observation of Haiti under US occupation. Emily Greene Balch
visited Haiti in 1926 as head of an unofficial commission of six Americans appointed
by the Women's International League for Peace and Freedom to survey the results of
eleven years of US control. This volume is the report of the delegation, with separate
chapters written by commission members Balch, Charlotte Atwood, Zonia Baber, Paul
H. Douglas, Mrs Addie Hanton, and Mrs. J. Harold Watson. The work covers the
background to the occupation, its political history, the land situation, agriculture,
health and sanitation, education, public works, race relations, public order, the
judiciary and civlil liberty, and the press and prisons. In most of these areas,
the writers deplore the outcome of US interference, their consensus being that the
occupation brought Haiti material progress but political and psychological disaster.
Appendices include a discussion of international law as applied to the United States
intervention in Haiti, a chronological summary of Haitian history, and a letter from
Normil Sylvain, giving a Haitian's view of the occupation.

253 The press and American intervention in Haiti and the Dominican Republic, 1904-1920.
John W. Blassingame. *Caribbean Studies*, vol. 9, no. 2 (July 1969), p. 27-43.

Studies the reaction of the American press towards US intervention in Haiti and the Dominican Republic, thereby filling a gap in the history of US relations with the Caribbean. Blassingame studied American newspapers dating from 1904 to 1920, in order to determine the editorial positions taken towards US imperialism. He found that during the period 1904-19, most journals endorsed the government's activities; it was only in 1920 that a shift towards criticism of US involvement occurred, a change spearheaded by *The Nation*.

254 The American occupation of Haiti, I.
Paul H. Douglas. *Political Science Quarterly*, vol. 42, no. 2 (June 1927), p. 228-58.

Factual, detailed and enlightening, this two-part article by Senator Douglas is required reading for students of the US occupation of the Haitian Republic. In this first segment, Douglas outlines the steps taken to secure and perpetuate US dominance in Haiti and discusses US – Haitian relations, 1910-1915; the consolidation of US control in Haiti, 1915-1917; and the structure of the Haitian government under the occupation, 1917-1926.

255 The American occupation of Haiti, II.
Paul H. Douglas. *Political Science Quarterly*, vol. 142, no. 3 (Sept. 1927), p. 368-96.

In the second half of his criticism of US imperialism, Senator Douglas contrasts the real services that the Americans have rendered in Haiti with the abuses that they have inflicted on the Haitian population. He then summarizes the economic and financial policies followed by the United States in Haiti.

256 The National Railway of Haiti: a study in tropical finance.
Paul H. Douglas. *The Nation*, vol. 124, no. 3211 (Jan. 1927), p. 59-61.

A courageous exposé by US senator Paul H. Douglas of the questionable financial transactions behind the concession for the construction of a railway between Cape Haitien and Port-au-Prince. The scheme was initiated by American adventurer James P. McDonald, whose bankruptcy involved the National City Bank of New York in claims on the Haitian government for interest payments on bonds for the line. When the Haitians balked at continuing payments on the unfinished railway – having contracted for a workable line, rather than three disconnected sections of track – the United States governement intervened in Haiti. Douglas calculates that the railway cost the Haitians eight million dollars, although in 1920 the bonds were worth only $700,000 on the Paris Bourse. According to Douglas 'Unknown individuals or the National City Bank . . . made more than $2,000,000' on financial transactions stemming from the unusable railway.

257 **The death of Charlemange.**
Harry A. Franck. *The Century*, vol. 100, no. 1 (May 1920), p. 23-35.

A one-sided and bluntly racist view of Charlemagne Peralte and the Cacos Rebellion of 1918. Franck's explanation of Peralte's motives in organizing and leading an uprising against US occupation of his country is expressed thus: 'wounded in his pride and denied his expected source of income (because he was not able to obtain elective office) . . . (Peralte) gathered a band of malcontents and penniless cacos . . . and played the patriotic card'. Most of the article recounts how Captain Herman H. Hannekin of US Marine Corps tracked and finally shot Peralte in the autumn of 1919, an episode that James Weldon Johnson called 'a black smirch on American arms and traditions'. Franck's article is reprinted in his *Roaming through the West Indies* (q.v.).

258 **Les blancs débarquent.** (The whites have landed.)
Roger Gaillard. Port-au-Prince: R. Gaillard, 1981-1983. 7 vols. in 8.
maps. bibliog.

Examines the American occupation from a Haitian point of view. The volumes are titled thus: Vol. 1, pt. 1: La république exterminatrice: une modernisation manquée (1880-1896); vol. 1, pt. 2: La république exterminatrice: déroute de l'intelligence; vol. 2: Les cents jours de Rôsalvo Bobo: une mise à mort politique (1914-1915); vol.3: Premier ecrasement de cacoisme (1915); vol. 4: La république autoritaire (1916-1917); vol. 5: Hinche mise en croix (1917-1918); vol. 6: Charlemagne Peralte, le caco (1918-1919); vol. 7: La guerilla de Batraville.

259 **The conquest of Haiti and Santo Domingo.**
Ernest H. Gruening. *Current History*, vol. 15, no. 6 (March 1922),
p. 885-96.

In this account, written during the US occupation, Gruening, the managing editor of *The Nation*, exposes the details of America's seizure of political and military control in Haiti, condemning US intervention in the region as ruthless and unjustified, 'the gravest breach of fundamental American traditions in (American) history'.

260 **Through Santo Domingo and Haiti: a cruise with the Marines; report of a visit to these island republics in the summer of 1919.**
Samuel Guy Inman. New York: Committe on Co-operation in Latin America, 1919. 96p. bibliog.

A contemporary account by an American scholar of the early US occupation in Haiti.

261 **Self-determining Haiti: I. The American occupation.**
James Weldon Johnson. *The Nation*, vol. 111, no. 2878 (Aug 1920),
p. 236-38.

The first of a series of four articles written by Johnson, an eminent black American and former US consul in Venezuela and Nicaragua. The series was instrumental in arousing criticism in the United States against continued American occupation of Haiti. In his opening essay, Johnson describes the harsh and humiliating conditions imposed on the Haitians by US military authorities.

262 **Self-determining Haiti: II. What the United States has accomplished.**
James Weldon Johnson. *The Nation*, vol. 111, no. 2879 (Sept. 1920),
p. 265-67.

In his second article, Johnson weighs up the benefits of US involvement in Haiti – a highway, improved sanitation, a hospital – against the offences committed by the military. He also provides an account of the Cacos Rebellion of 1918 and of the death of Charlemagne Peralte that questions other versions of these events.

263 **Self-determing Haiti: III. Government of, by, and for the National City Bank.**
James Weldon Johnson. *The Nation*, vol. 111, no. 2880 (Sept. 1920),
p. 295-97.

The subtitle of his third article sums up what Johnson considered to be the underlying reason for the presence of US Marines in the republic of Haiti. This essay comprises a detailed presentation of how the financial interests of the National City Bank of New York were involved in Haiti.

264 **Self-determining Haiti: IV. The Haitian people.**
James Weldon Johnson. *The Nation*, vol. 111, no. 2882 (Sept. 1920),
p. 345-47.

In the last article of this series, Johnson describes the chic and cultured life of urban Port-au-Prince and praises the cleanliness, industry and thrift of the Haitian people.

265 **Self-determining Haiti; four articles reprinted from *The Nation* embodying a report of an investigation made for the National Association for the Advancement of Colored People, together with official documents.**
James Weldon Johnson. New York: The Nation, 1920. 48p.

Johnson's reports from Haiti (see items nos. 261-64), originally published in *The Nation*, were reprinted in this rare pamphlet.

266 **The American intervention in Haiti and the Dominican Republic.**
Carl Kelsey. *Annals of the American Academy of Political and Social Science*, vol. 100, no. 189 (March 1922), p. 113-202.

A lengthy and detailed report on the island in 1921.

267 **The US 'colonial experiment' in Haiti.**
Rayford W. Logan. *Word Today*, vol. 17, no. 10 (Oct. 1961),
p. 435-46.

Considers the achievements of the Americans in Haiti since the treaties of 1916 and 1917, in which the United States promised 'to aid the Haitian Government in the proper and efficient development of its agricultural, mineral, and commercial resources and in the establishment of the finances of Haiti on a firm and solid basis'. Most of the attempts made by the United States to fulfil these commitments have been unsuccessful. Logan blames this failure on the inability of the United States 'to recognize the magnitude of the task', and on American unwillingness 'to provide the necessary funds and technical assistance to achieve a modest amelioration of Haiti's plight'.

268 **The United States Mission in Haiti, 1915-1952.**
Rayford W. Logan. *Inter-American Economic Affairs*, vol. 6, no. 4 (spring 1953), p. 18-28.
Written from an American perspective, Logan comments on the US intervention in Haiti between 1915-1934. He summarizes the consequences of this intervention by means of a series of 'snapshots' of the island republic in 1926, 1934 and 1942 and notes that, at the time of writing in 1952, much remains to be accomplished.

269 **Garde d'Haiti, 1915-1934: twenty years of organization and training by the United States Marine Corps.**
James H.McCrocklin. Annapolis, Maryland: US Naval Institute, 1956. 262p. map. bibliog.
The author, a US Marine Corps officer, states in his preface: 'This work is largely prepared from material contained in the Historial Archives of the United States Marine Corps, mainly on a report dated 31 July 1934, by a board headed by Major Franklin A. Hart, Garde d'Haiti (now General, U.S.M.C., Ret.). It is specifically limited to a consideration of the Gendarmerie d'Haiti and those American Marines who served it'.

270 **Administering the protectorates: the occupation of Haiti and the Dominican Republic.**
Richard Millett, G. Dale Gaddy. *Revista/Review Interamericana*, vol. 6, no. 3 (fall 1976), p. 383-402.
This scholarly, well-documented article, based largely on archival sources and on personal interviews, analyses the US government's use of military personnel as administrators in Haiti and the Dominican Republic. It is apparent that both failure by the State Department to inform Marine and Naval commanders of the goals of US intervention in the two republics, and the continued absence of any specific policy on how the occupations were to be conducted, led to confusion and the abuse of power by the military. The reader will find the authors' contrast of the structure of US control in Haiti with that which was imposed on the Dominican Republic enlightening.

271 **Haiti under American control, 1915-1930.**
Arthur C. Millspaugh. Boston, Massachusetts: World Foundation, 1931. 253p. Reprinted, Westport, Connecticut: Negro Universities Press, 1970.
Presents a pro-American assessment of US intervention in Haiti, written by the man who was financial adviser to, and general receiver of, Haiti for the United States from 1927 to 1929. The main text is followed by a 56-page appendix that provides the texts of communications of the US State Department, the Treaty of 16 September 1915, and subsequent agreements signed between Haiti and the United States.

272 **The American withdrawal from Haiti, 1929-1934.**
Dana G. Munro. *Hispanic-American Historial Review*, vol. 49, no. 1
(Feb. 1969), p. 1-26.
Examines the last years of the US occupation of Haiti. The article is detailed in its
description of how the US government implemented its termination of the nation's
protectorate status and withdrew from the island. Munro was US High Commissioner
in Haiti between 1930 and 1934, and as such was instrumental in managing this final
stage.

273 **The Banana Wars: a history of United States military intervention in
Latin America from the Spanish-American War to the invasion of
Panama.**
Ivan Musicant. New York: Macmillan, 1990. 470p. map. bibliog.
The author explains that 'in their military and naval aspects, the founding and policing
of (America's) Central American and Caribbean realm, de facto and de jure, are
colloquially termed the Banana Wars . . . the classic period [of which] occurred
roughly in the first third of the twentieth century.' In chapter 5, 'Haiti 1915-1934', (p.
157-234), Musicant provides the first military history in English of the two Cacos Wars
fought in Haiti during the United States military occupation, in which American
Marines defeated Haitians led by Charlemagne Peralte. The book is based on both
primary and secondary sources.

274 **The Afro-American response to the occupation of Haiti, 1915-1934.**
Brenda Gayle Plummer. *Phylon*, vol. 43, no. 2 (June. 1982),
p. 125-43.
Plummer uses primary sources in an attempt to provide a fresh insight into the role
played by the American black community and its leaders in ending the American
military occupation of Haiti. Black disapproval and political pressure to end the
occupation grew steadily throughout the intervention period and were instrumental in
convincing Washington to return sovereignty to Haiti in 1934.

275 **Race, nationality, and trade in the Caribbean: the Syrians in Haiti,
1903-1934.**
Brenda G. Plummer. *The International History Review*, vol. 3, no. 4
(Oct. 1981), p. 517-39.
Discusses the activities of Syrian merchants in Haiti during the first three decades of
the twentieth century. In the author's view, the Syrians were supported by the
Americans as 'their' men in Haiti; the means by which the United States penetrated
the Haitian market. Syrian control of mid-level commerce in Haiti aroused xenophobic
sentiments and the Haitian government made several attempts to expel the Syrians.
Plummer's description of how the American government handled this issue is revealing
of the tenor of United States policy in the Caribbean at this time.

276 **The United States occupation of Haiti, 1915-1934.**
Hans Schmidt. New Brunswick, New Jersey: Rutgers University
Press, 1971. 303p. map. bibliog.
The best, and most recent history of US intervention in, and occupation of, the Haitian
Republic. It is based on archival records available to researchers only since 1950, in

particular the Naval Records Collection in the US National Archives. The work covers the background of United States–Haitian relations prior to the intervention; the decision to intervene; the intervention itself; Haiti under US occupation; the reorganization of the country; racial and cultural tensions (which included the introduction of 'Jim Crow' segregation into Haiti); results of the occupation; the US withdrawal from Haiti; and the aftermath of US involvement. Schmidt is critical of American actions during the occupation and concludes that Haiti profited little from almost almost twenty years of direct and complete American control.

277 **W. Cameron Forbes and the Hoover Commissions to Haiti, 1930.**
Robert M. Spector. Lanham, Maryland: University Press of America, 1985. 258p. bibliog.

In 1930, W. Cameron Forbes, an investment banker and the former governor-general of the Philippines, headed President Herbert Hoover's Commission for Study of Conditions in Haiti, which recommended Haitianization of the island's administration and the phased withdrawal of the Americans (see item no. 280). Spector draws on primary sources in order to detail this last phase of the American occupation of Haiti.

278 **W. Cameron Forbes in Haiti: additional light on the genesis of the 'Good Neighbor Policy'.**
Robert M. Spector. *Caribbean Studies*, vol. 6, no. 2 (July. 1966), p. 28-45.

The report issued by the Forbes Commission (see item no. 280) was instrumental in crystallizing Hoover's determination to withdraw US troops from the republic and to adopt a new policy towards Latin America. This article, written by a historian, discusses the work of the Forbes Commission in Haiti, and reveals much concerning backstage political manoeuvring.

279 **Old gimlet eye: the adventures of Smedley D. Butler as told to Lowell Thomas.**
Lowell Thomas. New York: Farrar & Rinehart, 1933. 310p
(Reprinted, Quantico, Virgina: Marine Corps Association, 1981).

A legendary figure in the history of the US Marine Corps, Major Smedley Darlington Butler (1881-1940) was first commandant of the Gendarmerie d'Haiti, 1915-1918. His experiences in the US forces in occupied Haiti bulk large in these colourful memoirs.

280 **Report of the President's commission for the study and review of conditions in the Republic of Haiti, March 26, 1930.**
US Commission for Study and Review of Conditions in Haiti.
Washington, DC: US Government Printing Office, 1930. 45p.
(Department of State Publication no. 56; Latin American Series, no. 2).

This is the Forbes Commission Report (see item no. 277) that recommended the reestablishment of the authority of the Haitian government in Haiti and US withdrawal. The delegation, appointed by President Hoover to study the Haitian situation, was chaired by W. Cameron Forbes, former US Governor-General of the Philippines. Other members of the committee were Elie Vezina, Henry P. Fletcher, James Kerney and William Allen White.

281 **Inquiry into occupation and administration of Haiti and Santo Domingo: hearings before a Select Committee on Haiti and Santo Domingo, United States Senate, 67th Congress, 1st and 2nd sessions.**
US Congress. Senate Select Committee on Haiti and Santo Domingo. Medill McCormick, chairman. Washington, DC: US Government Printing Office, 1922. 37p. pamphlet (67th Congress. 2nd Session, Senate Report 794) and 2 vols. map.

These volumes, known as the McCormick Committee Report, present primary evidence on the abuses committed in Haiti under US occupation, and a transcription of testimony given at Senate hearings which were held between 5 August 1921 and 16 June 1932.

282 **The United States Marines in the Dominican Republic, Haiti, and Nicaragua: a bibliography of published works and magazine articles.**
United States Marine Corps.   Washington, DC: Historical Branch, G.3, Headquarters, US Marine Corps., 1958. 61. (Marine Corps Historical Reference Series, no. 2).

Includes a list of eleven unannotated items about the Marines in Haiti.

283 **The white king of La Gonâve.**
Faustin Wirkus, Taney Dudley, with an introduction by William B. Seabrook.   Garden City, New York: Garden City Publishing Co., 1931. 333p. map.

A Kiplingesque account which claims to be the true story of the reign of a US Marine crowned King by the inhabitants of Île de la Gonâve during the US occupation.

284 **A Marine tells it to you.**
Frederic M. Wise, Meigs O. Frost.   New York: Sears, 1929. 366p. (Reprinted, Quantico, Virginia: Marine Corps Association, 1981).

Several pages of Colonel Wise's autobiographical narrative of his twenty-one years' service in the US Marine Corps are devoted to his experiences in Haiti during the Cacos Rebellion. Another book in which the US occupation in Haiti is presented from a Marine's point of view is *Marine! The life of Lt. Gen. Lewis B. (Chesty) Puller, USMC (ret.)* by Burke Davis (Boston, Massachusetts: Little, Brown, 1962). Puller began his military career as a Private in Haiti in 1919. For a completely fictional account, see the adventure novel *Knights in the cockpit: a romantic epic of the flying Marines in Haiti* by Irwin R. Franklyn (New York: L. MacVeagh, Dial Press, 1931).

America's policy-making in Haitian education, 1915-1934.
See item no. 703.

The press in Haiti.
See item no. 866.

Haiti 1934-1957

285 **Révolution et contre-révolution en Haiti de 1946 à 1957.** (Revolution
and counter-revolution in Haiti from 1946 to 1957.)
Colbert Bonhomme. Port-au-Prince: Imprimerie de l'Etat, 1957.
349p.
A history often cited by reviewers as one of the best studies of the 1946-57 period.

286 **Haiti: the calvary of a soldier.**
Demosthenes Petrus Calixte. New York: Wendell Malliet, 1939.
125p. (Reprinted, New York: Negro Universities Press, 1969).
Calixte was commander of the Garde d'Haiti following the US occupation. In these
memoirs, written in exile in the United States, he accuses the Stenio Vincent
government under which he served of being corrupt and tyrannical, but denies the
charge of having plotted its overthrow in December 1937.

287 **Carribbean caudillo: Magloire of Haiti.**
Herbert Gold. *The Nation*, vol. 180, no. 6 (Feb. 1955), p. 118-20.
Paints a depressing picture of the Haitian situation under the presidency of Paul
Eugene Magloire, whom the author depicts as an example of the politics of *doublure* –
a black figurehead acting as a puppet for mulatto interests. Gold, an American writer,
stresses the corruption and political oppression which was rife in Magloire's Haiti.

288 **Haiti since 1930.**
David Nicholls. In: *Cambridge history of Latin America. Vol. 7: Latin
America since 1930, Mexico, Central America and the Caribbean.*
Edited by Leslie Bethell. New York; Cambridge, England:
Cambridge University Press, 1990, p. 545-77.
Provides a concise summary of the 1930-88 era and emphasizes the decline and
deterioration of Haiti's economy. A survey of Haiti's political and cultural history, and
of its international relations with the Catholic Church and the United States are also
included. A bibliographical essay (p. 714-17) evaluates the material which is available
for further study of the period.

Haiti 1957-

289 **Haiti: the Duvaliers and their legacy.**
Elizabeth Abbott. New York: McGraw-Hill, 1988. 381p. bibliog.
Abbott is a historian and professional journalist, the senior editor of Haiti's only
English Language monthly newspaper, the *Haiti Times*. She is also the sister-in-law of
Lieut.-General Henri Namphy, a major figure in post-Duvalier politics. As such she is
well placed to provide an independent observation of Haitian politics. Although
Abbott provides little political analysis, her work supplies many astonishing details of
life in Haiti both under the Duvaliers and after their fall

290 **The crisis of the gods: Haiti after Duvalier.**
Joan Dayan. *The Yale Review*, n.s., vol. 77 (spring 1988), p. 299-331.
Documents the author's sojourn in post-Duvalier Haiti from April 1986, to January 1988, during the Namphy régime. Dayan's article centres on the attempts to destroy Haiti's national culture through open assults on Voodoo temples, priests and devotees which were perpetrated by the government, the Roman Catholic church and by Protestant sects.

291 **Papa Doc: the truth about Haiti today.**
Bernard Diederich, Al Burt, with a foreword by Graham Greene.
New York: McGraw-Hill, 1969. 393p.
Presents a well-informed report of the first ten years of the François Duvalier regime. Diederich, a New Zealander, was the founder and editor of Port-au-Prince's English-language weekly, the *Haiti Sun*. Of particular interest in the volume are accounts of anti-Duvalier guerrilla activities, including the three invasions launched by Haitian exiles from Dominican territory in 1964.

292 **Papa Doc, Baby Doc: Haiti and the Duvaliers.**
James Ferguson. Oxford; New York: B. Blackwell, 1987. 171p. map. bibliog.
A popular account of the rise and fall of the Duvalier dictatorship. Ferguson uses eyewitness recollections in order to provide a vivid analysis of the kleptocratic reigns of the megalomanical François Duvalier and the corrupt Jean-Claude, a 'kleptocracy' being, essentially, a rule by thieves. The book includes an account of the final usurpment of the Duvalier régime.

293 **Duvalier, Caribbean cyclone: the history of Haiti and its present government.**
Jean Pierre O. Gingras. New York: Exposition Press, 1967. 163p. bibliog.
Following an overview of the history of Haiti based on printed sources, Gingras devotes the major part of his book to a denunciation of François Duvalier, who has 'wiped out all the bridges that linked Haiti with the free civilized world'.

294 **Merci Gonaïves.** (Thank you, Gonaïves.)
Danny Lyon. Clintondale, New York: Black Beauty Books, 1988. 62p.
The title of this volume refers to the small Haitian town of Gonaïves whose citizens sparked the revolt that led to the collapse of the Duvalier government. Lyon's work forms a photographic chronicle of the February 1986 Revolution.

295 **Haiti: the tragic island.**
O. Ernest Moore. *Revista/Review Interamericana*, vol. 1, no. 3 (fall 1980), p. 305-19.
Examines the condition of Haiti at the end of the 1970s. After a brief overview and an analysis of what are depressing statistics – in almost every sphere of civilized life, Haiti holds the lowest rank among Western hemisphere countries – Moore, an economist

who was an advisor to the Haitian government, 1951-1959, describes the state of political and economic repression existing under the Jean-Claude Duvalier régime.

296 **Haiti: family business.**
Rod Prince, with additional material by Jean-Jacques Honorat.
London: Latin American Bureau (Research and Action) Ltd., 1985.
86p. map. bibliog. (Latin American Special Brief).
Written in 1985 before the collapse of the Duvalier family dictatorship, this report gathers together a variety of facts and figures in an attempt to detail the dismal effects of two generations of Duvalier rule on Haiti's economy, social conditions and international relations.

297 **Caribbean exile invasions: a special regional type of conflict.**
Robert D. Tomasek. *Orbis*, vol. 17, no. 4 (winter 1974), p. 1354-82.
Attempts and plans by groups of Haitian exiles groups to invade their homeland and overthrow the François Duvalier régime are among those examined in this analysis of armed conflicts in the post-war Caribbean. A valuable chart, 'Synopsis of Caribbean invasions', appended to the text, provides details of anti-Duvalier exile invasions that occurred in 1959, 1963 and 1967.

298 **Under a grudging sun: photographs from Haiti Libéré 1986-1988.**
Alex Webb. New York; London: Thames and Hudson, 1989. 85p.
The author, a photojournalist, provides a largely pictorial account of Haiti's revolutionary period, the *dechoukaj* ('uprooting'), that began with Jean-Claude Duvalier's flight in February 1986. He records the popular jubilation at the collapse of the Duvalier government in February 1986, and the horrors of the massacres that occurred during the November elections in 1987.

Haiti since 1930.
See item no. 288.

Population and Fertility

20th century

299 **Fertility and family planning in Haiti.**
James Allman. *Studies in Family Planning*, vol. 13. 8/9 (Aug-Sept. 1982), p. 237-45.

Discusses the slowly emerging population policy of the Haitian government: 'This paper will consider levels and trends in fertility and some of the factors – including union patterns, desired family size, infant mortality levels, and breastfeeding patterns – that determine the current situation. It will then examine knowledge and use of contraception and the impact of the recently established national family planning program'. Allman uses the data drawn from the 1977 *Haitian Fertility Survey* (q.v.).

300 **Fertility, mortality, migration, and family planning in Haiti.**
James Allman, John May. *Population Studies*, vol. 33, no. 3 (Nov. 1979), p. 505-21.

Analyses Haiti's population dynamics, based on data from the 1971 Census and the Multi-Round Demographic Survey conducted between 1971 and 1975. The article covers fertility; bio-medical, socio-economic, and cultural factors affecting fertility; internal and international migration; mortality; and Haiti's family planning and population policy.

301 **Mortality and acceptability of family planning in a Haitian community.**
John A. Ballweg, Ryland E. Webb, Gisele Biamby. *Community Health*, vol. 5, no. 6 (May-June 1974), p. 304-11. bibliog.

A report of a study conducted in the Haitian village of Collin, twenty kilometres south of Port-au-Prince. Interview techniques were used to correlate participants' knowledge and their use of family planning methods with their pregnancy histories. The interviewers sought to determine whether the perception of a high likelihood of infant death played a role in a high pregnancy rate. From the results of the study this did not seem to be the case; rather, the authors conclude that 'without the resources to prevent pregnancies (women) are compelled to accept a greater number (of children) than they consider ideal'.

302 **Morphology, serology, dermatoglyphics, and micro-evolution of some village populations in Haiti, West Indies.**
A. Basu, K. K. Namboodiri (et al.). *Human Biology*, vol. 48, no. 2 (May 1976), p. 245-69.
'During the spring of 1968 and 1969, a population genetics survey was conducted in four villages on the island of Grande Cayemite and the mainland town of Pestel, Haiti, West Indies'. This article reports the analysis of the data drawn from the survey. 'The genetic data confirms the history and appearance (of the population) in indicating about 80 per cent Negro ancestry and some French and less American Indian.'

303 **Rural Haitian women: an analysis of fertility rates.**
H. Berggren, N. Marthy, S. J. Williams. *Social Biology*, vol. 21, no. 4 (winter 1974), p. 363-78.
Asserts that the following factors influence fertility among Haitian women: childhood mortality; sterility; maternal health and nutritional status; marital stability; age at marriage; lactation patterns; and preferences concerning family size.

304 **Trends, age patterns and differentials in childhood mortality in Haiti (1960-1987).**
George Bicego, Anouch Chahnazarian, Kenneth Hill, Michel Cayemittes. *Population Studies: a Journal of Demography*, vol. 45, no. 2 (July 1991), p. 235-52.
Data collected in the *Enquête mortalité, morbidité et utilisation des services* in 1987 made this article possible. The authors review earlier work on child mortality in Haiti, then present and interpret the new data. They conclude that 'child-mortality declines in Haiti have approximately kept pace with those elsewhere in the Caribbean, but it remains a high-mortality pocket in Latin America'.

305 **Distribution of population on Hispaniola.**
Donald R. Dyer. *Economic Geography*, vol. 30, no. 4 (Oct. 1954), p. 335-46.
The completion of the 1950 Haitian census, the first trustworthy enumeration of the country's population, was central to this study. Covering both Haiti and the Dominican Republic, the article discusses diversity of land features, regional distribution of population, urban and rural settlement, and population along the international border. This study is now, of course, primarily of historical interest, but it should be noted that Dyer's concluding prediction of a Haitian population of 5,900,000 in 1980 was correct.

306 **The handbook of national population censuses: Latin America and the Caribbean, North America, and Oceania.**
Edited by Doreen S. Goyer, Eliane Domschke. Westport, Connecticut: Greenwood Press, 1983. 711p. map.
The 'Haiti' chapter, p. [209]-13 of this reference work, describes the country's two population censuses: that of August 8 1950, and that of August 31 1971. The quality of the data collected is discussed, certain features of the censuses are commented on, and publication details are provided for each report.

307 **Recensement général de la République d'Haiti, août 1950.** (General
census of the Republic of Haiti, August 1950.)
Haiti. (Republic). Port-au-Prince: Institut Haïtien de Statistique,
1951-1959. maps. 5 vols. in 7.
This is Haiti's first reliable census: Vol. 1: *Département du Nord-ouest*; vol. 2, pts. 1
and 2: *Département du Nord*; vol. 3: *Département de l'Artibonite*; vol. 4: *Département
de l'Ouest*; vol. 5, pts. 1 and 2: *Département du Sud*.

308 **Recensement général de la population et du logement, août 1971.**
(General census of population and housing, August 1971.
Haiti. (Republic). Port-au-Prince: Institut Haïtien de Statistique,
1978-79. 7 vols.
These are the multi-volume results of the census of 1971, presented in tabular form.

309 **Resultats préliminaires du recensement général (septembre 1982).**
(Preliminary results of the general census [September 1982]).
Haiti (Republic). Institut Haïtien de Statistique et d'Informatique.
Port-au-Prince: L'Institut, 1983. 60p. maps.
Haiti's most recent population census, undertaken in 1982, was not entirely successful.
This item reports preliminary statistics on housing, households, and population in a
tabular format.

310 **World population growth and aging: demographic trends in the late
twentieth century.**
Nathan Keyfitz, Wilhelm Flieger. Chicago: University of Chicago
Press, 1990. 608p.
Detailed population data and forecasts for Haiti, 1950 to 2020/25, are tabulated on
p. 185 of this volume, accompanied by excellent graphs which visually summarize
demographic information on births, age distribution, death rate, fertility and aging.

311 **Women in perdition: ritual fertility control in Haiti.**
Gerald F. Murray. In: *Culture, nataility and family planning.* Edited
by John F. Marshall, Steven Polgar. Chapel Hill, North Carolina:
University of North Carolina Press, 1976, p. 59-78.
Discusses traditional practices for the regulation of fertility in Haiti.

312 **Haiti.**
Aaron Segal. In: *Population policies in the Caribbean.* Edited by
Aaron Segal. Lexington, Massachusetts: Lexington Books, 1975,
p. 197-204.
In spite of its date of publication, Segal's essay retains its usefulness. It provides
information on fertility, contraception and on government policy on population
limitation in Haiti.

313 **Evaluation des données de l'Enquête haitienne sur la fecondité.**
(Evaluation of data from the Haitian Fertility Survey.)
Camille Tardieu. Voorburg, Netherlands; London: World Fertility
Survey, 1984. 60p. bibliog. (Scientific Reports/World Fertility Survey,
no. 50).
Evaluates Haitian fertility statistics gathered by the World Fertility Survey.

314 **The Haitian fertility survey 1977: a summary of findings.**
World Fertility Survey. Voorburg, The Hague, Netherlands:
International Statistical Institute, 1981. (World Fertility Survey).
This country survey, conducted in 1977, provides the first reasonably accurate data on
fertility and its determinants in Haiti. The summary of findings covers fertility rates
and fertility in relation to infant mortality, family size, gender preference, knowledge
of contraception, contraceptive use and other factors. It concludes that the desired
average total family size in Haiti is 3.58 children.

Pre-20th century

315 **Demographic statistics in Haiti.**
Robert Bazile. In: *The Haitian potential; research and resources of
Haiti.* Edited by Vera Rubin, Richard P. Schaedel. New York:
Teachers College Press, 1975, p. 3-10. (Publications of the Center for
Education in Latin America).
Provides both a valuable history and a discussion of Haitian demographic activities and
population surveys, 1804-1967.

316 **James Redpath and American Negro colonization in Haiti, 1860-1862.**
Willis D. Boyd. *The Americas: a Quarterly Review of Inter-American
Cultural History*, vol. 12 (Oct. 1955), p. 169-82.
A good article on a subject upon which little has been written: the efforts of the
eccentric and energetic Scots immigrant James Redpath to resettle free American
blacks in Haiti during the 19th century. The essay is based on research in primary
sources.

317 **Forgotten venture: migration of US Negroes to Hispaniola in [the] early
nineteenth century.**
Guillermo Cabrera Leives. *Americas*, vol. 4, no. 6 (June 1952),
p. 16-19.
Briefly examines the efforts in 1824 of Haitian president Jean-Pierre Boyer to induce
free American blacks to emigrate to Haiti and to the Dominican Republic, then under
Haitian control. Boyer sent Jonathan Granville as his emissary to the United States to
further his emigration project. Most of the article is concerned with settlements on the
Dominican side of Hispaniola, where a Dominican-American presence still survives.

80

See also the article 'La immigración de negres norteamericanos en Haiti en 1824' [The immigration of North American blacks to Haiti in 1824] by Jean Stephens in *Eme-eme: estudios dominicos*, vol. 3, no. 14 (Sept.-Oct. 1974), p. 40-71.

318 **Les juifs dans les colonies françaises au XVIIIe siècle.** (Jews in the French colonies during the eighteenth century.)
Abraham Cahen. *Revue des Etudes Juives*, vol. 4 (1882), p. 126-45; 236-48.

Drawing on primary material in the French National Archives, Cahan provides important information on the history of the Jewish community in Saint-Domingue, notably the extraordinary monetary exactions demanded of the Jews of Cap François by the Comte d'Estaing, Governor-General of France's overseas islands in the latter half of the eighteenth century.

319 **Essays in population history: Mexico and the Caribbean.**
Sherburne F. Cook, Woodrow Borah. Berkeley, California: University of California Press, 1971-1979. 3 vols. bibliog.

In Chapter six of volume one, *The aboriginal population of Hispaniola*, the authors review Spanish accounts contemporary with early explorations. They conclude that at the time of its discovery, the island was far more densely populated than had been previously believed. Using mathematical techniques, they estimate a pre-Columbian population figure of seven to eight million inhabitants for Hispaniola.

320 **British West Indians in Haiti in the late nineteenth and early twentieth centuries.**
Peter D. Fraser. In: *After the crossing: immigrants and minorities in Caribbean Creole societies*. Edited by Howard Johnson. London: Frank Cass, 1988, p. 79-94.

Using British Foreign Office records as his source, Fraser has written the first study of the community of British subjects who resided in independent Haiti. Emigrating from Jamaica and other West Indian islands of the British empire, many were labourers, but several represented the middle class. They were particularly active in the affairs of Haiti's Protestant denominations. Fraser covers their economic and political activities, as well as their relationship with the host society.

321 **On the contact population of Hispaniola: history as higher mathematics.**
David Henige. *Hispanic American Historial Review*, vol. 58, no. 2 (May 1978), p. 217-37.

Discusses the current revision of population figures and the changing interpretation of the size of the New World population at the entry of Europeans into the Western Hemisphere. In particular, Henige examines the estimate of the aboriginal population of Hispaniola which Sherbourne Cook and Woodrow Borah presented in their *Essays in population history: Mexico and the Caribbean* (q.v.). Henige evaluates the validity of the assumptions upon which Cook and Borah base their figures, discussing the three main sources used in formulating their determinations; the testimonies of Christopher Columbus and of Bartolome de las Casas and the 1496 *repartimiento*. Henige is critical of Cook's and Borah's methodology, warming that available sources do not permit a reliable population estimate for pre-Columbian Hispaniola.

322 **Un cimetière juif au Cap-Haïtien (Haiti).** (A Jewish cemetary at Cap Haïtien (Haiti).)
Zvi Liker. *Revue des Etudes Juives*, vol. 136, fasc. 3-4 (July-Dec. 1977), p. 425-7.

Few traces remain today of the Jewish cemetery that once existed in the Calvaire neighbourhood of Cap Haitien. However, in eighteenth-century Saint-Domingue the cemetery was the final resting place for the deceased of a structured Jewish community, established by Jewish merchants of Portuguese extraction from Curaçao. Loker provides the facts available about this community.

323 **Were there Jewish communities in Saint Domingue (Haiti)?**
Zvi Loker. *Jewish Social Studies*, vol. 45, no. 2 (spring 1983), p. 135-46.

Supplies documentary proof that a Jewish community existed at Cap François (Cap Haitien) in the second half of the eighteenth century, identifying the Portuguese–Jewish families mentioned in contemporary records as being active in the French colony.

324 **The emigration of black Americans to Haiti, 1821-1863.**
Leon D. Pamphile. *The Crisis*, vol. 90, no. 9 (Nov. 1983), p. 43-44.

Presents a brief overview of a number of nineteenth-century efforts to persuade blacks from the United States to emigrate to Haiti. Pamphile notes that a good number of black Americans did settle in the republic, and among the enduring contributions brought by them to Haiti was Protestantism.

325 **The population of Hispaniola at the time of Columbus.**
Angel Rosenblatt. In: *The native population of the Americas in 1492*. Edited by William M. Denevan. Madison, Wisconsin: University of Wisconsin Press, 1976 (1992. 2nd ed.), p. 43-66.

The aboriginal population of Hispaniola at the time of the discovery is a controversial subject. In this essay, a revised and expanded translation of his *Población de America en 1492: viejos y nuevos cálculos* (Mexico City: El Colegio de Mexico, 1967), Rosenblatt quotes a comparatively low population level of 100,000 for the island and defends this estimate, explaining his calculations and the sources from which he derived his figures.

326 **Afro-American emigration to Haiti during the American Civil War.**
William Seraille. *The Americas: a Quarterly Review of Inter-American Cultural History*, vol. 35, no. 2 (Oct. 1978), p. 185-200.

When, needing agriculturalists, Haitian President Geffrard invited American blacks to emigrate to Haiti in 1859, American black leaders were divided on whether or not to advocate the project. Based on research in archives and newspaper files, this article discusses the debate within both black and white communities in the United States in response to the proposed emigration to Haiti. Eventually, approximately 2,500 American blacks did go to Haiti at this time, many settling at St. Marc.

Emigration

General

327 **Haitian migration: 30 years assessed.**
James Allman. *Migration Today*, vol. 10, no. 1 (1982), p. 6-12.
bibliog.
Allman analyses Haitian international migration between 1950 and 1980, covering migration to the United States, the Dominican Republic, Canada, the Bahamas and several other countries. He reviews available sources of data on migration, considers current policies and predicts future trends. Tables of statistics, population figures and a bibliography listing sources for migration data are also included.

328 **A bibliography of Caribbean migration and Caribbean immigrant communities.**
Compiled and edited by Rosemary Brana-Shute, with the assistance of Rosemarijn Hoefte.   Gainesville, Florida: Reference and Bibliographic Dept., University of Florida Libraries in co-operation with the Center for Latin American Studies, University of Florida, 1983. 339p. (Bibliographic Series, no. 9).
Approximately 180 references to Haitian migration can be found among the 2,585 unannotated citations on post-slave-trade population movements to, from and within the Caribbean area which comprise this bibliography. The references were gathered through database searches and cite books, periodical articles, essays and unpublished papers. The main listing is alphabetical by author with topical and geographical indexes.

329 **La femme Haïtienne en diaspora.** (The Haitian woman in the diaspora.)
Le Comité ad hoc des femmes Haïtiennes.   Montreal: Centre
International de Documentation et d'Information Haïtienne,
Caraibéene et Afro-Canadienne; New York: Women's International
Resource Exchange, 1986. 21p.

Assesses the social and economic problems of Haitian emigrée women, both the
difficulties that drive them from Haiti and the adverse conditions in foreign
environments with which they must contend.

330 **Aiding migration: the impact of international development assistance on
Haiti.**
Josh DeWind, David H. Kinley III.   Boulder, Colorado: Westview
Press, 1988. 196p. bibliog.

A research paper published in co-operation with the Immigration Research Program,
Center for Social Sciences, Columbia University. DeWind and Kinley explore the
paradox that international economic assistance aimed at improving conditions and
ameliorating the lives of people within Haiti actually contributes to the desire to leave
and provides the means for further emigration out of the country.

Haitians in the West Indies

331 **Haitians in the Bahamas face a new wave of massive deportations.**
Max Dominique, CS, SP.   *Migration Today*, vol. no. 5 (1985), p. 30-2.

Haitians, who now constitute 20 per cent of the Bahamian population, were once
welcomed as cheap labour. Now, however, high unemployment has sparked periodic
efforts by the Bahamian government to repatriate the Haitians. Dominique's article
exposes the abuses involved in the series of deportations that took place in 1985.

332 **The Haitian problem: illegal migration to the Bahamas.**
Dawn I. Marshall.   Mona, Kingston, Jamaica: Institute of Social and
Economic Research, University of the West Indies, 1979. 239p. maps.
bibliog.

This is the first monograph to cover the post-1956 illegal entry of an ever-increasing
number of Haitians into the Bahamas and to provide the first hard data on this
immigration. Marshall firstly depicts the lifestyle of a typical migrant in Haiti, then
traces the history of Haitian migration to the Bahamas and the conditions under which
Haitians live in the islands. She closes with a case study of a Bahamian immigrant
community. The data collected for the volume is presented in easily comprehensible
tables.

333 Haitian emigration in the early twentieth century.

Glenn Perusek. *International Migration Review*, vol. 18, no. 1 (spring 1984), p. 4-18. bibliog.

A detailed study of the migration of Haitian labourers to Cuba and the Dominican Republic during the first decades of the twentieth century. Perusek advances a new theory to explain this population movement, locating its impetus in the catastrophic factors in the migrant's country of origin, rather than in the more usual attraction of the receiving country.

334 Haitian migrants and backyard imperialism.

Gayle Plummer. *Race & Class*, vol. 26, no. 4 (spring 1985), p. 35-43.

Traces the international migration of Haitian workers from 1902 onwards – first to Cuba, then to the Dominican Republic and, mostly recently, to the United States. Plummer emphasizes her view that the American government's Caribbean policy is above all aimed at using Haiti as a supplier of cheap labour.

Haitians in the Dominican Republic

335 A Dominican harvest of shame.

Marcy Fink. *Caribbean Review*, vol. 8, no. 1 (Jan-March 1979), p. 34-8.

Ninety per cent of sugar cane cutters in the Dominican Republic are Haitian migrants. This article details the historical background of Dominican–Haitian relations and discloses the inhuman conditions under which Haitians labour in Dominican cane fields.

336 Neoslavery in the cane fields: Haitians in the Dominican Republic.

Paul R. Latortue. *Caribbean Review*, vol. 14, no. 4 (fall 1985), p. 18-20.

A concise history of the migration of Haitian works to the Dominican Republic beginning in 1915. Latortue's depiction of the work situation on the sugar plantations supports the use of the term 'neoslavery' with regard to the harsh conditions endured by Haitian cane-cutters in return for minimal wages.

337 Bitter sugar: slaves today in the Caribbean.

Maurice Lemoine, translated from the French by Andrea Johnston.
London: Zed Press; Chicago: Banner Press, 1985. 308p. maps.

Contains text and photographs detailing the shocking conditions endured by Haitian contract labourers in the cane fields of the Dominican Republic. More documentation of the abuse of Haitian sugar workers can be found in *Sold like cattle: Haitian workers in the Dominican Republic*, a dossier compiled by the World Council of Churches (Geneva: World Council of Churches, 1980).

Emigration. Haitians in the West Indies.
Haitians in the Dominican Republic

338 **La inmigración haitiana.** (Haitian immigration).
Frank Marino Hernández. Santo Domingo: Editiones Sargoza, 1973.
98p. bibliog.
Examines Haitian emigration to the Dominican Republic, written from a Dominican perspective.

339 **Migrant workers in the Dominican Republic: a case for human rights action.**
Geneva: World Council of Churches, 1978. 47p. bibliog.
Contains documents 'which demonstrate the systematic denial of human rights to tens of thousands of Haitian sugar cane workers in the Dominican Republic. Much of the material is reprinted, although this report represents the first collection of this material'. The articles include: 'Exploitation of Haitian sugar workers in the Dominican Republic'; 'The Haitian cane-culture: notorious Dominican racket; and 'Haitian workers in the Dominican Republic: still a source of cheap labour'.

340 **Sugar and modern slavery: a tale of two countries.**
Roger Plant. London; Atlantic Highlands, New Jersey: Zed Books, 1987. 177p. map. bibliog.
In this report, sponsored by Britain's Anti-Slavery Society, Plant not only investigates the appalling conditions under which Haitian migrant workers labour on the Dominican Republic's sugar plantations, but also sets the Haitians' present situation in the larger context of the world sugar market and the multinational organization of sugar production. The volume's bibliographical essay supplies suggestions for further reading.

341 **A troubled year: Haitians in the Dominican Republic.**
New York: Human Rights Watch, 1992. 54p.
This publication, issued in conjunction with the National Coalition for Haitian Refugees, documents the continuing mistreatment of Haitian workers in the Dominican Republic in 1992. Forced to cut sugar cane for low wages on Dominican government plantations, Haitians are often expelled from the Dominican Republic without due process of law.

342 **Immigracion, haitianos, esclavitud.** (Immigration, Haitians, slavery.)
Ramon Antonio Veras. Santo Domingo, Dominican Republic: Taller, 1983. 179p. (Biblioteca Taller, no. 152).
Exposes the slave-like conditions under which Haitian migrants labour in the Dominican Republic's sugar cane fields. This book is based on a conference paper originally presented at the Coloquio sobre Migraciones y Relaciones Internacionales en el Caraibe in October 1981.

Haitians in the United States

20th century

343 **A reporter at large: the Haitians of New York.**
Jervis Anderson. *The New Yorker*, vol. 51 (31 March 1975), p. 50ff.
Reports on New York City's community of exile Haitians during the mid-1970s.
Anderson describes their political and intellectual groups, newspapers, radio station
and social life. He sketches notable personalities within the community and discusses
the problems faced by the Haitians.

344 **The cultural meaning of social class for Haitians in New York City.**
Susan Huelsebusch Buchanan. *Ethnic Groups*, vol. 5, nos. 1 & 2 (July
1983), p. 7-29. bibliog.
Examines the way in which Haitian emigrants define their social reality in the context
of New York City. Continuing to view their community primarily in terms of the socio-
cultural divisions which had existed in Haiti, the Haitians persist in classifying their
community into *elit* (elite) and *pep-la* (the people), assigning membership in these
categories according to such factors as wealth, ancestry, birth place and residence, and
education and comportment.

345 **Language and identity: Haitians in New York City.**
Susan Huelsebusch Buchanan. *International Migration Review*,
vol. 13, no. 2 (summer 1979), p. 298-313. bibliog.
Provides a unique insight into the persistence of class stratification in emigré Haitian
society by means of a sociological case study of the struggle over which primary
language – French or Haitian Creole – was to be used in the Roman Catholic Mass at a
church in New York City. Buchanan describes the language situation in Haiti and the
identity and status conflicts which are experienced by Haitian immigrants in New York;
conflicts that were expressed in this bitter debate over language usage.

346 **Risk factors for AIDS among Haitians residing in the United States:
evidence of heterosexual transmission.**
The Collaborative Study Group of AIDS in Haitian-Americans.
JAMA: Journal of the American Medical Association, vol. 257, no. 6
(June 1987), p. 1035-47.
Summarizes the epidemiology of AIDS among Haitian emigrants in the United States.

347 **Haitians.**
Frederick J. Conway, Susan Huelsebusch Buchanan. *Refugees in the
United States: a reference handbook*. Edited by David W. Hanies.
Westport, Connecticut: Greenwood Press, 1985. p. 95-109.
A concise summary of Haitian immigration to the United States as of 1985. Following
a background sketch of Haiti's language, culture, and political history, the authors
assess the status of Haitian refugees in the United States: their characteristics;

adaptation to American culture; and the policies of the Carter and Reagan administrations in regard to the Haitian 'boat people'.

348 **The new American immigration: evolving patterns of legal and illegal emigration: a bibliography of selected references.**
Francesco Cordasco. New York; London: Garland Publishing, 1987.
418p. (Garland References Library of Social Science, v. 376).

This bibliography of 2,328 references is organized in four main categories: American immigration before 1965: history and backgrounds; American immigration after 1965: general studies and related references; Illegal immigrants in the United States; and Miscellanea. Citations are for books, periodical articles, government documents and unpublished materials. Cordasco has brought together a vast amount of material – including many references to Haitian immigration – but unfortunately the work lacks a detailed subject index, making it difficult to locate items about a specific immigrant group.

349 **'I never knew they existed': the invisible Haitian migrant worker.**
Tito Craige. *Migration World*, vol. 15, no. 2 (1987), p. 17-21.

Basing his article on interviews with fifty-nine Haitian migrant farmworkers in North Carolina in 1984, Craige depicts the harsh, impoverished lives of the Haitian refugees who harvest that state's tobacco, vegetable and apple crops.

350 **Haitian family patterns of migration to South Florida.**
Stephen M. Fjellman, Hugh Gladwin. *Human Organization*, vol. 44, no. 4 (winter 1985), p. 301-12. bibliog.

Draws on the histories of seven Haitian migrant families in order to illustrate how the organization of the Haitian extended family makes it possible for Haitians not only to survive but even to prosper, in spite of harsh conditions, as emigrants to the United States. Among the topics discussed are the multinational family, sequential migration, the role of women in migration, problems with the United States immigration authorities, and personal and financial difficulties.

351 **Haitian immigrants in Boston, a commentary.**
Pierre-Michel Fontaine. In: *Caribbean immigration to the United States*. Edited by Roy S. Bryce-Laporte, Delores M. Mortimer. Washington, DC: Smithsonian Institution, Research Institute on Immigration and Ethnic Studies, 1976, p. 111-29. (RIIES Occasional Papers, 1).

By 1976, between 10,000 and 15,000 Haitian immigrants to the United States had settled in the Boston area. This article discusses their adaptation to their new environment and the racial/ethnic problems that they have encountered.

352 **Refugee *refoulement*: the forced return of Haitians under US – Haitian interdiction agreement.**
Maryse Fontas, Laura B. Sherman, edited by Arthur C. Helton. New York: Lawyers Committe for Human Rights, 1990. 64p.

In 1981 the Reagan administration established the Haitian Migrant Interdiction Program to deter Haitian 'boat-people' from entering the United States. The authors of this report examine the implementation of the programme and detail cases in which they believe that Haitians' rights as refugees have been violated.

353 **Haitians: America's boat people.**
Migration Today, vol. 7, no. 4 (Sept. 1979), p. 1-48.

This special issue of the periodical which covers national and international population movements contains six articles on Haitians in the United States: 'Haitian refugees: (Haiti's) missing persons' (Michelle Bogre); 'The Haitian niche in New York City' (Michel Laguerre); 'Haitian women in New York' (Susan H. Buchanan); 'Haitian emigration to New York' (Franck Laraque); 'Haitians in the arts' (Rocco Galatioto and Susan Buchanan); and 'Haitians in Miami' (Bryan O. Walsh).

354 **Profiles of undocumented aliens in New York City: Haitians and Dominicans.**
Charles B. Keely, Patricia J Elwell, Austin T. Fragomen, Jr., Silvano M. Tomasi. Staten Island, New York: Center for Migration Studies, 1978. 16p (Center for Migration Studies. Occasional Papers and Documentation Series, no. 5).

Presents six pages of text and nine pages of tabulated information on personal and family background characteristics, labour, and tax payment and social service usage for fifty-four Haitian and seventeen Dominican aliens in New York City. The data was gathered by means of personal interviews.

355 **American odyssey: Haitians in New York City.**
Michel S. Laguerre. Ithaca, New York: Cornell University Press, 1984. 198p.

A thorough study of Haitians in New York City. Now numbering more than 300,000 and growing rapidly, Haitians account for a substantial segment of the city's foreign population.

356 **Haitian-Americans.**
Michel S. Laguerre. In: *Ethnicity and medical care*. Edited by Alan Harwood. Cambridge, Massachusetts: Harvard University Press, 1981, p. 172-210. bibliog. (A Commonwealth Fund Book).

This medico-anthropological study of Haitian communities in the United States focuses on those emigrés who have come to the United States since the advent of the Duvalier régime in 1957. Laguerre provides a general demographic picture of these immigrants, then discusses their methods of dealing with disease: their beliefs as to natural and supernatural causes of illness; their problems in dealing with the mainstream US medical system; and their typical responses to medical treatment.

357 **Haitian migrants and Haitian Americans: from invisiblity into the spotlight.**
Robert Lawless. *The Journal of Ethnic Studies*, vol. 14, no. 2 (summer 1986), p. 29-70. bibliog.
A bibliographical essay evaluating numerous publications on Haitian emigrants and Haitian-Americans. Six works are reviewed in detail: Michel Laguerre's *American odyssey* (q.v.), Susan Buchanan's doctoral dissertation *Scattered seeds*; Takle Mariam Woldemikael's PhD dissertation *Maintenance and change of status in a migrant community*; Jake Miller's *Plight of Haitian Refugees* (q.v.), and Alex Stepick's articles 'Haitians released from Krome' and 'The business community of Little Haiti'. The main text is followed by a bibliography listing approximately 200 books, articles, reports and dissertations on Haitian immigrants.

358 **Human rights, US foreign policy and Haitian refugees.**
Gilbert Loescher, John Scanlan. *Journal of Interamerican Studies and World Affairs*, vol. 26, no. 3 (Aug. 1984), p. 313-56. bibliog.
Criticizes the refugee admission policy followed by the American government in regard to Haitian refugees. The authors of this article see United States immigration policy as politically driven, contending that 'the principal reason for the special immigration animus against Haitians, particularly as it has displayed itself in the handling of political asylum claims, has been the close political relationship between the US and the Duvaliers'. They trace American foreign policy interests in Haiti from the Eisenhower through the Reagan administrations, providing a detailed and documented review of this aspect of Haitian immigration.

359 **The plight of Haitian refugees.**
Jake C. Miller. New York: Praeger, 1984. 222p.
This monograph on Haitian refugees includes a chapter on Haitian emigrés in the Dominican Republic, Cuba, Jamaica, the Bahamas, France and Canada, but it is for the most part a study of the Haitians who flee to the United States: their dangerous journey and less than welcome reception there.

360 **An ethnic 'boiling pot': Cubans and Haitians in Miami.**
Raymond A. Mohl. *Journal of Ethnic Studies*, vol. 13, no. 2 (summer 1985), p. 51-74. bibliog.
Pages 63-67 of this article summarize the situation of Haitian immigrants to Miami as of the early 1980s, where Haitians number approximately 50,000 but were a relatively unknown ethnic group.

361 **The new Haitian immigration: a preliminary bibliography.**
Raymond A. Mohl. *Immigration History Newsletter*, vol. 17 (May 1985), p. 1-8.
A brief list of items pertaining to Haitian immigration to the United States.

362 **Actes du colloque sur l'enfant Haïtien en Amérique du Nord: santé,**
scolarité, adaptation sociale: 23, 24, 25 octobre 1981. (Proceedings of a
conferences on the Haitian child in North America: health, school
attendence, social adaptation: October 23, 24, 25 1981.)
Emile Olliver, Charles Pierre-Jacques (et al.).   Montreal: Centre de
Recherches Caraïbes, Université de Montreal, 1982. 132p. bibliog.

Two of the nineteen papers presented at this conference on the problems of Haitian
immigrant children in the United States and Canada are in English and examine
Haitian students in the Boston Public Schools. The two papers, which complement
each other, are Mary Murphy's 'Seventeen Haitian children: their learning styles and
the education implications: psycho-educational perspective', and Louise S. Tardif's
'Seventeen Haitian children: their learning styles and the educational implications:
social perspectives'.

363 **Unwelcome immigrants: the labor market experiences of 1980 (Mariel)**
Cuban and Haitian refugees in South Florida.
Alejandro Portes, Alex Stepick.   *American Sociological Review*,
vol. 50, no. 4 (Aug. 1985), 493-514. bibliog.

A scholarly article in which two sociologists contrast the employment situations of
Mariel Cubans and Haitians, two refugee groups recently arrived in the United States.
Portes and Stepick determine that traditional sociological theories – classical
assimilation and labour market segmentation – are disconfirmed as predictors
concerning the entry of these two foreign minorities into the United States labour
market; rather, the Mariel refugees' employment opportunities are enhanced by the
existence of an Cuban enclave in South Florida. Lacking an enclave option, the
Haitians are forced to accept secondary and informal employment, although most
remain unemployed.

364 **The Negro immigrant: his background, characteristics and social**
adjustment, 1899-1937.
Ira De Augustine Reid.   New York: Columbia University Press, 1939,
261p. bibliog. (Studies in History, Economics and Public Law, edited
by the Faculty of Political Science of Columbia University, no. 449).
(Reprinted, New York: AMS Press, 1968).

Information on pre-Second World War Haitian emigration to the United States can be
found on p. 94-100 of this work.

365 **Ethnic groups are made, not born: the Haitian immigrant and American**
politics.
Nina Glick Schiller.   In: *Ethnic encounters: identities and contexts*.
Edited by George L. Hicks, Philip E. Leis.   North Scituate,
Massachusetts: Duxbury Press, 1977, p. 23-25. bibliog.

Focuses on the interaction between an organization of Haitian immigrants – the
Haitian-American Citizens Council – and an American institution – the Democractic
Party – in order to detect the processes by which emigrants gain political leverage.
Schiller demonstrates how the Haitians' assumption of a common identity in the
United States is a function of America's pluralistic politics: the Haitians, divided by

class and colour in Haiti, are united in the United States in response to the Democractic Party's willingness to provide them with access to political power if they share a group identity.

366   **'Everywhere we go, we are in danger': Ti Manno and the emergence of a Haitian transnational identity.**
Nina Glick-Schiller, Georges Fouron.   *American Ethnologist*, Vol. 17, no. 2 (May 1990), p. 329-47. bibliog.

Ti Manno was Antoine Rossini Jean-Baptiste, a popular Haitian musician, whose death sparked the short-lived Ti Manno movement. (The movement was an effort organized by prominent Haitian personalities to pay Ti Manno's hospital bills shortly before his death.) The authors examine his lyrics and the developments of the movement in an attempt to gain an insight into the identity formed by Haitian immigrants in the United States. They argue that Haitians evolve a transnational identity in reponse to their experience of the realities of race and class in both Haiti and the United States.

367   **Exile, ethnic, refugee: the changing organizational identities of Haitian immigrants.**
Nina G. Schiller, Marie Lucie Brutus, Carolle Charles, Adrian DeWind, Georges Fouran, Luis Thomas.   *Migration World*, wold. 15, no. 1 (1987), p. 7-11.

A study based on field-work conducted in New York City in 1969-71 and 1985-86. The authors trace the changing self-definitions of Haitians immigrants who entered the United States between 1957 and 1986, focusing on the question of whether the Haitians view themselves as political refugees. They also examine how political and economic conditions in both Haiti and the United States have shaped the Haitians' self-perceptions.

368   **The Haitians: the cultural meaning of race and ethnicity.**
Susan Buchanan Stafford.   In: *New Immigrants in New York City*.
Edited by Nancy Foner.   New York: Columbia University Press, 1987, p. 131-58. bibliog.

Buchanan states that her essay 'examines shifts in the symbolic meaning of race and ethnicity' among Haitian immigrants in New York City, and that it also demonstrates that 'meaning and perception have practical consequences for behaviour and social relationships'. The article provides a clear picture of New York's Haitians as of 1974-77: their settlement patterns, social organization, incorporation into American society, and interaction with American blacks and with other Caribbean immigrant groups.

369   **Flight into despair: a profile of recent Haitian refugees in South Florida.**
Alex Stepick, Alejandro Portes.   *International Migration Review*, vol. 20, no. 2 (summer 1986), p. 329-50. bibliog.

A survey by two professional sociologists, based on data derived from interviews with Haitians who had recently arrived in South Florida. The authors describe the Haitians' background, arrival and early resettlement patterns, educational level, English language competence, knowledge about the United States, employment status, occupation, income and use of public assistance.

370 **Haitian boat people: a study in the conflicting forces shaping US immigration policy.**
Alex Stepick. *Law and Contemporary Problems*, vol. 45, no. 2 (spring 1982), p. 161-96.
A lengthy presentation of Haitian immigration in the context of American immigration law and policy. Among the topics explored are the Haitians and the courts, Haitian contacts with the United States Immigration and Naturalization Service, and the 1979 case of the Haitian Refugee Center v. Civiletti. Proposed legislation relating to immigration is also discussed.

371 **Haitian refugees in the United States.**
Alex Stepick, with the assistance of Dale Frederick Swartz. London: Minority Rights Group, 1986. 20p. bibliog. Updated ed. (Minority Rights Group. Report no. 52).
Examines the validity of the claim by Haitian refugees to political asylum in the United States, as opposed to the American government's contention that the Haitians are economic migrants. Also included are: a brief review of the political, economic and human rights situation in Haiti as of 1984; the Haitian diaspora in the Dominican Republic, the Bahamas, and the United States; and Haitian immigration cases decided in United States courts as of the early 1980s. The bibliography lists many reports compiled by groups and organizations monitoring Haitian conditions.

372 **Mangoes don't grow in Brooklyn.**
Bill Thompson. *Revista/Review Interamericana*, vol. 1, no. 2 (winter 1971-72), p. 84-90.
Bill Thompson teaches English to Haitians in Brooklyn, New York. In this article he sympathetically describes the hardships faced by these Caribbean emigrants in the harsh and gritty atmosphere of the metropolis.

373 **Trying times: Haitian youth in an inner city high school.**
Paule Verdet. *Social Problems*, vol. 24, no. 2 (Dec. 1976), p. 228-33.
Paule Verdet is a French sociologist at Boston University who volunteered in 1974 to teach English and mathematics to Haitian students at an inner city secondary school. Her classes were conducted in French as part of a billingual programme. She describes the difficulties faced by Haitians in the American school system, where their language problems are complicated by poor communication patterns and cultural differences as regards the management of educational studies.

374 **Becoming Black American: Haitians and American institutions in Evanston, Illinois.**
Tekle Mariam Woldemikael. New York: AMS Press, 1989. 191p (Immigrant Communities and Ethnic Minorities in the United States and Canada, 54).
The material for this study was assembled as part of the author's PhD thesis in sociology. Woldemikael conducted research within the Haitian immigrant community in Evanston, Illinois, to investigate how Haitians 'deal with the contradiction between their own self-definition, based on Haitian history, culture and nationality, and the

racial identity imposed on them by most American institutions'. Woldemikael observed the Haitians in various milieux – domestic, educational, and religous – in order 'to explore the consequences of the interactions between dominant white, subordinated black Americans, and triply-subordinated Haitian immigrants'.

375 **Opportunity versus constraint: Haitian immigrants and racial ascription.**
Tekle M. Woldemikael. *Migration Today*, vol. 13, no. 4 (1985), p. 7-12.

In this case study of Haitians in a small midwestern American city, Woldemikael explores 'the triple interaction between dominant whites, subordinate black Americans and doubly subordinated black immigrants', commenting in particular on the strained relations between Haitians and American blacks.

376 **The Haitians versus the United States: the courts as last resort.**
Naomi Flink Zucker. *The Annals of the American Academy of Political Science and Social Science*, vol. 467 (May 1983), p. 151-62.

Criticizes the policy of the Reagan administration not to admit Haitians to the United States as political refugees. Although American courts have generally ruled in favour of Haitian immigrants' right to remain in the United States, government policy has not changed. Zucker describes the various court cases in which Haitian immigrants have been involved, and argues for fairer treatment for the refugees. The article is based on research using government documents, newspaper accounts and interviews.

Pre-20th century

377 **The role of Haitian volunteers at Savannah in 1779: an attempt at an objective view.**
George P. Clark. *Phylon*, vol. 41, no. 4 (Dec. 1980), p. 356-66.

Clark searched for documentation which would substantiate the claim that black Chasseurs Volontaires brought from Saint-Domingue by the Comte d'Estaing played a significant role in the siege of Savannah in 1779. After examining a number of both printed and archival sources, Clark states that 'there is no real substantiation for a Haitian role at Savannah notably more meritorious than that of other units', but comments that the heroic myth, tracable to T.G. Steward's 1899 publication *How the black St. Domingo Legion saved the patriot army in the siege of Savannah, 1779* (q.v.) still survives.

378 **Chicago's Haitian ancestor.**
Mercer Cook. *Americas*, vol. 4, no. 2 (Feb. 1952), p. 24-27, 41.

Cook dispels legend and conjecture in his presentation of the biographical facts about Jean Baptiste Paul Dessables (also known as Jean Baptiste Pointe du Sable), a fur trader from Saint-Domingue. He established a trading post on the shores of Lake Michigan in 1779 at a place that the Indians called 'Checagou', and thus is credited with being Chicago's first settler.

379 **Jean Baptiste Pointe de Sable: founder of Chicago.**
Shirley Graham. New York: J. Messner, 1953. 180p.
Writing for secondary school students, Graham recounts the life of Jean Baptiste Pointe de Sable, the Saint-Dominguan black who founded a trading post at what was later to become Chicago.

380 **Memoir of Pierre Toussaint: born a slave in St Domingo.**
Harriet Farnham Lee. Boston, Massachusetts: Crosby, Nichols & Company, 1854. 124p. (Reprinted, Westport, Connecticut: Negro Universities Press, 1970).
Pierre Toussaint (1766-1853) was brought to New York from Haiti as a slave in 1787. Given his freedom, Toussaint, a devout Roman Catholic, became known for his industrious life and charitable deeds. Lee's book about Toussaint is less a biography than an anti-slavery tract, written to support the abolitionist movement of the time. It is interesting to note that Toussaint may have been the model for Harriet Beecher Stowe's fictional character Uncle Tom in *Uncle's Tom's Cabin*.

381 **Pierre Toussaint, a citizen of old New York.**
Arthur T. Sheehan, Elizabeth Odell Sheehan. New York: P. J. Kenedy, 1955. 257p. bibliog.
A fictionalized biography that emphasizes the sunnier aspects of Toussaint's life. The book was published in Great Britain as *Black pearl: the hairdresser from Haiti* (London: Harvil Press, 1956). The Sheehans have also written a children's book about Toussant: *Pierre Toussaint, pioneer in brotherhood* (New York: P. J. Kenedy, 1963).

382 **How the black St. Domingo Legion saved the patriot army in the siege of Savannah, 1779.**
T. G. Steward. Washington DC: American Negro Academy, 1899. 15p. maps. (American Negro Academy. Occasional Papers, no. 5). Reprinted, New York: Arno Press, 1969.
This pamphlet by a black American army chaplain was the first to laud the military performance of black troops from Saint-Domingue in the siege of Savannah, Georgia, during the American Revolution.

383 **The other Toussaint: a modern biography of Pierre Toussaint, a post-revolutionary black.**
Ellen Tarry. Boston, Massachusetts: St. Paul Editions, 1981. 377p. bibliog.
A hagiography that bears the imprimatur of the Roman Catholic Church. Haitian-born Pierre Toussaint (1799-1853) is a candidate for canonization, and Tarry's work is not a scholarly biography but an account that emphasizes Toussaint's pious life in the United States.

Haitians in Canada

384 **The Haitians in Quebec.**
Paul Dejean, translated from the French with a foreword by Max
Dorsinville. Ottawa: Tecumseh Press, 1980. 158p. (Tecumseh Titles
in Canadian Studies).

Originally published in French in 1978 by the Presses de l'Université du Quebec in
collaboration with the Bureau de Communauté Chrétienne de Haïtiens de Montréal,
this is a sociological study of the Haitian immigrant population in French-speaking
Quebec. Dejean discusses immigration from Haiti to Canada, both legal and illegal,
and the situation of the Haitians in Quebec.

385 **Exiles in a cold land: Montreal's Haitian community faces a double
barrier of prejudice.**
Janice Hamilton. *Canadian Geographic*, vol 110 (Dec. 1990-
Jan. 1991), p. 34-42.

A report on the problems faced by Haitians as a black minority in Montreal, Quebec.
In another article dealing with the racial discrimination in that city, 'Toward a fare
solution', *Maclean's*, vol. 101 (11 April 1989), p. 53, Michael Rose describes how
Montreal's Haitian taxicab drivers have overcome discrimination in employment by
forming their own company, Metro Montreal Taxi.

386 **Haitian immigration to Quebec.**
Herard Jadotte. *Journal of Black Studies*, vol. 7, no. 4 (June 1977),
p. 485-500. bibliog.

A theoretical article that makes use of the Marxist concept of class struggle in its
attempt to analyse the influx of Haitians to Quebec province, Canada, since the mid-
1960s. Jadotte, a Haitian scholar who arrived in Montreal in 1967, examines Haitian
immigration in the context of the post second World War internationalization of labour
and in the light of the immigration policy adopted by the Canadian government to
meet the country's need for manpower.

Haitians in France

387 **Les Haïtiens en France. (Haitians in France).**
Roger Bastide, Françoise Morin, François Raveau, with the
collaboration of MM. Achard and Lerman. Paris: Mouton, 1974.
229p (Publications de l'Institut d'Etudes et de Recherches
Interethniques et Interculturelles, 4).

This is a psychological study of middle-class Haitians and Haitian students living in
France in the early 1970s. From their data, the authors construct four 'types' of
Haitians residing in France: 'Westernized'; 'in search of identity'; 'self-sufficient'; and
'pragmatists'.

Folklore

General

388 **Anthologie du folklore Haïtien.** (Anthology of Haitian folklore.)
Remy Bastien.   Mexico City: Sociedad de Alumnos de las Escuela
Nacional de Antropoligica e Historia, 1946. 118p. bibliog. (*Acta
Anthropologica*, vol. 1 no. 4).
A collection of Haitian folk-tales, proverbs and riddles in French. Introduced by the
author, the volume also provides a one-page bibliography.

389 **Social anthropology; recent research and recent needs.**
Remy Bastien.   In: *The Haitian potential; research and resourses of
Haiti.*   Edited by Vera Rubin, Richard P. Schaedel.   New York:
Teachers College Press, 1975, p. 11-16. (Publications of the Center for
Education in Latin America).
Reviews recent anthropological research in, and about, Haiti, in the context of past
ethnological projects.

390 **The drum and the hoe: life and lore of the Haitian people.**
Harold Courlander.   Berkeley, California: University of California
Press, 1960. 371p. bibliog. Reprinted, 1973. (California Library Reprint
Series).
An outstanding work in English on Haitian folklore and folk culture, based on material
gathered by its author in Haiti during nine field trips undertaken between 1937 and
1955. This book is a treasury of information on the folk-tales, games, proverbs, arts,
and religion of the Haitian peasant, but its greatest importance lies in its record of the
folk music in Haiti: more than 186 songs and drum rhythms are notated on p. 203-313
of the volume.

391 **Folk-lore of the Antilles, French and English.**
Elsie Clews Parsons.   New York: Stechert, for the American Folklore
Society, 1933-1943. 3 vols. (Memoirs of the American Folk-lore
Society, vol. 26, pts. 1-3). bibliog. (Reprinted, Millwood, New York:
Kraus Reprint Co., 1976).
Haitian materials – tales, riddles and proverbs collected by Parsons in Haiti in 1924,
1925 and 1927 – are found in the second and third volumes of this set. In Volume 2
(p. 470-596), eighty-five Haitian folk-tales are recorded in their original Creole;
English summaries of these stories, with bibliographical references, are provided in the
third volume. Also in the last volume are riddles (p. 447-53) and proverbs (p. 484-87),
transcribed in Creole without translations.

392 **Panorama du folklore Haïtien (presence Africaine en Haïti).** (A
panorama of Haitian folklore [the African presence in Haiti]).
Emmanuel C. Paul.   Port-au-Prince: Imprimerie de l'Etat, 1962. 323p.
(Reprinted, Port-au-Prince: Les Editions Fardin, 1978).
In the first part of this French-language work, Paul covers oral literature (tales,
proverbs and riddles); folk songs; folk dances; musical instruments; games; festivals
and carnival; and traditions pertaining to collective labour. The second part of the
volume is devoted to the Voodoo religion: its structure and dogma; its mythology and
rituals; and its preliminary, initiatory and funerary rites. The study is especially
noteworthy for its extensive material on Haiti's carnival.

393 **Ainsi parla l'oncle: essais d'ethnographie.** (Thus spake the uncle:
ethnographic essays.)
Jean Price-Mars, with an introduction to the new edition by Robert
Cornevin.   Port-au-Prince: Imprimerie de Compiegne, 1928. 243p.
(Bibliothèque Haïtienne). New ed., Montreal: Lemeac, 1973. 316p.
map. bibliog. (Collection Caraïbes).
A scholarly anthropological study of Haitian folklore and the Voodoo religion. The
work's influence exceeded its actual ethnographic content, and it became a manifesto
for a politico-literary movement that stressed the African heritage of the Haitians. The
1973 edition has a 42-page introduction by Robert Cornevin, discussing the book and
its significance.

394 **So spoke the uncle = Ainsi parla l'oncle.**
Jean Price-Mars, translated from the French and with an introduction
by Magdaline W. Shannon.   Washington DC: Three Continents Press,
1983. 252p. map. bibliog.
The first English translation of Price-Mars' seminal 1928 work, *Ainsi parla l'oncle*
(q.v.). Shannon's 28-page introduction places this important book in its context.

395 **Quelques moeurs et coutumes des paysans haïtiens: travaux pratiques d'ethnographie sur la region de Milot à l'usage des étudiants.** (Manners and customs of the Haitian peasants: field-work in ethnography in the Milot region for the use of students.)
Jean-Baptiste Romain. Port-au-Prince: Imprimerie de l'Etat, 1959.
264p. map. bibliog. (Revue de la Faculté d'Ethnologie, no. 2).
(Reprinted, Norwood, Pennsylvania: Norwood Editions, 1975).

A valuable compilation in French of ethnographic information on the social and religious life of the rural population in the Milot region of northern Haiti, based on anthropological research undertaken in 1944 and 1945. Chapters cover the customs followed in family and kinship groups, the folk knowledge common among Milot's inhabitants, the region's oral literature of tales and proverbs, and its religious and artistic expression.

Proverbs

396 **Recueil de proverbes créoles.** (A Collection of Creole proverbs.)
Jean Joseph Audain. Port-au-Prince: J. J. Audain, 1877. 2e éd. rev. et augm. 40p.

Audain was the first to collect and classify the proverbs of Haiti. This book lists 1,011 proverbs in Haitian Creole.

397 **The wit and wisdom of the Haytians.**
John Bigelow. New York: Scribner & Armstrong, 1877. 112p.

Lists proverbs collected by the author in Haiti in 1854, during the empire of Faustin Soulouque, and first published in a series of articles in *Harper's New Monthly Magazine* in 1875. Characterizing the proverbs of Haiti as novel and distinctive, Bigelow lists proverbs in Creole, translates them into English, explains their meanings, and draws parallels between Haiti's proverbs and other sayings worldwide.

398 **Proverbes créoles, avec leur traduction littérale ou leurs équivalents en français.** (Creole proverbs with their literal translation or their equivalents in French.)
Edmond Chenet. Port-au-Prince: Imprimerie Edmond Chenet, 1896. 205p.

A comprehensive collection of 1,456 proverbs.

399 **3333 proverbs in Haitian Creole: the 11th Romance language.**
Nestor A. Fayo. Port-au-Prince; Fardin, 1980. 428p.

This volume contains three thousand, three hundred and thirty-three proverbs in Haitian Creole with English translations.

400 **The wisdom of the Haitian peasant, or some Haitian proverbs considered.**
James W. Ivy. *Journal of Negro History*, vol. 26, no. 4 (Oct. 1941), p. 485-98.
A short study of approximately sixty Haitian proverbs, mainly those that originated on the island and are characteristic of the *genre*. Ivy describes them as being 'flavoured with the soil of the island . . . frequently profound in their widom . . . terse . . . with a salty peasant humor, now and then scatological'. The proverbs are quoted in Haitian Creole, with their equivalents and their meaning in English.

Folk-tales

401 **The woe shirt: Caribbean folk tales.**
Paulé Bartón, translated from the Creole by Howard Norman.
St Paul, Minnesota: Graywolf Press, 1982. 62p.
Inspired by folklore, these are original tales told by a contemporary Haitian peasant.

402 **Les contes haïtiens.** (Haitian tales.)
Suzanne Comhaire-Sylvain. Wetteren, Belgium: Imprimerie De Meester, 1937. 2 vols. maps. bibliog. (Reprinted, New York: AMS Press, [n.d.] 2 vols. in 1). (The Folktale).
A scholarly dissertation, presented as the author's thesis at the University of Paris, on the major themes of the Haitian folk-tale and their relationship to motifs found in the folk-tales of the Americas, Africa and Western Europe.

403 **Creole tales from Haiti.**
Suzanne Comhaire-Sylvain. *Journal of American Folklore*, vol. 50, no. 197 (July-Sept. 1937), p. 207-95. bibliog.
A valuable contribution to the study of Haitian folklore, this entire issue of the *Journal of American Folklore* is devoted to the Creole folk-tale. The twenty tales presented are grouped into two classes: tales with human characters (with a subclass, tales without supernatural elements); and tales of men and supernatural beings. Each story is first transcribed in Creole, then translated into English. Music for folksongs found in the tales is included. The source for each tale is given in a footnote, and an unannotated bibliography of West Indian and African folk-tales and folk-songs is provided.

404 **Uncle Bouqui of Haiti.**
Harold Courlander, illustrated by Lucy Herndon Crockett. New York: William Morrow, 1942. 126p.
Presents English translations of Haitian folk-tales centring around the figure of Uncle Bouqui, a regular character in such tales: his outstanding characteristics are stupidity and stubbornness.

405 Children of Yayoute: folk tales of Haiti.
François Marcel-Turenne des Pres. Port-au-Prince: Deschamps, 1949.
180p.
Contains English-language versions of Haitian folk tales.

406 Folk tales of Haitian heroes.
George E. Simpson, J. B. Cineas. *Journal of American Folklore*,
vol. 54, nos. 213-14 (July-Dec. 1941), p. 176-85.
This article summarizes twenty-three folk-tales about Henry Christophe, Jean-Jacques
Dessalines and Toussaint Louverture collected by the authors in Haiti in 1937.
Nineteen of the legends concern Henry Christophe, whose dramatic career obviously
captured the imagination of the Haitian peasant.

407 *Loup garou*, and *loa* tales from northern Haiti.
George E. Simpson. *Journal of American Folklore*, vol. 55, no. 218
(Oct.-Dec. 1942), p. 219-27.
The author explains that in Haiti 'loups garous are sorcerers who have the power to
change themselves into dogs, horses, trees, and other animals and objects', and that
stories about them are taken very seriously. Simpson summarizes fourteen examples of
such tales recounted by Haitian informants in 1937: 'A loup garou had a burning skin';
'A loup garou tries to pay the annual debt for her power'; 'A loup garou disguises as a
lighter mapou tree'; 'A loup garou disguises as a beggar'; 'Rescued from the loups
garous by loa Saint James'; 'A loup garou disguises as a pig'; 'A loup garou disguises as
a white horse'; 'Punishment for annoying a loa'; 'A zange disguises as a snake';
'Abandoning a house to the rainbow loa'; 'The rainbow loa's cap'; 'A peasant's
attempt to seize the rainbow loa's cap'; 'Swimming in a zange's pond'; and 'Loa
President Clermeil, father of light colored children'.

408 Traditional tales from Haiti.
George E. Simpson. *Journal of American Folklore*, vol. 56, no. 222
(Oct.-Dec. 1943), p. 255-65.
Following a short discussion of the dying custom of storytelling in rural Haiti, Simpson
recounts seven folk-tales collected in 1937: 'Tar baby: cat as thief'; 'Why cat does not
eat young cocks'; 'Enfant terrible: the-one-who-is-always-right'; 'Cricket, fortune
teller', 'A magic cane'; 'Changing a baby into a turkey'; and 'Magic flight'.

409 The singing turtle, and other tales from Haiti.
Philippe Thoby-Marcelin, Pierre Marcelin, illustrated by George Ford,
translated from the French by Eva Thoby-Marcelin. New York:
Farrar, Straus & Giroux, 1971. 115p. (An Ariel Book).
This is an illustrated collection of eighteen Haitian folk-tales, translated from the
authors' *Contes et legendes d'Haiti* (Paris: Nathan, 1967).

410 **The magic orange tree, and other Haitian folktales.**
Collected and told by Diane Wolkstein, drawings by Elsa Henriquez.
New York: Knopf, 1978. 212p. (Reprinted, New York: Schocken
Books, 1980).

An attractively illustrated collection of Haitian folk-tales, narrated in English for
children. Similar presentations, certain to delight young readers, are Harold
Courlander's *Piece of fire and other Haitian tales* (New York: Harcourt, Brace,
Jovanovich, 1964) and Gyneth Johnson's *How the donkeys came to Haiti, and other
folk tales* (Old Greenwich, Connecticut: Devin, 1949).

Folk-music, folk-songs, folk-dances

411 **The voice of Haiti: original ceremonial songs, Voodoo chants, drum
beats, stories of traditions, etc. of the Haitian people.**
Edited by Laura Bowman, LeRoy Antoine. New York: Clarence
Williams Music Publishing Co., 1938. 41p. bibliog.

Provides the words of a variety of Haitian songs in both French and English. The
Haitian national anthem, 'La Dessalinienne', with piano score is also included.

412 **Haiti singing.**
Harold Courlander. Chapel Hill, North Carolina: University of North
Carolina Press, 1939. 273p. bibliog. (Reprinted, New York: Cooper
Square Publishers, 1973). (Library of Latin-American History and
Culture).

First published in 1939, Courlander's collection of 185 Haitian folk-songs is still the
basic work on Haitian folk-music in English. Lyrics are given in both Creole and
English; melodies are provided for 126 songs, and drum music for two dances – 'Quitta
Mouille' and 'Juba' – is included. The volume also contains background chapters on
Haitian culture and a short bibliography.

413 **Haiti's political folksongs.**
Harold Courlander. *Opportunity: Journal of Negro Life,* vol. 19,
no. 4 (April 1941), p. 114-8.

Political folk-songs have a long tradition in Haiti, going back to the songs sung by the
runaway slaves or maroons. In republican Haiti, they became an outlet for outspoken
political commentary. Strongly biased, they dwell on the faults and virtues of
candidates for office, constituting a folk-history of Haitian politics. Courlander's article
gathers together a number of these songs which have been translated into English.

414 **Musical instruments of Haiti.**
Harold Courlander. *Musical Quarterly,* vol. 37, no. 3 (July 1941),
p. 371-83.

The major part of this article is a detailed list and description of the types of drums
played in Haiti. Other instruments discussed include: the *ganbo*, or bamboo stamping
tube; the rattle (both the common rattle or *tcha-tcha* and the sacred rattle or *asson* of
the Voodoo priest); the *marimba*; several varieties of horns; scrapers; claves; and
whistles and bells. Photographs are included of the tambour *maringouin* (the mosquito
drum or earth bow), *ganboes*, a Voodoo 'orchestra', and a Mardi Gras band.

415 **Dances of Haiti.**
Katherine Dunham, photographs by Patricia Cummings. Los
Angeles: Center for Afro-American Studies, UCLA, 1983. 78p.
(A CAAS Special Publication).

A seminal work on Haitian dance, based on investigative field work conducted in Haiti
by Dunham for her doctoral thesis in anthropologoy in 1937. This work is a revised
version of two earlier editions: the first published in Spanish and English as *Danzas de
Haiti* (Mexico City: Bellas Artes Press, 1947); then in French as *Danses de Haïti* (Paris:
Fasquel, 1957), with a foreword by Claude Levi-Strauss (translated into English for
this edition by Jeanelle Stovall). Dunham provides background information on Haiti
and the Vodun cult, then details the sacred and secular dances of Haiti; their
categories, equipment and the organization and function of dance groups.

416 **La méringue, danse nationale d'Haïti.** (The merengue, Haiti's national
dance.)
Jean Fouchard. Port-au-Prince: Editions H. Deschamps, 1988. 147p.
(Regards sur le temps passé, vol. 7).

A history of the merengue, Haiti's national dance.

417 **Haitian folk songs.**
New York: Folkway Records Corporation, 1953 (Sound recording).
1 disc. (Folkways 6811).

A recording of Haitian Creole folk songs sung by Lolita Cuevas, with guitar by Frantz
Casseus. A four-page insert with programme notes by folklorist Harold Courlander
and Creole texts of the songs with English translations accompanies the disc.

418 **Les danses folkloriques Haïtiennes.** (Haitian folk dances.)
Michel Lamartinière Honorat. Port-au-Prince: impr, de l'Etat, 1955.
155p. bibliog. (Publications de Bureau d'ethnologie de la République
d'Haiti, serie 2, no. 11).

Analyses the movement patterns of Haitian folk and Voodoo dances.

419 **Africanisms in New World negro music.**
Alan Lomax. In: *The Haitian potential; research and resources of Haiti.* Edited by Vera Rubin, Richard P. Schaedel. New York: Teachers College Press, 1975, p 38-58. (Publications of the Center for Education in Latin America).
A detailed study, linking Haitian rural songs to African traditional music.

420 **Peasant children's games in northern Haiti.**
George E. Simpson. *Folk-Lore*, vol. 65, no. 2 (Sept. 1954), p. 65-73.
'A description of ten children's games from the Bassin section of Plaisance'. The author believes these games, some sung in French rather than Creole, 'have changed little since Colonial times'. The games included are: 'Lago-lago'; 'Marie-Lor'; 'Ca-cache-mamba'; 'Zombi-mann-mannian'; 'Ma commère, prends poule'; 'Les petits oiseaux' (Rich and poor); 'A ce jeu, je vous embrasse'; 'Mariera qui voudra; 'Trois fois, passez la!'; and 'Les oignons quitte bon marché'. The words of the songs are translated into English.

421 **Peasant songs and dances in northern Haiti.**
George E. Simpson. *Journal of Negro History*, vol. 25, no. 2 (April 1940), p. 203-15.
Simspon first describes the context in which the peasants of northern Haiti utilize music at *coumbites* (work-bees) and *bals* (social gatherings). He then transcribes seven *coumbite* and four *bal* songs in both Creole and English versions, accompanying the verses with notes explaining allusions in the songs or the occasions upon which they were sung. He also notes the dances of the peasants, briefly describes several, and adds some information about the music played at bals. The article is based on observations made in 1937.

422 **Dances of the Bahamas & Haiti.**
Lavinia Williams. New York: City College of New York, 1980. 12p. (City College Papers, no. 15).
Transcript of a lecture delivered February 21 1980, at the City College of New York by a dance instructor. Williams first explains the Voudou context of Haitian dance, then enumerates the types of dance found in Haiti: sacred dances performed as part of the Voudou ritual and profane dances of either African or European origin. She ends with an account of a possession experience.

423 **Rara in Haiti.**
Dolores Yonker. In: *Caribbean festival arts; each and every bit of difference.* Edited by John W. Nunley, Judith Bettelheim. Seattle, Washington: The Saint Louis Art Museum in association with University of Washington Press, 1988, p. 147-55.
'Rara' is a festival unique to Haiti It is celebrated in the Haitian countryside during Lent by roving bands of dancers and musicians who solicit contributions for their performances. Yonker's essay describes the customs of this festival, the organization of Rara groups, and the music and dances performed by celebrants. Accompanying photographs· depict Rara participants in full sequinned and tinselled costume.

The Zombie

424 **The persistence of folk belief: some notes on cannibalism and zombis in Haiti.**
Erika Bourguignon. *Journal of American Folklore*, vol. 72, no. 283 (Jan.-March 1959), p. 36-46. bibliog.

In this article Bourguignon does not attempt to prove or disprove the factual validity of the existence of zombies, cannibalism, or the transformation of humans into animals in Haiti; rather she 'attempts to find out just what it is that the Haitian peasant believes with reference to these subjects', before tracing the ramifications of such beliefs, and determining their psychological implications. From her analysis Bourguignon concludes that 'the themes of feeding and eating and oral aggression are among the many strands of the interconnections' of these beliefs, and 'on the interpersonal level, the beliefs in question express both fear and hostility of others, particularly of strangers and those who have power'. A short bibliography is appended.

425 **The ethnobiology of the Haitian zombie; on the pharmacology of Black Magic.**
E. Wade Davis. *Caribbean Review*, vol. 12, no. 3 (Summer 1983), p. 18-21 and ff.

A popular article explaining the 'zombie poison' in layman's terms. Davis identifies the flora and fauna combined in the preparation of the drug, then discusses methods of administering the poison, the victim's symptoms and the poison's antidote. See also entry nos. 426 and 427.

426 **Passage of darkness: the ethnobiology of the Haitian zombie.**
Wade Davis.   Chapel Hill, North Carolina: University of North Carolina Press, 1988. 344p. bibliog.

An extensive investigation of the phenomenon of the Haitian zombie. David drew upon insights from ethnology, pharmacology and sociology as part of a field investigation in Haiti called 'The Zombie Project' – a search for a hypothesized powder that turns humans into robotlike slaves. Davis states in the introduction, that his book results from his participation in this project between 1982 and 1984, during which time 'the identity of the folk toxin (responsible for zombification) was established, but perhaps more significantly, the interdisciplinary approach that led to its discovery and a glimpse at the process of zombification also suggested cultural aspects of great importance. Evidence suggests that zombification is a form of social sanction imposed by recognized corporate bodies – the poorly known and clandestine secret Bizango societies – as one means of maintaining order and control in local communities.' See also entry 425 and 427.

427　**The serpent and the rainbow.**
　　　Wade Davis.　New York: Warner Books, 1985. 371p. bibliog.
Ethnobotanist Wade Davis recounts his real-life adventures in Haiti as a participant in 'The Zombie Project', a search for the ingredients of the rumoured compound that turns men into the 'living dead'. His quest takes him from nightclubs to Voodoo temples and into the clandestine world of Haiti's secret societies. Not surprisingly, a film version of this book appeared in 1988. See also entry nos. 425 and 426.

428　**On the nature of zombie existence; the reality of a Voudon ritual.**
　　　Bernard Diederich.　*Caribbean Review*, vol. 12, no. 3 (Summer 1983), p. 14-17 and ff.
Reports on the work of Dr. Lamarque Douyon, a Haitian psychiatrist and expert on the zombie phenomenon. Diederich describes Douyon's recent work with two apparently genuine zombies, 'Ti-Femme' (Francina Illeus) and Clairvius Narcisse, and his researches into drugs prepared by Voodoo practitioners that may be the cause of zombification.

429　**Chemistry of voodoo.**
　　　Mark Kemp.　*Discover*, vol. 10, no. 1 (Jan. 1989), p. 26-28.
In this short article, Kemp casts doubts on Wade Davis's (q.v.) hypothesis of a pharmacological explanation for physical zombification and on the scientific validity of Davis's work with tetrodotoxin.

430　**The myth of the zombi.**
　　　Maximilien Laroche.　In: *Exile and tradition: studies in African and Caribbean literature.* Edited by Rowland Smith.　New York: Africana, 1976, p. 44-61. (Dalhousie African Studies Series).
A perceptive contribution to understanding Haiti and the Haitians. Laroche analyses the transformation of the fundamentally religious figure of the African 'living-dead' into what he defines as the essentially economic figure of the Haitian zombie: 'the symbol of a condition brought about in an unknown way, but reversible by human will', – a condition in which mind and soul are subdued but capacity to work remains, corresponding to the situation faced by the Africans enslaved on the plantations of Saint-Domingue.

Religion

Roman Catholicism

431 **The church in Haiti – land of resistance.**
Jean-Bertrand Aristide. *Caribbean Quarterly*, vol. 37, no. 1 (March 1991), p. 108-13.

Jean-Bertrand Aristide, a former Roman Catholic priest, was elected President of Haiti in December 1990, took office in February 1991, and was exiled as the result of an army coup in September of that same year. In this article written shortly after his inauguration, he outlines his vision of the role of the Church in Haiti.

432 **The Catholic Church in Haiti (1704-1785): selected letters, memoirs, and documents.**
Edited and introduced by George Breathett. Salisbury, North Carolina: Documentary Publications, 1983. 202p. bibliog.

This is not a history but a collection of translated documents that illustrate the day-to-day concerns of Catholic missionaries in eighteenth-century Saint-Domingue. Breathett states in his preface that the materials translated by him are selected from *Documents inédits, concernant les missions religieux à Saint Domingue*, contained in the *Archives Nationale de France (Colonies), Paris, France, Series F5A, Register 4*. The documents include letters and inventories of church possessions that reveal everyday life in a French colony during the ancien régime.

433 **Catholic missionary activity and the Negro slave in Haiti.**
George Breathett. *Phylon*, vol. 23, no. 3 (Third Quarter [Fall] 1962), p. 278-85.

The French took seriously their mandate to Christianize the black slaves in their West Indian colonies, and the work of the Jesuits, Dominicans, Capuchins and Trinitarians who undertook this task played a significant role in the development of Saint-Domingue. Breathett relates the history of these missionaries from the seventeenth century to the beginnings of Haitian independence in the early nineteenth century. As they attempted to instruct the slaves in the Roman Catholic religion, these clergymen oftern came into conflict with slave-owners over the existing abuses of the slave system. In the eighteenth century the Jesuit Order was most successful in converting slaves – so much so that in 1763 the colonial government, alarmed at growing Jesuit influence, secured the Order's expulsion from Saint-Domingue.

434 **Notes sur l'histoire religieuse d'Haïti de la révolution au concordat (1789-1860).** (Notes on the religious history of Haiti from the Revolution to the Concordat [1789-1860].)
Adolphe Cabon. Port-au-Prince: Petit Seminaire, College Saint-Martial, 1933. 520p.

Written by a priest, this is the definitive history of the Roman Catholic Church's relations with Haiti, 1789-1860. The work first appeared in the *Bulletin de la quinzaine*, the fortnightly review of the archdiocese of Port-au-Prince.

435 **The Haitian schism: 1804-1860.**
Jean L. Comhaire. *Anthropological Quarterly*, vol. 29, (n.s. vol. 4), no. 1 (Jan. 1956), p. 1-10.

A good presentation in English of a neglected topic in the history of the Roman Catholic Church in Haiti. Comhaire examines the fifty-six-year period following Haitian independence during which the country had no formal relations with Rome. He focuses on attempts by the papacy to resolve the situation and re-establish its authority in the former French colony – efforts culminating in the Concordat of 28 March 1860, which instituted relations between the Holy See and Haiti and legalized Catholic public life in the republic. The article also briefly discusses Protestantism, Freemasonry and Voodoo in 19th-century Haiti.

436 **The status of the Church in Saint-Domingue during the last years of the French monarchy, 1781-1793.**
William A. Trembley. *Caribbean Studies*, vol. 1, no. 1 (April 1961), p. 11-18.

A detailed research paper on the Roman Catholic Church in Saint-Domingue during the final years of the colonial period. The *Ordonnance du Roi concernant les missions dans les colonies françaises de l'Amérique*, issued 24 November 1781, promulgated new regulations for Saint-Domingue's clergy. Trembley traces the strains between the Church and successive French governments – whether royal or republican – that developed because of the new rules. Trembley's article provides valuable information on an aspect of the stormy revolutionary period about which there has been little written in English.

Protestantism

437 **Beyond all this: thirty years with the mountain peasants of Haiti.**
Mildred Anderson. Grand Rapids, Michigan: Baptist Haiti Mission,
1979. 216p.
An account of American Baptist missions in Haiti, centring around the lengthy service
of Bertha Holdeman (1888-1979).

438 **Pentecostalism in Haiti: healing and hierarchy.**
Frederick James Conway. In: *Perspectives on Pentecostalism: case
studies from the Caribbean and Latin America.* Edited by Stephen D.
Glazier. Washington, DC: University Press of America, 1980,
p. 7-20.
A case study of Protestant evangelicalism in Haiti.

439 **Defender of the race: James Theodore Holly, black nationalist bishop.**
David M. Dean. Boston, Massachusetts: Lambeth Press, 1979. 150p.
map. bibliog.
Dean skilfully combines the biography of Bishop James Theodore Holly (1829-1911)
with the history of the Episcopal Church in Haiti. Holly was born into a free black
family in Washington DC. Ordained an episcopal priest, he espoused the cause of
emigration for American blacks. In 1861 he led a group of American emigrants to
Haiti, founding the *Eglise Orthodox Apostolique Haitienne* there, and, in 1874, became
Haiti's first Episcopal bishop.

440 **The growing church in Haiti.**
Harmon A. Johnson. Coral Gables, Florida: West Indies Mission,
1970. 88p. bibliog.
Reports on religious missions in Haiti sponsored by American Protestant denominations.

441 **Vodou et Protestantisme.** (Voodoo and Protestantism.)
Alfred Metraux. *Revue de l'Histoire des Religions,* vol. 144, no. 2
(Oct.-Dec. 1958), p. 198-216.
Discusses Voodoo and Protestantism in the Marbial Valley.

442 **La protestantisme Haïtien.** (Haitian Protestantism.)
Catts Pressoir. Port-au-Prince: Imprimerie de la Société Biblique et
des Livres Religieux d'Haïti, 1945. vol. 1; Port-au-Prince: Imprimerie
du Seminaire Adventiste, 1977. vol. 2.
A standard work in French on the history of the Protestant Churches in Haiti.

Voodoo

General

443 Strange altars.
Marcus Bach.   Indianapolis, Indiana: Bobbs Merrill, 1952. 254p.
Relates the author's experiences with Haitian Voodoo. Bach was assisted in his contacts with the cult and its practitioners by Stanley Reser, an American resident of Haiti.

444 African civilisations in the New World.
Roger Bastide, translated from the French by Peter Green, with a foreword by Geoffrey Parrinder.   New York: Harper & Row, 1971. 232p. bibliog.
The section 'Haitian Voodoo' (p. 138-51) is a précis of the history and benefits of the cult, and includes clear definitions of Voodoo terms. Bastide makes some interesting comments on the possible migration of Voodoo from Haiti to the slave plantations of Cuba and the United States.

445 Mama Lola: a Vodou priestess in Brooklyn.
Karen McCarthy Brown.   Berkeley, California: University of California Press, 1991. 405p. bibliog. (Comparative Studies in Religion and Society, 4).
An ethnographic study of Voodoo as practised in the Haitian diaspora – in this case, Brooklyn, New York. Brown, a white scholar, details the life of an immigrant Haitian Vodou priestess or *manbo*, Alourdes Kowalski. Her book is both a descriptive anthropological study and an autobiographical account of her personal relationship with 'Mama Lola' and the Vodou cult.

446   **Voudoun fire: the living reality of mystical religion.**
      Melita Denning, Osbourne Phillips, photographs by Gloria Rudolph,
      illustrated by Matthew Wood, Nan Bruno.   St. Paul, Minnesota:
      Llewellyn Publications, 1979. 161p.
      This is largely a photographic study of Haiti's Voodoo cult.

447   **Une explication philologique du Vodu; communication faite à la Société
      d'histoire et de géographie d'Haïti.** (A philological explanation of
      Voodoo; a communication made to the Society of the History and
      Geography of Haiti.)
      J. C. Dorsainvil.   Port-au-Prince: V. Pierre-Noel, 1924. 40p.
      Dorsainvil uses the etymological evidence of the names of Voodoo deities to link the
      Haitian cult to what he believes to be its Dahomean (Benin) origin.

448   **Àshe, traditional religion and healing in sub-Saharan Africa and the
      Diaspora: a classified international bibliography.**
      John Gray.   New York: Greenwood Press, 1989. 518p. (Bibliographies
      and Indexes in Afro-American and African Studies, no. 24).
      The 'Haiti' chapter of this bibliography p. 343-74), provides a substantial list of more
      than 450 items in English, Spanish, Portuguese and French on Haitian Voodoo and
      folk medicine. Citations are provided for books, essays, periodical articles, newspaper
      accounts, doctoral dissertations, MA and BA theses and book reviews on such subjects
      as Voodoo and politics, sacred music, religious art, the zombie, and traditional
      healing. This bibliography is especially valuable for the number of French, Canadian
      and Haitian periodicals indexed, among them Haiti's leading anthropological journal
      the *Bulletin du Bureau d'Ethnologie*.

449   **Kongo in Haiti: a new approach to religious syncretism.**
      Luc De Heusch.   *Man*, n.s., vol. 24, no. 2 (June 1989), p. 290-303.
      bibliog.
      According to Heusch, Voodoo, Haiti's popular religion, owes its origins to African
      sources – its Christian symbolism is purely superficial. In this article, he compares and
      contrasts the manifestations of two Voodoo cults: the Rada cult, which goes back to
      Dahomey (Benin); and the Petro cult, which has its roots among the Kongo people
      whose kingdom was at the mouth of the Zaïre river. Each cult has its own altar in
      Voodoo temples. The Petro gods are linked to fire and magic; the Rada deities are
      more peaceful and benevolent, although some have violent Petro counterparts.

450   **Les daimons du culte Voudo.** (The daimons of the Voodoo cult.)
      Arthur C. Holly.   Port-au-Prince: Imprimerie Edmond Chenet, 1918.
      523p.
      Holly's preface to this book is an early defence of Voodoo.

451 **Dieu dans la Vaudou Haitien.** (God in Haitian Voodoo.)
Laennec Hurbon, preface by Genevieve Calame-Griaule. Paris:
Payot, 1972. 268p. bibliog. (Bibliothèque Scientifique). (Reprinted,
Port-au-Prince: Deschamps, 1987).

Written by a Haitian author, this is a contribution to the study of Voodoo. In a review
in *Social and Economic Studies*, vol. 22, no. 2 (June 1973), p. 305-06, David Nicholls
describes this book as 'a most important and interesting study of the Voodoo cult . . .
certainly one of the most thought-provoking and intelligent studies of the Voodoo
religion to have been published'.

452 **Tell my horse: voodoo and life in Haiti and Jamaica.**
Zora Neale Hurston; with a new foreword by Ishmael Reed. New
York: Harper & Row, 1938, 1990. 311p. bibliog.

Hurston was awarded a Guggenheim Fellowship in March 1936, to study West Indian
Obeah practices. She spent April 1936, to March 1937, in Jamaica and Haiti, returning
to Haiti in the summer of 1937. This book records her experiences on the two islands
during this time. Two sections of the book are devoted to Haiti: Part 2 'Politics and
personalities of Haiti', which describes incidents and events of 1937 Haiti; and Part 3,
'Voodoo in Haiti', a popular presentation of Hurston's firsthand observation of the
Voodoo cult. The volume includes an Appendix, 'Songs of worship to Voodoo gods'
and 'Miscellaneous songs', and an afterword, 'Zora Neale Hurston "A negro way of
saying"', by Henry Louis Gates, Jr.

453 **The invisibles: Voodoo gods in Haiti.**
Francis Huxley. New York: McGraw-Hill, 1966. 247p.

Readers will be fascinated by Huxley's anecdotal, atmospheric account of his first hand
investigations into Haitian Voodoo. The book includes two useful appendices: a
glossary of Voodoo terms and definitions and a list of Haitian plants credited with
medicinal properties.

454 **Etudes sur le vodou haïtien: bibliographie analytique.** (Studies on
Haitian Voodoo: an analytical bibliography.)
Michel S. Laguerre. Montreal: Centre de recherches caraïbes, 1979.
50p.

A classified bibliography on Voodoo. Laguerre is also the compiler of a bibliography
on Voodoo in Haitian Creole: 'You lis liv sou Vodous' ('A selective bibliography on
Voodoo'), *Sel*, vol. 6, no. 42 (1978), p. 34-38.

455 **The place of Voodoo in the social structure of Haiti.**
Michel S. Laguerre. *Caribbean Quarterly*, vol. 19, no. 3 (Sept. 1973),
p. 36-49.

Outlines how the role of the Voodoo religion in the cultural and political life of Haiti
has shifted in response to specific historical pressures. During the colonial slave era,
Voodoo was the carrier of a Messianic message and contributed to revolutionary
cohesion: Voodoo leaders emerged as those having a divine mission to save the black
race. During the 1804-60 Great Schism, Voodoo filled the gap vacated by the Roman
Catholic Church, becoming the religion of the masses and a familiar cult. When the

Church was officially reinstated after the Concordat of 1860, Voodoo was disestablished and became the religion of the non-Europeanized Haitian, as opposed to the Roman Catholic clergy and their supporters. The US occupation revived the Messianic aspect of Voodoo, and in 1928 Price-Mars rehabilitated the folk-religion for the Haitian intellectual. Later, François Duvalier cleverly manipulated Voodoo for his political ends. In contemporary Haiti, Voodoo has an independent status and is a public religion, officially tolerated.

456 Voodoo heritage.
Michel S. Laguerre, with a foreword by Vera Rubin.   Beverly Hills, California: Sage, 1980. 231p. bibliog. (Sage Library of Social Research, vol. 98).

A sociological analysis of the oral tradition of the Voodoo cult. Laguerre records over 300 songs and prayers of a Voodoo congregation in Port-au-Prince and interprets their contents. In a review of this book in the March 1980 issue of *Caribbean Studies*, Nelida Agosto writes that 'this is the first time such an analysis has been undertaken', adding that 'these songs are certainly a key to the understanding of Voodoo as a living religion with living gods'.

457 Voodoo in Haiti.
Alfred Metraux, translated from the French by Hugo Charteris.   New York: Oxford University Press, 1959. 400p. bibliog. (Reprinted, New York: Schocken Books, 1972).

Written by a well-known ethnographer with extensive experience in the Haitian countryside, this book is often cited as an authoritative source on the Voodoo folk religion. Metraux's book covers the history, social framework, metaphysics, rituals and magical practices of the cult, and also includes a chapter discussing Voodoo in relation to Christianity. The lengthy, unannotated bibliography lists works in French and English. It was first published in French as *Le Vaudou Haïtien* in 1958. The 1972 paperback reprint of the English translation has a new introduction by the distinguished American anthropologist Sidney W. Mintz.

458 Myths of voodoo worship and child sacrifice in Hayti.
William W. Newell. *Journal of American Folklore*, vol. 1, no. 1 (April-June 1888), p. 16-30.

This early contribution to the professional study of folklore is largely of historical interest. Newell draws his conclusions about Voodoo from printed materials and locates a European source for Voodoo in an imaginary sect of witches called the Vaudois. He also disputes Sir Spenser Buckingham St. John's assertion that cannibalism is practised in Haiti.

459 Reports of voodoo worship in Hayti and Louisiana.
William W. Newell. *Journal of American Folklore*, vol. 2, no. 4 (Jan.-March 19889), p. 41-7.

Continues the discussion of Haitian Voodoo that Newell began in his earlier article, 'Myths of voodoo worship and child sacrifice in Hayti' (q.v.). He reiterates his belief that Haitian Voodoo is derived, in the main, from European witchcraft superstitions, questions the validity of popular reports of Voodoo worship, and denies that cannibalism is part of the cult's ritual.

460 **Spirit cult in Hayti.**
Elsie Clews Parsons. *Journal de la Société des Américanistes de Paris*, n.s., vol. 20 (1928), p. 157-79.
Provides comments on Voodoo, written by an American anthropologist.

461 **Secret of Voodoo.**
Milo Rigaud, translated from the French by Robert B. Cross, photographs by Odette Mennesson-Rigaud. New York: Arco, 1969. 219p. (Reprinted, San Francisco: City Lights Books, 1985).
An esoterist's interpretation of Voodoo, first published in Paris in 1953 as *La tradition Vaudou et le Vaudou Haïtien: son temple, ses mystères, sa magie.*

462 **Black religions in the New World.**
George E. Simpson. New York: Columbia University Press, 1978. 415. maps. bibliog.
This major contribution to the study of Afro-American New World religions incorporates Simpson's extensive research on Haitian Voodoo.

463 **Religious cults of the Caribbean: Trinidad, Jamaica, and Haiti.**
George E. Simpson. Rio Piedras, Puerto Rico: Institute of Caribbean Studies, University of Puerto Rico, 1980. 3rd enlarged ed. 347p. bibliog. (Caribbean Monograph Series, no. 15).
In this enlarged edition of Simpson's study of Afro-Caribbean religions (first published in 1965 as *Shango cult in Trinidad*), part three, 'Haiti', presents five of Simpson's essays on Haitian Voodoo: 'The Vodun cult in Haiti', p. 231-33; 'The belief system of Haitian Vodun', p. 234-56; 'The Vodun service in northern Haiti', p. 257-72; 'Four Vodun ceremonies', p. 273-86; and 'Vodun and Christianity', p. 287-88.

464 **Voodoos and obeahs: phases of West Indian witchcraft.**
Joseph J. Williams. New York: L. MacVeagh, Dial Press, 1932. 257p. bibliog. (Reprinted, New York: AMS Press, 1970).
One of the earliest studies of Voodoo, treated in conjunction with Jamaican Obeah. Williams posited an origin for Voodoo in African ophiolatry.

465 **The black pope of voodoo (part I).**
Faustin E. Wirkus, [Henry Wysham Lanier]. *Harpers Magazine*, vol. 168 (Dec. 1933), p. 38-49.
Writing in the first person, Wirkus describes his experiences with Haitian Voodoo and his search for the 'Man of Trou Forban', whom he describes as 'the carefully hidden high priest' of the Voodoo religion.

466 **The black pope of voodoo (part II).**
Faustin E. Wirkus, [Henry Wysham Lanier]. *Harpers Magazine,*
vol. 168 (Jan. 1934), p. 189-98.
Wirkus continues his search for the 'all-powerful Pope of Voodoo (see also item
no. 465), who is called simply 'The Man'. His quest takes him from Haiti to New
York's Harlem, then back to Haiti where he finally encounters 'The Man', whom he
believes to be the supreme pontiff of Voodoo and who guards a secret temple.

Rituals and beliefs

467 **Authentic Voodoo is synthetic.**
Michelle Anderson. *The Drama Review,* vol. 26, no. 2 (summer
1982), p. 89-110.
Anderson's aim, when she went to Haiti in the summer of 1980, was – in her own
words – 'to find Voodoo'. In this account she describes three Voodoo performances
that she observed. Each is typical of a particular form into which the Voodoo ritual has
evolved: at Mariani she viewed a theatrical Voodoo show produced for a tourist
audience; at Jacmel, she watched a Voodoo ritual performed for both tourists and
Haitians; and at Nansouci she gained access to a Voodoo rite attended only by
Haitians. Anderson's comparison and interpretation of these performances is
informative.

468 **Religion and justice in Haitian Vodoun.**
Erika Bourguignon. *Phylon,* vol. 46, no. 6 (Dec. 1985), p. 292-95).
Little attention has been paid to the idea of Voodoo as a moral system; thus, this
article in which Bourguignon discusses the concept of justice in Haitian Voodoo is a
welcome addition to the literature on the subject. Bourguignon relates Voodoo to
magic and notes the 'ethos of suspicion' that characterizes the world of Voodoo where
'Obedience and respect for seniority . . . are the primary moral law, and punishment
for its infractions must then be justice . . . Justice is concerned with the maintenance of
(a harsh *status quo*) keeping any one individual from gaining wealth at the expense of
others. For all personal gain, it is believed, can only occur at the expense of others'.

469 **Ritual and myth in Haitian Vodoun.**
Erika Bourguignon. *African religious groups and beliefs; papers in
honor of William R. Bascom.* Edited by Simon Ottenberg. Meerut,
India: Archana Publications for Folklore Institute, 1982, p. 290-304.
bibliog.
Bourguignon notes that in spite of Haiti's flourishing Afro-American Voodoo cult,
African myths are conspicuous by their absence in collections of Haitian folk
narratives. In this article, she seeks to determine the role of myth in Voodoo ritual by
examing the mythic content of a narrative related by a houngan (devotee) in Port-au-
Prince, then linking this material to Voodoo ritual and its informing social reality. Her
analysis explains the meaning of her informant's discourse, demonstrating how Haitian
spirits act in the here-and-now, rather than in a 'mythic time'. She also describes how

narrative material is organized according to African principles, which are central to the beliefs concerning Haitian deities.

470 **The center and the edges: God and person in Haitian society.**
Karen McCarthy Brown. *Journal of the Interdenominational Theological Center*, p. 22-39.

A study of the *vèvè*, the cornmeal drawings sketched on the earthen floor that are an important part of Voodoo ceremonies. Brown explores the *vèvè* 'primarily as self-images [in order] to draw from them something of the Haitian idea of self', which, in Haitian context, 'is more of a sociological than a psychological enterprise'. While Brown's paper concentrates on a single visual relationship, that between the centre and the edges of the veve, it also includes analyses and discussions of other aspects of the Voodoo ceremony, such as the *pwe* (drawings of dots, stars and crosses), the *poteau-mitan* (the centre pole of the ceremonial spaces), and the possession experience. Brown concludes by contrasting the Haitian idea of self with that of the American concept.

471 **Who is that fellow in the many-colored cap? Transformations of Eshu in Old and New World mythologies.**
Donald Cosentino. *Journal of American Folklore*, vol. 100, no. 397 (July-Sept. 1987), p. 261-75.

Cosentino studies how the trickster deity Eshu Elegba, who originated among the Yoruba of Nigera, was transformed in Haiti into 'Papa' Legba, first among loa (supernatural beings) in Haitian Voodoo. 'Papa' Legba, in his turn, expanded and split into two significant divine offshoots, Carrefour and Ghede. Based on research conducted in Haiti in 1986, Cosentino's explanation of Eshu's mutations illuminates Haitian religious imaging and mythopoesis.

472 **Gods of the Haitian mountains.**
Harold Courlander. *Journal of Negro History*, vol. 23, no. 3 (July 1944), p. 339-72.

An informative article describing the hundreds of supernatural beings – the loa – of the Haitian folk-religion. The latter part of the essay is a dictionary of the Voodoo pantheon, identifying the loa and supplying information on their origins, names, habits, habitats, rites, cycles and families.

473 **The potency of dance: a Haitian examination.**
Yvonne Daniel. *The Black Scholar*, vol. 2, no. 8 (Nov.-Dec. 1980), 61-73. bibliog.

Based on research conducted in Haiti in the 1970s, this article focuses on a single Voodoo dance, Petro, in order to explicate the role of dance in an Afro-Caribbean society. Daniel examines the cultural complex of which dance is the centrepiece, provides a firsthand description of the Petro cult and its rituals, then summarizes the place of Voodoo dance in Haitian social life and culture.

474 **The faces of the gods: Vodou and Roman Catholicism in Haiti.**
Leslie G. Desmangles. Chapel Hill, North Carolina: The University
of North Carolina Press, 1992. 218p. map.
This is the first full-length study in English to focus on the incorporation of elements
drawn from Roman Catholicism into the beliefs and rituals of Haitian Voodoo.
Desmangles utilizes the concept of symbiosis to explain the relationship of two
religious traditions – European and African – in Haitian Voodoo, where constituents
of both co-exist, juxtaposed, but not fused. Desmangles finds the source of this
relationship in Haitian history. His book also includes a discussion of the situation that
currently obtains between Roman Catholicism and Voodoo in Haiti.

475 **The Vodoun way of death: cultural symbiosis of Roman Catholicism and
Vodoun in Haiti.**
Leslie G. Desmangles. *Journal of Religious Thought*, vol. 36, no. 1
(1979), p. 5-20.
Analyses the inclusion of elements drawn from Roman Catholicism in Voodoo funeral
rites. In an earlier essay, 'Baptismal rites: religious symbiosis of Vodoun and
Catholicism in Haiti', in *Liturgy and cultural religious traditions*, edited by Herman
Schmidt and David Power (New York: Seabury Press, 1977, p. 51-61), he applies the
concept of symbiosis to a comparison of Voodoo and Catholic baptismal ceremonies.

476 **Lemba, 1650-1930: a drum of affliction in Africa and the New World.**
John M. Janzen. New York: Garland, 1982. 383p. bibliog. (Critical
Studies on Black Life and Culture, vol. 19).
Lemba is identified as being a 'major historic African cult of healing, trade, and
marriage relations [that] came into being in the seventeenth century'. Chapter eight of
this study, 'Lemba in the New World' links Lemba to the Petro complex of rites
practised as part of Haiti's Voodoo religion. Janzen analyses a Lemba-Petro rite
observed in the 1930s by Melville Herkovits and described in Herskovits's *Life in a
Haitian Valley* (see item no. 570) and a similar ritual, also from the 1930s, witnessed by
Jean Price-Mars and detailed in Mars's 'Lemba-Petro, un culte secret' (see item
no. 483). Janzen concludes by indicating retentions and variations between Haitian
Lemba-Petro and African Lemba.

477 **Voodoo and magic practices.**
Jean Kerboull, translated from the French by John Shaw. London:
Barrie & Jenkins, 1978. 192p. bibliog.
A discussion of the links between Haitian magic and French magic.

478 **Ritual goat sacrifice in Haiti.**
Ari Kiev, MD. *American Imago*, vol. 19, no. 4 (winter 1962),
p. 349-59. bibliog.
Kiev examines Freudian theory in an attempt to gain an insight into both the personal
and the societal meaning of ritual animal sacrifice in Haiti, examining 'the Voodoo
ritual of goat sacrifice in the light of psychoanalytic theory of repetition and
commemoration of the primal murder of the father', but also hypothesizing that 'the
ritual sacrifice is relevant to the immediate reality situation as well'. He describes the
poisoning of a goat by a Voodoo priest as a sacrifice to the Petro spirit Angelus and

117

interprets the ceremony as both satisfying unconscious symbolic needs and reinforcing the houngan's social control over his congregation.

479 **The meaning of Africa in Haitian Vodu.**
Serge Larose. In: *Symbols and sentiments; cross-cultural studies in symbolism.* Edited by loan Lewis. New York: Academic Press, 1977, p. 85-116. bibliog.

In Haiti, *L'Afrique Guinee*, the idea of Guinea or Africa, is a dominant symbol, standing for tradition, ancestral rituals, and legitimate spiritual power. 'Africa' stands in opposition to other Haitian cult groups that are preoccupied with 'magical' powers and the practice of sorcery. Larose explains the beliefs and rituals centred around 'Guinea', and discusses other concepts important to understanding the Voodoo world view, such as the *demembre*, the *loas*, and the *points*. The article ends with a description of a Voodoo ritual through which the *loas* of a deceased person are transmitted to living family members.

480 **Notes sur l'usage de chromolithographies catholiques par les voduisants d'Haïti.** (Notes on the use of Catholic religious prints by the practitioners of Voodoo in Haiti.)
Michel Leiris. In: *Les Afro-Américains.* Dakar: Institut Français d'Afrique Noire, 1953, p. 201-07. (Mémoires de l'Institut Français d'Afrique, no. 27) (Reprinted, Amsterdam: Swets & Zeitlinger, 1968).

Leiris elucidates the process through which attributes of Catholic saints are identified with those of Voodoo deities, enabling Voodoo cultists to use Catholic religious prints as representations of the *loa*.

481 **Ritual performance and religious experience: a service for the gods in Southern Haiti.**
Ira P. Lowenthal. *Journal of Anthropological Research*, vol. 34, no. 3 (fall 1978), p. 392-414. bibliog.

An ethnographic re-examination of Haitian Voodoo and its importance in Haitian society. Basing his study on his field-work in the rural Fond-des-Nègres region in Southern Haiti in 1974, Lowenthal makes an in-depth analysis of a single type of ritual event – the *sevis Iwa* (service for the *loa*) – in order 'to come to terms with some of [Haitian Voodoo's] most essential features as a coherent system of belief and worship'. The research value of this article is enhanced by its author's review of the modern literature of Voodoo, which he classifies according to the analytic approach adopted as either culture-historical, functional or psychological.

482 **The concept of soul in Haitian Vodu.**
Alfred Metraux. *Southwestern Journal of Anthropology*, vol. 2, no. 1 (spring 1946), p. 84-92.

Defines and clarifies the Haitian popular concept of the soul, a complex idea central to Voodoo. Metraux discusses the soul and witchcraft, outlines beliefs about the soul after death, and describes a ceremony held to strengthen an enfeebled soul.

483 **Lemba-Petro, un culte secret.** (Lemba-Petro, a secret cult.)
Jean Price-Mars. *Revue de la Société d'Histoire et de Géographie d'Haïti*, vol. 9, no. 28 (1938) p. 12-31.

Describes a clandestine Lemba-Petro ceremony that Price-Mars happened upon in the Cul-de-Sac Valley in the 1930s. Readers may also be interested in an article by Lorimer Denis and François Duvalier: 'Une cérémonie du culte Pétro', *Les Griots*, vol. 2. no. 2 (Oct.-Nov.-Dec. 1938, 1st year).

484 **Vè-vè; diagrames rituels du Voudou.** (Vè-vè; ritual Voodoo diagrams).
Milo Rigaud. New York: French & European Publications, 1974. 587p.

A *vè-vè* is a magical design that is an important part of a Voodoo ceremony. Drawn on the ground, usually with cornflour, it symbolizes and invokes the particular deity for whom the ceremony is performed. Rigaud's book consists largely illustrations of these designs accompanied by text in French, English and Spanish.

485 **The feasting of the gods in Haitian vodu.**
Odette M. Rigaud, translated from the French by Alfred Metraux, Rhoda Metraux. *Primitive Man*, vol. 19, nos. 1-2 (Jan.-April 1946), p. 1-58.

Provides a highly detailed description of an important Voodoo ceremony, the *mange loa*, or feasting of the gods. Rigaud gathered the data for this article prior to 1943. The ceremony described is a *mangé loa* offered by a 70-year-old market women, Mariline, in Port-au-Prince. The reasons for the ceremony, preliminary preparations, invocations to the gods, songs, food offerings, *vèvè* diagrams, animal sacrifices, prayers, possession experiences, and preparation of food for the deities are all meticulously noted.

486 **Le sacrifice du tambour-assotor.** (The sacrifice of the tambour-assotor.)
Jacques Roumain. Port-au-Prince: Imprimerie de l'Etat, 1943. 71p.
(Publications du Bureau d'Ethnologie de la République d'Haïti, no. 1).

An ethnographic account of a ceremony connected with a type of Voodoo drum. Readers may also wish to consult Bruce W. Merwin's 'A Voodoo drum from Hayti', *University of Pennsylvania Museum Journal*, vol. 8 no. 2 (1917), p. 123-25.

487 **A salute to the spirits.**
Sal Scalora. *Americas*, vol. 45, no. 2 (Mar.-Apr. 1993), p. 26-33.

A unique article on the brillant flags that are ceremonially unfurled in Voodoo rituals. The boldly coloured, sequinned and beaded flags depict the personages and legends of the Voodoo cosmos, and Scalora illustrates his article with striking full-colour photographs of flags representing St. Jacques (Ogoun), Erzulie Freda, and the Creation myth. The text of the article describes the flags and how they are made.

Voodoo. Rituals and beliefs

488 **The belief system of Haitian Vodun.**
George E. Simpson. In: *Peoples and cultures of the Caribbean.* Edited
by Michael M. Horowitz. Garden City, New York: Natural History
Press, 1971, p. 491-521.
This article supplies a detailed summary of the faith of Voodooists. Simpson describes
the contemporary beliefs of the cult as of 1945, beliefs about the *loa* and the dead, and
about the relations between *fidele* and *loa.* The article includes a list of Voodoo deities
and a chart that lists information on their individual cults, giving for each: his or her
name; physical characteristics; the attire of the *serviteurs*; their abode; their favourite
foods, drinks and colours; their sacred days; and the powers and behaviour of
serviteurs when possessed. Simpson's work is based on interviews with Voodoo cultists,
and is outdated only in its conclusion that the Roman Catholic Church and the Haitian
government's campaign against Voodoo would succeed in their attempts to eclipse the
power of the folk-religion. This article is reprinted in Simpson's *Religious cults of the
Caribbean: Trinidad, Jamaica, and Haiti* (see item no. 463).

489 **Four Vodun ceremonies.**
George E. Simpson. *Journal of American Folklore*, vol. 59, no. 232
(April-June 1946), p. 154-67.
Contains highly detailed descriptions of four Voodoo rituals which focus on the
relationship between a devotee or a *houngan* and his 'spirit' or *loa*: the ceremony of
degradation, which removes the spirit from a deceased *houngan* to an appropriate
successor; the ceremony of renunciation, which is performed when a devotee wishes to
renounce his *loa*; and the ceremony of dismissal, during which a *loa* is sent away. The
article includes Creole texts and English translations of the songs and chants that
accompany these rites and a diagram of the throwing of the sacred shells which is part
of the degradation ceremony. This article has been reprinted in Simpson's *Religious
cults of the Caribbean: Trinidad, Jamaica, and Haiti* (see item no. 463).

490 **Haitian magic.**
George E. Simpson. *Social Forces*, vol. 19, no. 1 (Oct. 1940),
p. 95-100.
Simpson gathered his data for this short article on the types of magic practised in
northern Haiti from peasants living near the village of Plaisance in 1940. The article
also describes how *houngans* acquire their supernatural powers and includes definitions
of Voodoo terms.

491 **Magical practices in northern Haiti.**
George E. Simpson. *Journal of American Folklore*, vol. 67, no. 266
(Oct.-Dec. 1954), p. 395-403.
Based on field-work in Haiti, Simpson describes several Voodoo rites and rituals in
detail: the *change tête* rite, in which a victim is killed by black magic; the *lave-tête*, a
kind of baptism for a new cult member; the baptism of Voodoo drums; and a ritual to
stop the dead from persecuting a family. He also describes three Voodoo altars and
recounts some interesting peasant beliefs about plants and animals. At the end of the
article, Simpson repeats a number of anecdotes told to him by Haitian peasants that
demonstrate the kinds of empirical evidence which serve to reinforce and perpetuate
the Voodoo magico-religious world view in Haiti.

120

492 **Two Vodun related ceremonies.**
George E. Simpson. *Journal of American Folklore*, vol. 61, no. 239
(Jan.-March 1948), p. 49-50.

The main ceremony described in this article is a celebration in 1937 of the birthday of
Saint John, also known in Voodoo parlance as Frère Ti-Jean or Agoun-Tonnerre, by
Madame Ti-Nomme, a Voodoo priestess. The second ceremony is the 'Ceremony of
drawing the cakes' which took place during an interlude in the Saint John celebration.
Simpson was an observer at these rituals and his account of the rites, songs, dances and
chants of the participants is richly detailed.

493 **The Vodun service in northern Haiti.**
George E. Simpson. *American Anthropologist*, vol. 42, no. 2, pt. 1
(April-June 1940), p. 236-54).

This article is an elaborately detailed description of the central Voodoo ritual, the
service, based on a ceremony witnessed by Simpson in northern Haiti on July 17, 1937,
and on data supplied by informants. Chants and songs sung in the service are included,
as well as descriptions of spirit possession among the *serviteurs*, and an account of the
sacrifice of a goat and several chickens. This article has been reprinted in Simpson's
Religious cults of the Caribbean: Trinidad, Jamaica, and Haiti (see item no. 463).

494 **Flash of the spirit: African and Afro-American art and philosophy.**
Robert Farris Thompson. New York: Random House, 1983. 317p.

In chapter three of this, 'The Rara of the universe: Vodun religion and art in Haiti',
p. 161-91, Thompson views Haiti's religion as 'one of the signal achievements of
people of African descent in the western hemisphere: a vibrant, sophisticated synthesis
of the traditional religions of Dahomey, Yorubaland, and Kongo with an infusion of
Roman Catholicism [and with] a remarkable tradition of sacred art'. Thompson
examines the influence of classical African religions on Haitian ritual art, and discusses
religious objects, especially Vodun flags and *vèvès* (ground paintings).

495 **Haiti-dance.**
Lavinia Williams Yarborough. Frankfurt-am-Main: Brönners
Druckerei, 1959. 49p.

An illustrated pamphlet in English identifying specific Haitian Voodoo dances.

Dances of Haiti.
See item no. 415.

Les danses folkloriques Haïtiennes.
See item no. 418.

Dances of the Bahamas & Haiti.
See item no. 422.

Spirit possession

496 **Haitian Voodoo: social control of the unconscious.**
Nelida Agosto Munoz. *Caribbean Review*, vol. 4, no. 3 (July-Sept. 1972), p. 6-10.

This article focuses on spirit possession, the most striking element in Haitian Voodoo. The author argues that it is the social context provided by Voodoo that makes this state of dissociation meaningful for the cultists: the religious framework within which the trance state occurs allows the devotee to socialize suppressed impulses through a display of ritually learned behaviour patterns in a supportive, controlled environment. Agosto stresses the importance of kinaesthetic stimulation in inducing a *crise de possession*, and makes some interesting comparisons between Voodoo possession and neurosis.

497 **Possession.**
Erika Bourguignon. Prospect Heights, Illinois: Waveland Press, 1991. Rev. ed. 78p.

A general study of spirit possession from an anthropological perspective, with Haitian Voodoo serving as the main illustration. The volume's second chapter is a case study of possession belief and possession trance in Haiti, describing the ritual in detail. In the third chapter, the author attempts an explanation of trance phenomena.

498 **Divine horsemen: the living gods of Haiti.**
Maya Deren. London: Thames & Hudson, 1953. 350p. bibliog. (Myth and Man). (Reprinted, New Paltz, New York: McPherson, 1983).

An account by an American non-professional anthropologist and photographer who became a devotee of the Voodoo cult and a *serviteur*, experiencing spirit possession during Voodoo ceremonies. Her book is a full discussion of Voodoo – its cosmography, mythology, theology, rituals, dances, music and ceremonies – but the reader will be most interested in her description of her experiences as the *cheval* of the Voodoo goddess Erzulie.

499 **Vodou et nevrose.** (Voodoo and neurosis.)
J. C. Dorsainvil. Port-au-Prince: Imprimerie 'La Presse', 1931. 175p.

One of the first attempts at a medical explanation of possession phenomena in Haitian Voodoo. Dorsainvil maintains that the possession experience is pathological.

500 **A research model on trance and possession states in Haitian Vodun.**
Emerson Douyon. In: *The Haitian potential; research and resources of Haiti*. Edited by Vera Rubin, Richard P. Schaedel. New York: Teachers College Press, 1975, p. 167-72. (Publications of the Center for Education in Latin America).

Douyon, a psychologist, believes that trance and possession states hold the key to the Haitian's psychology. In this essay, he suggests eight experimental studies that could be undertaken to investigate the Voodoo trance phenomenon. Douyon is also the author of 'L'examen au Rorscharch des Vaudouisants haïtiens', in *Trance and possession states,* edited by Raymond Prince (Montreal: R. M. Bucke Memorial Society, 1968), p. 97-119.

501 **Spirit possession in Haiti.**
Ari Kiev. *American Journal of Psychiatry*, vol. 118, no. 2 (Aug. 1961), p. 133-38.
Explores spirit possession as it occurs in Haitian Voodoo and describes three episodes of possession: that of a *houngan* or Voodoo priest; that of a Voodoo adept; and that of a non-adept. From his scrutiny of these cases, Kiev concludes that Voodoo possession is culturally sanctioned in Haiti, where it serves as an acceptable way of 'going crazy', allowing the expression of suppressed behavioural patterns. He notes that Voodooists themselves distinguish between legitimate possession within the context of the cult and non-legitimate possession or *folie*.

502 **Voodoo possession: a natural experiment in hypnosis.**
Kent Ravenscroft, Jr. *International Journal of Clinical and Experimental Hypnosis*, vol. 13, no. 3 (July 1965), pr. 1957-82.
In this lengthy scientific study of the central experience of the Voodoo devotee, the author 'attempts to present Haitian Vodun possession in a form allowing comparison with familiar clinical and experimental hypnotic phenomena'. The article is quite valuable for its detailed description of the *crise de possession*: the major part of the article describes its induction, phases, variations and termination. Ravenscroft also places the Voodoo trance in its social framework, detailing Voodoo beliefs, the Voodoo hierarchy, and the introduction of the Haitian child to Voodoo. The article is based on field-work undertaken in 1961.

Therapeutics

503 **The power to heal: reflections on women, religion and medicine.**
Karen McCarthy Brown. In: *Shaping new vision; gender and values in American culture.* Edited by Clarissa W. Atkinson, Constance H. Buchanan, Margarat R. Miles. Ann Arbor, Michigan: UMI Research Press, 1987, p. 123-41.
Brown presents a case study of healing in Haitian Voodoo, describing how 'Mama Lola', a *manbo* in Brooklyn, New York, treated a client 'hungry for family' (lonely). Brown analyses the Haitian view of healing power and compares Haitian therapeutic practices with Western medicine.

504 **Voodoo death.**
Walter B. Cannon. *American Anthropologist*, vol. 44, no. 2 (April-June 1942), p. 169-81. (Reprinted, *Psychosomatic Medicine*, vol. 19, no. 3 (May-June 1957), p. 182-90).
Although this article mentions Haiti only in passing, students of Voodoo may be interested in reading the opinion of a professional physiologist on the possible physical

causes of a death brought on by black magic. Cannon gives instances of the Voodoo death phenomenon as it occurs in primitive cultures in Africa, South America, New Zealand and Australia. He then discusses the symptoms exhibited by Voodoo victims in medical terms and suggests possible scientific explanations for the demise of victims of Voodoo curses.

505 **Primitive medicine in Haiti.**
Thomas W. Dow. *Bulletin of the History of Medicine*, vol. 39, no. 1 (Jan.-Feb. 1965), p. 34-52.

A straightforward article, informative on the magico-religious framework within which the *houngan* – the Voodoo priest-diviner-doctor – treats disease. Dow summarizes the belief system of Voodoo, describes a Voodoo ceremony, and details Voodoo methods of diagnosis and therapy. The article is based on interviews and firsthand observation by its author in Haiti in 1962.

506 **Voodoo and sudden death: the effects of expectations on health.**
Efrain A. Gomez. *Transcultural Psychiatric Research Review*, vol. 19, no. 2 (1982), p. 75-92. bibliog.

Although not specifically on Haiti, this is a useful review that summarizes the literature on the phenomenon of 'death by magic'. Noting that Cannon's classic paper, 'Voodoo death' (q.v.) is still pertinent, Gomez concludes that 'the role played [in the sudden-death phenomenon] by predisposing, contributory, and precipitating factors are still unclear'.

507 **Folk psychiatry in Haiti.**
Ari Kiev. *Journal of Nervous and Mental Disease*, vol. 132, no. 3 (March 1961), p. 260-65.

Examines theories of personality and of psychiatric illness held by adherents of the Haitian Voodoo cult, and scrutinizes those therapies which are prescribed by *houngans* for cultists whom Westerners would describe as mentally ill. Noting similarities between Voodoo treatments and Western medicine, Kiev makes the point that, as the modern psychiatric clinic becomes more common in underdeveloped countries, psychiatrists should be aware of the assumptions and bases of such folk medical systems as Voodoo.

508 **Psychotherapy in Haitian Voodoo.**
Ari Kiev. *American Journal of Psychotherapy*, vol. 16, no. 3 (July 1962), p. 469-76.

In this article, Kiev, a psychiatrist, examines the nature of the forms of psychiatric treatment provided by the Haitian folk-religion. After a brief account of the types of mental illness prevalent in Haiti, Kiev discusses the aetiology of such illness according to Voodoo belief, then describes the treatments dispensed by the *houngans*. A detailed account of a Voodoo ritual performed for a woman with a history of mania is given. Kiev concludes that 'tentatively, it appears that the Voodoo priest is successful sufficiently often to warrant more examination of his techniques'.

Social Conditions

General

509 **A case study: the problems of slavery and the colonization of Haiti.**
Jean Casimir.   In: *Africa in Latin America; essays on history, culture, and socialization.* Edited by Manuel Moreno Fraginals, translated from the Spanish by Leonor Blum.   New York, Holmes & Meier, 1984, p. 306-27.

Casimir, a Haitian sociologist and historian, presents a theory of Haitian society which focuses on the presence of slaves and maroons in the colonial society from which the country's peasantry evolved at independence. According to him, many current Haitian problems date back to Haiti's early despotic village production system, which was an African response to the slave era. Casimir is especially interesting in his analysis of the role of the military in Haiti and its tyranny over the rural peasantry.

510 **Life in a Haitian valley.**
Melville J. Herskovits, with an introduction to the reprint by Edward Brathwaite.   New York: Knopf, 1937. 350p. bibliog. Reprinted, Garden City, New York: Doubleday, 1971. 371p. bibliog. (Anchor Books A805). (Reprinted, New York: Octagon Books, 1975).

When it was published in 1937, this book broke new ground in the study of Haitian society and culture and, especially, in the study of the Voodoo folk-religion, which it treated in a dispassionate way, setting it in its cultural context. The field-work on which Herskovits based his book was conducted in 1934 in the small rural community of Mirebalais in the Artibonite Valley. For a critique of Herskovits' work, discussing *Life in a Haitian valley* against the background of its time and from a later perspective, see Sidney W. Mintz's 1964 study, 'Melville J. Herskovits and Caribbean Studies: a retrospective tribute', *Caribbean Studies*, vol. 4, no. 2 (July 1964), p. 42-51. In this essay, Mintz points out the concepts that Herskovits advanced in the book and evaluates his methodology.

511 **Anthropology and the UNESCO pilot project of Marbial (Haiti).**
Alfred Metraux. *America Indigena*, vol. 9, no. 3 (July 1949),
p. 183-94.

Alfred Metraux, an American anthropologist of Swedish origin who was the first
director of the UNESCO Marbial Valley project, describes the anthropological field
survey to be undertaken prior to the commencement of the project, whose aim was to
upgrade Haitian agriculture and ameliorate social conditions in Haiti in the late 1940s.
He states the philosophy behind the survey, the methods that will be utilized, and the
areas to be investigated: life cycles, marketing systems, crafts and skills, diet and food
habits, social structure, child care, popular religion, and folklore.

512 **Making a living in the Marbial Valley: report.**
Alfred Metraux. Paris: UNESCO, 1951. 217p. (Occasional Papers in
Education, 10).

This report, prepared in collaboration with E. Berrouet and Jean and Suzanne
Comhaire-Sylvain, was generated by an intensive case study of social, cultural and
economic conditions among the peasants of the Marbial Valley, 1948-1950, by a team
of UNESCO experts directed by Alfred Metraux (q.v.).

513 **The concept of community development in Haiti and Venezuela.**
Richard P. Schaedel. In: *The Haitian potential; research and resources
of Haiti*. Edited by Vera Rubin, Richard P. Schaedel. New York:
Teachers College Press, 1975, p. 23-37. (Publications of the Center for
Education in Latin America).

This sociological study compares the Community Development Service in Haiti with
the Central Office for Planning and Coordination in Venezuela.

514 **Acculturation in northern Haiti.**
George E. Simpson. *Journal of American Folklore*, vol. 64, no. 254
(Oct.-Dec. 1951), p. 397-403.

A summary article in which Simpson, drawing on his own field-work in Haiti and also
on data provided by the research efforts of other scholars, discusses the process of
acculturation in Haiti. He notes how folklore functions to inculcate the Haitian child
with the social values admired by the Haitian peasants.

Social structure

515 **Class structure and acculturation in Haiti.**
Erika Bourguignon. *Ohio Journal of Science*, vol. 52, no. 6 (Nov. 1952), p. 317-20.
An anthropologist's comments on Haiti's social structure.

516 **Haitian social structure in the nineteenth century.**
Jean Casimir-Liautaud. In: *Working papers in Haitian society and culture.* Edited by Sidney W. Mintz. New Haven, Connecticut: Yale University, Antilles Research Program, 1975, p. 35-49. (Occasional Papers, no. 4).
One of the few available historical studies of Haiti's social structure. Liautaud is also the author of 'Two classes and two cultures in contemporary Haiti', in *Contemporary Carribean: a sociological reader*, edited by Susan Craig (Maracas, Trinidad and Tobago: College Press, 1981-82), vol. 2, p. 181-210.

517 **Urban stratification in Haiti.**
Jean Comhaire-Sylvain, Suzanne Comhaire-Sylvain. *Social and Economic Studies*, vol. 8, no. 2 (June 1959), p. 179-89. map. bibliog.
Presents an in-depth study of class structure in Port-au-Prince, based on an analysis of statistics. The authors conclude from their data that 'considering such factors as occupation, income, housing, education, family composition, ancestry, religion, entertainment, transport, language, and perhaps political attitudes also, four distinct classes can be distinguished in Port-au-Prince, with housing the most conspicuous index'.

518 **Class parameters in Haitian society.**
Maurice De Young. *Journal of Inter-American Studies*, vol. 1, no. 4 (Oct. 1959), p. 449-58.
De Young defines the parameters of Haiti's social strata in terms of three basic status pyramids: economic, social-occupational, and political. From the results of this study, he concludes that earlier sociologists were wrong in asserting that there was no emerging middle class in Haiti. On the contrary, not only does this class exist, it is one of Haiti's most important groups, and includes François Duvalier among its members.

519 **Idéologie de couleur et classes sociales en Haiti.** (Ideology of colour and social class in Haiti.)
Micheline Labelle. Montreal: Presses de l'Université de Montreal, 1978. 393p. bibliog. (Collection Recherches Caraïbes).
A scholarly study by an anthropologist which analyses the connection between colour and social class in Haiti.

Social Conditions. Social structure

520 **The military and society in Haiti.**
Michel S. Laguerre. Knoxville, Tennessee: University of Tennessee Press, 1993. 223p. maps.
This history of the Haitian military assesses its place in Haiti's social structure and its relation to civil authorities. The Haitian army's traditional involvement in politics has posed a threat to civil authority since Haitian independence in 1804.

521 **Urban life in the Caribbean: a study of a Haitian urban community.**
Michel S. Laguerre. Cambridge, Massachusetts: Schenkman Pub. Co., 1984. 214p. maps. bibliog.
A ground-breaking study of the urban community of Upper Belair, the oldest neighbourhood in Port-au-Prince. Based on research conducted in 1974-76, Laguerre covers the physical and social setting of this community, and its economic strategies, family organization, political life, and the place of voodoo in the lives of its residents. In his preface, Laguerre states that 'it is [his] assumption that a study of the internal organization of Upper Belair as a reflection of the dependence of the community upon the local elite will enable us to unveil the very dynamics of urban life in one of the oldest Caribbean cites'.

522 **The Haitian people.**
James G. Leyburn, with an introduction to the revised edition by Sidney W. Mintz. New Haven, Connecticut: Yale University Press, 1941. 342p. bibliog. Rev. ed., 1966. (Caribbean Series, 9). Reprinted, Westport, Connecticut: Greenwood Press, 1980.
Although now over fifty years old, Leyburn's work remains important for the study of Haitian culture and society. It provides 'a connected story of the growth of (Haiti's) social institutions out of the backgrounds of slavery and French colonial life', and describes the economic, political, religious, marital and class organization and functioning of the Haitian social system. Sections cover caste and class, religion, sexual relations, home life, politics and economics, and the problems of modern Haiti (as of 1940). Pages 238-41 provide an annotated list of Haiti's eighteen constitutions, from Toussaint Louverture's constitution of 1801 to the 1932 constitution adopted under the Stenio Vincent administration. For a review of Leyburn's book from a Haitian perspective, see Jean Price-Mars's 'Classe ou caste? Etude sur *The Haitian People* de James G. Leyburn', in *Revue de la Société Haïtienne d'Histoire et de Géographie*, vol. 13, no. 42 (July 1942), p. 1-50.

523 **Caste and class in Haiti.**
John Lobb. *American Journal of Sociology*, vol. 46, no. 1 (July 1940), p. 23-24.
This older article analyses the Haitian social structure in terms of two clearly delineated groups, the *élite* and the *noirs*, separated by physical characteristics, family position and intellectuality. Lobb concludes that former caste demarcations are in the process of being replaced in Haiti by more flexible class distinctions, and predicts the emergence of a middle class.

524 **Class structure and class conflict in Haitian society.**
Roland Wingfield, Vernon J. Parenton. *Social Forces*, vol. 43, no. 3
(March 1965), p. 338-47.
The authors identify four classes in Haiti: the urban traditional mulatto bourgeoisie;
the emerging middle class; the urban proletariat; and the peasant masses. They note
great disparity between the 'haves' and the 'have-nots' of Haitian society, akin to
colonial days' with six per cent of the population holding the power and wealth of the
country. However, class conflict in Haiti is within the privileged sector, between the
traditional mulatto bourgeoisie and the new middle class.

Family, kinship and sexuality

525 **Sexual unions in rural Haiti.**
James Allman. *International Journal of Sociology of the Family*,
vol. 10, no. 1 (Jan.-June 1980), p. 15-39. bibliog.
Reviews the historical background of Haitian family structure before analysing the
current sexual unions of 747 rural Haitian women in conjunction with socio-economic
factors, based on data collected for the 1977 Haitian Fertility Survey Pretest. The
article ends with a discussion of the norms governing sexual behaviour and mating
relationships in Haiti's rural areas.

526 **La familia rural Haitiana, Valle de Marbial.** (The rural Haitian family,
Marbial valley.)
Rémy Bastien. Mexico City: Libra, 1951. 184p. maps. bibliog.
A major study of the organization and life cycle of the Haitian peasant family, based
on data gathered in the Marbial Valley UNESCO Pilot Project in Fundamental
Education. This work is often cited as the most extensive study of the structure of the
Haitian rural family; it has recently been translated from Spanish to French by Linette
and André-Michel d'Ans as *Le paysan haïtien et sa famille: vallée de Marbial* (q.v.).
There is as yet no English translation.

527 **Haitian rural family organization.**
Rémy Bastien. *Social and Economic Studies*, vol. 10, no. 4 (Dec.
1961), p. 478-510.
A substantial factual article, based primarily on data collected in the Marbial valley
during the ethnographical investigation carried on April-October 1948, supplemented
with data from other regions of Haiti and from the urban centre of Port-au-Prince.
Bastien covers the history of the formation of family tradition in Haiti, land tenure in
the Marbial valley, the household in Marbial (the *lakou*), kinship terminology and
relationships, social and ritual kinship, mating, marriage and family life.

528 **Le paysan haïtien et sa famille: vallée de Marbial.** (The Haitian peasant and his family: Marbial Valley.)
Rémy Bastien, translated from the Spanish by Linette and André-Michel d'Ans; introduction by André-Michel d'Ans. Paris: Karthala, 1985. 217p. maps. bibliog.

The translators of Rémy Bastien's *La familia rural Haitiana, Valle de Marbial* (q.v.), have contributed greatly to Haitian studies by making this work accessible in French. André-Michel d'Ans' introduction aids the reader by placing Bastien's ethnological research, which was undertaken in 1948, in its historical and intellectual context.

529 **Courtship, marriage and plasaj at Kenscoff, Haiti.**
Suzanne Comhaire-Sylvain. *Social and Economic Studies*, vol. 7, no. 4 (Dec. 1958), p. 210-33.

A detailed descriptive article on sexual unions in Haiti, in which Comhaire-Sylvain discusses customs relating to marriage, *plasaj*, and polygamy. The work was based on research conducted in the Kenscoff district, fifteen miles southeast of Port-au-Prince.

530 **The household at Kenscoff, Haiti.**
Suzanne Comhaire-Sylvain. *Social and Economic Studies*, vol. 10, no. 2 (June 1961), p. 192-222.

Discusses five types of households common in rural Haiti, providing details on the roles of family members.

531 **On truth and fiction.**
Herbert Gold. *The Nation*, vol. 249, no. 21 (Dec. 18, 1989), p. 759-61.

A touch of surrealism informs novelist's Gold's sketch of an evening spent in a Haitian homosexual milieu.

532 **Ticouloute and his kinfolk: the study of a Haitian extended family.**
Michel S. Laguerre. In: *The extended family in black societies.* Edited by Demitri Shimkin, Edith M. Shimkin, Dennis A. Frate. The Hague: Mouton, 1978. p. 407-45. bibliog. (World Anthropology).

A case-study of Haitian family relations. Laguerre states that 'this study analyzes the structure and functioning of a Haitian extended family, relating these phenomena both to individual characteristics and to the historical development of Haitian family patterns. This study differs from previous research, which has dealt primarily with rural families in the context of the *lakou*, or kin-based compound, by considering diverse social environments and their correlates in the household of a single large family'. Laguerre draws his data from a sample of ten households, all linked by kinship, located in four environment, three in Haiti – rural, village, and urban (Port-au-Prince) – and one in the United States (metropolitan).

533 **Kin groups in a Haitian market.**
Caroline J. Legerman. In: *Peoples and cultures of the Caribbean.*
Edited by Michael M. Horowiltz. Garden City, New York: Natural
History Press, 1971, p. 382-99.

Based on field-work conducted in Haiti in 1961, this article relates kinship and occupation through a study of the women selling eggs and live fowl in the Port-au-Prince market. The author indicates the relationship between the nature of the products and the organization of selling activities. A chart delineating the genealogical relationships in a Haitian market clarifies information provided in text. This article was first published in *Man* vol. 62 (1962), p. 145-49.

534 **Observations on family and kinship organization in Haiti.**
Caroline J. Legerman. In: *The Haitian potential; research and resources of Haiti.* Edited by Vera Rubin, Richard P. Schaedel. New York: Teachers College Press, 1975, p. 17-22. (Publications of the Center for Education in Latin America).

Presents the results of a study of marriage and mating patterns and family forms in Haiti, undertaken by the author between 1964 and 1965.

535 **Some aspects of hierarchical structure in Haiti.**
Rhoda Metraux. In: *Acculturation in the Americas; proceedings and selected papers of the 29th International Congress of Americanists, New York, 1949.* Edited by Sol Tax, with an introduction by Melville J. Herskovits. Chicago: University of Chicago Press, 1952, p. 1985-94. (Reprinted, New York: Cooper Square Publishers, 1967).

Studies the 'chronic political instability that characterizes Haitian public life', and states that the explanation for Haitian politics lies in the patterns of behaviour and the system of values inculcated in Haitian children by means of their family interactions.

536 **The Haitian family: implications for the sex education of Haitian children in the United States.**
Ketty Hippolyte Rey. New York: Committee of Family Life Education, Department of Public Affairs, Community Society of New York, 1970. 37 leaves.

A study of Haitian emigrants in the United States.

537 **Sexual and familial institutions in northern Haiti.**
George E. Simpson. *American Anthropologist*, (n.s.) vol. 44, no. 4, pt. 1 (Oct.-Dec. 1942), p. 513-52.

Despite being based on data gathered more than fifty years ago, this article retains its original interest. Simpson, with his usual thoroughness and attention to detail, describes and discusses *plasaj*, legal marriage, peasant habitations and plantations, the extended family, the status of women, the sexual division of labour, child rearing practices, birth control, prostitution, and peasant attitudes towards sex.

538   **Haitian attitudes towards family size.**
      J. Mayone Stycos.   *Human Organization*, vol. 23, no. 1 (spring 1964),
      p. 42-47.
Summarizes the results of unstructured interviews with forty-four Haitian males and
forty-five females from a rural village who were asked to comment on photographs of
Haitian families. From their responses the author, an American sociologist, concludes
that 'family size is a matter of very low salience for most of the Haitien men and
women interviewed, that norms concerning the appropriate family size seem non-
existent and inappropriate for most subjects, and that an attitude of religious fatalism
about number of children is characteristic'.

539   **A comparison of socialization and personality in two simple societies.**
      Frances W. Underwood, Irma Honigmann.   *American Anthropologist*,
      vol. 49, no. 4, pt. 1 (Dec. 1947), p. 557-77.
Compares the Kaska Indians of northwestern Canada with rural Haitians in the
Beaumont Plateau region of Haiti. The section on Haiti, 'Peasant child rearing in rural
southwestern Haiti', describes how the Haitians deal with the child's physiological
needs and how they train their children for social living. The authors draw some
conclusions about the formation of the adult Haitian's character from their analysis of
the child's experience of cultural patterns. The article is based on field-work completed
in 1944.

540   **Conjugal unions among rural Haitian women.**
      Stephen Williams, Nirmala Murthy, Gretchen Berggren.   *Journal of
      Marriage and the Family*, vol. 37, no. 4 (Nov. 1975), p. 1022-31.
      bibliog.
Provides results of a four-year longitudinal study of the potential impact of family
formation patterns on fertility in rural Haiti. The nature and stability of conjugal
unions entered into by 425 Haitian women in twenty-three villages were investigated.
The authors state that 'findings reflect relative instability of conjugal unions associated
with a pattern of serial union formation. Considerable time spent by women out of
active union combined with relatively late age at first entry into union appear to be
important dampers on fertility in this population'.

Women

541   **Femmes haïtiennes.** (Haitian women.)
      Collectif de femmes haïtiennes.   Montreal: Maison d'Haïti, avec la
      collaboration de Carrefour International, 1980. Rev. ed. 63p. bibliog.
Examines the place of women in Haitian society and the status of women's rights in the
contemporary Haiti. This is a revised, corrected, and expanded version of the 1976
edition published by Rasanbleman Fanam Ayisyen.

Haiti: the breached citadel.
See item no. 1.

Haiti future: views of twelve Haitian leaders.
See item no. 10.

La femme haïtienne en diaspora.
See item no. 329.

Haitians: America's boat people.
See item no. 353.

Social Welfare and Social Problems

General

542 **Crime and punishment in the Caribbean.**
Edited by Rosemary Brana-Shute, Gary Brana-Schute. Gainesville,
Florida: University Presses of Florida, 1980. 146p. maps.

This collection of essays on tropical crime, published for the Association of Caribbean
Universities and Research Institutes and the Center for Latin American Studies,
includes Max Carré's 'A profile of the state of criminology in Haiti'.

543 **Port-au-Prince: awakening to the urban crisis.**
Simon M. Fass. In: *Metropolitan Latin America: the challenge and the
response.* Edited by Wayne A. Cornelius, Robert V. Kemper.
Beverly Hills, California: Sage, 1978, p. 155-80. maps. bibliog. (Latin
American Urban Research, 6).

By means of a case study the authors appraise the urbanization process in
contemporary Port-au-Prince. Employment, housing, water and erosion controls,
sanitation, health, energy, and transportation are all examined.

544 **Symptoms of stress in four societies.**
George M. Guthrie, Anne Verstraete, Melissa M. Deines, Robert M.
Stern. *Journal of Social Psychology*, vol. 95, second half (April 1975),
p. 165-72.

This paper by four psychologists from Pennsylvania State University reports the results
of a survey to determine reactions to stressful situations. Questionnaires distributed
among sample groups of French, American Filipino and Haitian college students were
used to gather the information used in the study. Differences in reported frequency of
reactions were found for sex, level of industrialization, language and nationality.

545 **Assistance sociale en Haiti, 1804-1972.** (Social assistance in Haiti, 1804-1972.)
Augustin Mathurin. Port-au-Prince: Imprimerie des Antilles, 1972. 478p. bibliog.
A history of public and private social service in Haiti.

546 **Social programs throughout the world: 1991.**
Social Security Administration, US Department of Health and Human Service. Washington, DC: Government Printing Office, 1991. 319p. (SSA Publication no. 61-006).
Includes tabulated information on Haiti's social assistance programmes: administrative organization, coverage, source of funds, qualifying conditions, cash benefits, and permanent disability and medical benefits for insured workers and their dependents.

547 **Acute water shortage and health problems in Haiti.**
S. B. Thacker, S. I. Music (et al.). *The Lancet*, vol. 1, no. 8166 (March 1980), p. 471-73.
Briefly examines the impact of water restriction on disease. The study was undertaken in Port-au-Prince following the water shortage of February 1977, when the city was deprived of more than half of its water supply. Disease in children was found to be related to quantity of water used, the family's socio-economic status, the employment of head of household, and to family size.

Medicine and health care

548 **For the people for a change: bringing health to the families of Haiti.**
Ary Bordes, Andrea Couture. Boston, Massachusetts: Beacon Press; Toronto: Fitzhenry & Whiteside, 1978. 299p.
This book tells the history of Dr. Ary Bordes and the Family Hygiene Centre (10 Impasse Lavaud, Port-au-Prince). Based on taped interviews with Bordes, who had devoted his life to maternal–child health care and family planning in Haiti, the volume is an intelligent and factual presentation of a Haitian physician's contribution towards solving Haiti's health problems.

549 **Survie et santé de l'enfant en Haïti: résultats de l'enquête mortalité, morbidité et utilisation des services, 1987.** (Child survival and health in Haiti: results of the survey Mortality, morbidity, and utilization of services, 1987.)
Michel Cayemittes, Anouch Chahnazarian. Port-au-Prince: Editions de l'Enfance, 1989. 182p. bibliog.
During the summer of 1987, under the auspices of Haiti's Ministry of Public Health and Population, a survey of 4,026 Haitian households was undertaken by the Institut Haitien de l'Enfance, Pétionville, and Johns Hopkins University, Baltimore, Maryland,

135

Social Welfare and Social Problems. Medicine and health care

in order to determine trends in health care services for children and into child and
infant mortality. This volume reports the results of the survey.

550 **Brief comments on the occurrence, etiology, and treatment of**
indisposition.
Claude Charles. *Social Science and Medicine; Medical Anthropology*,
vol. 13B, no. 2 (April 1979), p. 135-36.
Notes on *indisposition* by a Haitian social anthropologist, who relates the explanations
of the causes of this psycho-physiological phenomenon which are commonly given by
Haitians. Non-professional methods of treatment of *indisposition* by Voodoo
practitioners are also mentioned.

551 **Innovation among Haitian healers: the adoption of oral rehydration**
therapy.
Jeannine Coreil. *Human Organization*, vol. 47, no. 1 (spring 1988),
p. 48-57. bibliog.
A study of the adoption of a modern medical technique by practitioners of traditional
and alternative medicine in the Montrouis region of Haiti. Coreil evaluates the
knowledge and use of ORT (Oral Rehydration Therapy) to treat childhood diarrhoea
by Haitian midwives, herbalists, shamans and by injection. She finds that these healers
selectively incorporate this simple and effective Western therapy into their traditional
practices.

552 **Bad blood, spoiled milk: bodily fluids as moral barometers in rural**
Haiti.
Paul Farmer. *American Ethnologist*, vol. 15, no. 1 (Feb. 1988),
p. 62-83. bibliog.
An ethnographic analysis of two physical syndromes which are widely experienced in
rural Haiti: *move san* (bad blood), and its corollary, *let gate* (spoiled milk), which
occurs when a pregnant or nursing mother is afflicted with *move san*. Farmer presents
two case studies of women suffering from *move san*, then examines the various
explanatory models devised to interpret the illness by the patient and those associated
with her – her mother and a confidante – and by a local healer and a professional
physician. He looks at explanations for the illness as the result of economic forces or as
a mental disorder, then argues that '*move san* is best understood as a disorder of
experience in which stories told by sufferers, and by their consociates, play a key role
in the shaping of that experience'.

553 **Who gave the world syphilis? The Haitian myth.**
Richmond C. Holcomb; with an introduction by C. S. Butler. New
York: Froben Press, 1937. 189p. bibliog.
Many believe that the current AIDS epidemic is Haitian in origin. This is not the first
time that Haiti has been blamed for causing worldwide infection. In the 16th century,
the virulent outbreak of syphilis in Europe was supposedly traced to sexual encounters
between the Spaniards and Amerindians on Hispaniola, an explanation disseminated
by Ruy Diaz de Isla in his *Tractado contra el mal serpentino* (Seville: Dominico
Robertis, 1539; out of print). Holcomb's book is a criticism of Diaz's views.

554 Obstacles to medical progress in Haiti.
Ari Kiev. *Human Organization*, vol. 25, no. 1 (Sept. 1966), p. 10-16.

Kiev finds that 'Voodoo exerts both therapeutic and anti-therapeutic effects' upon the Haitian through the prevalence of its belief system and practices in Haitian life. He examines these beliefs and practices in terms of their effect on the introduction of Western medical techniques into Haiti, finding that, while providing a certain security for the Haitian peasant, Voodoo beliefs militate against the attainment of ego maturity and scientific thinking. Nevertheless, those introducing Western techniques have little change of success unless a method can be found to integrate Western medicine into the peasant's traditional view of life. Of particular interest in this article are Kiev's descriptions of treatments by Voodoo priests, which he witnessed firsthand during Voodoo ceremonies.

555 Research and resources in psychiatry in Haiti.
Ari Kiev. In: *The Haitian potential; research and resources of Haiti.* Edited by Vera Rubin, Richard P. Schaedel. New York: Teachers College Press, 1975, p. 173-79. (Publications of the Center for Education in Latin America).

Suggests a range of psychiatric services and programmes that could be established in Haiti.

556 The Haiti Psychiatric Institute: Centre de Psychiatrie.
N. S. Kline, L. Mars. In: *Psychiatry in the underdeveloped countries.* Edited by N. S. Kline, L. Mars. Washington, DC: American Psychiatric Association, 1961. p. 48-51.

Information on the first modern psychiatric clinic in Haiti. Kline also co-authored (with M. Bordeleau) the article 'Experiences in developing psychiatric services in Haiti', in *World Mental Health*, vol. 14 (Nov. 1962), p. 1-13.

557 Diseases of the peasants of Haiti.
Camille Lherisson. *American Journal of Public Health*, vol. 25, no. 8 (Aug. 1935), p. 924-29. bibliog.

An early survey of Haiti's health problems, based on data collected between 1924 and 1929. Among the diseases prevalent in Haiti at this time were hookworm, cancer, skin disease, infectious diseases, tuberculosis, malaria, leprosy, and yaws – the latter being the most common disease in country districts.

558 Dr. Mellon of Haiti.
Peter Michelmore. New York: Dodd, Mead & Co., 1964; London: Gollancz, 1965. 176p.

Describes William Larimer Mellon and the Albert Schweitzer Hospital at Deschapelles. Inspired by Albert Schweitzer's medical work in West Africa, Mellon, a grand-nephew of financier Andrew Mellon, opened a hospital near St. Marc in 1956, in an attempt to bring Western medicine to the inhabitants of the region.

559 **Recent research in public health in Haiti.**
Pierre Noel. In: *The Haitian potential; research and resources of Haiti.* Edited by Vera Rubin, Richard P. Schaedel. New York: Teachers College Press, 1975, p. 157-66. (Publications of the Center for Education in Latin America).
Reviews public health research conducted in Haiti since the 1920s.

560 **History of Haitian medicine.**
Robert P. Parsons, foreword by Edward R. Stitt. New York: P. B. Hoeber, 1930. 196p. map. bibliog.
Reprinted with additions and corrections from *Annals of medical history* (n.s., vol. 1, no. 3, 1929), this chronicle of Haitian medicine to 1929 is the most complete account available in English. Parsons divides the medical history of the country into three periods – the French colonial era, the independence period, and the period of the US occupation – and describes how each administration dealt with the diseases endemic to the island: smallpox, yellow fever, malaria, tetanus, and intestinal parasites. According to Parsons, the state of public health in Haiti changed for the better only with the advent of the Americans, who introduced scientific medical concepts and practices to the Haitians. He supplies interesting facts about the dedicated American doctors who laboured to establish a medical care system and medical education in Haiti. These included Porter K. Lowell during the nineteenth century and Paul W. Wilson, Kent C. Melhorn, Richard H. Laning, and C. S. Butler during the US occupation.

561 *Indisposition* **in Haiti.**
Jeanne Philippe, Jean Baptiste Romain. *Social Science & Medicine; Medical Anthropology*, vol. 13B, no. 2 (April 1979), p. 129-33.
'*Indisposition* is a Haitian syndrome which falls between psychic and somatic ailments. The term *indisposition* is common in Haiti and the condition frequently discussed. Although identified in the Haitian community in Miami, it has not been extensively studied there or previously studied in Haiti. This article represents the authors' first attempt to examine the phenomenon in a Haitian context. It reports the results of a clinical study and responses to a questionnaire administered to sixty-nine people. . . . It is concluded that *indisposition* is one of several types of dissociative states commonly used by Haitians. A brief discussion relates the ease of dissociation to Haitian concepts of personality and the soul'.

562 **The psychopathology of Haitian females.**
R. Rowlands. *International Journal of Social Psychiatry*, vol. 25, no. 3 (autumn 1979), p. 217-23.
A study of mental disorders in Haitian women.

563 **Arztin auf Haiti.** (Doctor in Haiti.)
Margarete Schmidt-Schutt. Berlin-Grunewald: Herbig, 1950, c1942. 303p. map. (Reprinted, Munich: Deutsches Verlaghaus Bong, 1955).
In this autobiographical work, Schmidt-Schutt describes her experiences during three years (1923-26) spent practising as a primary care physician in Haiti.

564 **Syncrisis: the dynamics of health: vol. 6: Haiti.**
US Department of Health, Education and Welfare, Public Health
Service, Office of International Health, Division of Program Analysis.
Washington, DC: US Government Printing Office, 1976. Rev. ed. 88p.
bibliog.
'Syncrisis studies describe and analyze health problems in countries which are major
recipients of international assistance [They present] a concise, organized, and up-to-
date introduction to the health situation in the country and an orientation to the most
significant problems faced by the health system'.

Haitian-Americans.
See item no. 356.

AIDS

565 **La muerte vudu, la respuesta al stress, depresion y SIDA.** (Voodoo
death, the response to stress, depression and AIDS.)
Sanford I. Cohen. *Psicopatologia*, vol. 8, no. 1 (Jan.-March 1988),
p. 1-15.
Combines insights from biology, psychology and the social sciences to construct a
biopsychosocial model for AIDS research. The high incidence of deaths from HIV
infection in Haiti has been explained by such non-medical factors as belief in Voodoo
and the social and familial stigmatization of homosexuals. Cohen believes that these
stresses contribute to the fatalities from AIDS-related illnesses among Haitian patients
by weakening immunological responses.

566 **HIV and AIDS in Haiti: recent developments: special section: AIDS – the
first ten years.**
M. Desvarieux, J. W. Pape. *AIDS-Care*, vol. 3, no. 3 (1991),
p. 271-79.
A summary of the history of the decade-long Acquired Immune Deficiency Syndrome
(AIDS) epidemic in Haiti. By the beginning of the 1990s, heterosexual transmission
had overtaken homosexual contact and blood transfusion as the predominant mode of
infection by the HIV virus, with an increasing number of AIDS cases appearing among
women and children.

567 **AIDS and accusation: Haiti and the geography of blame.**
Paul Farmer. Berkeley, California: University of California Press,
1992. 338p. (Comparative Studies of Health Systems and Medical Care,
no. 33).
A monograph by a medical anthropologist on the social impact on Haiti and Haitians
of the belief that AIDS originated in Haiti.

Social Welfare and Social Problems. Nutrition

568 Sexual behavior, smoking, and HIV-1 infection in Haitian women.
Neal A. Halsey, Jacqueline S. Coberly, Elizabeth Holt. *The Journal of the American Medical Association*, vol. 267 (April 15, 1992), p. 2062-66. bibliog.
Discusses behavioural risk factors in relation to AIDS amongst women in Haiti.

569 **Transmission of HIV-1 infections from mothers to infants in Haiti: impact on childhood mortality and malnutrition.**
Neal A. Halsey, Reginald Boulos, Elizabeth Holt. *The Journal of the American Medical Association*, vol. 264 (Oct. 24-31, 1990), p. 2088-92. bioliog.
A study of what has become a major public health problem in Haiti: the increasing number of AIDS cases among Haitian children.

570 **A mask on the face of death.**
Richard Selzer. *Life*, vol. 10, no. 8 (Aug. 1987), p. 58-64.
In this popular article, Selzer, a professor of surgery, investigates sex and AIDS in Haiti, visiting Port-au-Prince's red-light district, an AIDS clinic and several hospitals. The article summarizes statistics on HIV infection in Haiti as of 1987.

Risk factors for AIDS among Haitians residing in the United States: evidence of heterosexual transmission.
See item no. 346.

Nutrition

571 **L'Alimentation et la nutrition en Haïti.** (Food and nutrution in Haiti.)
Ivan Beghin, William Fougere, Kendall W. King. Paris: Les Presses Universitaires de France, 1970. 248p. bibliog. (Etudes Tiers Monde: Croissance, Développement, Progrès).
This older monograph continues to be cited in matters regarding Haiti's nutritional problems.

572 **Nutrition research in Haiti.**
Kendall W. King. In: *The Haitian potential; research and resources of Haiti.* Edited by Vera Rubin, Richard P. Schaedel. New York: Teachers College Press, 1975, p. 147-56. (Publications of the Center for Education in Latin America).
Summarizes development in the knowledge of malnutrition in Haiti between 1958 and 1965, and of attempts during the same period to ameliorate the problem.

573 **Maternal nutrition and traditional food behavior in Haiti.**
     H. Jean C. Wiese. *Human Organization*, vol. 35, no. 2 (summer
     1976), p. 193-200.

An anthropological study of the effects of the hot/cold food system of humoral
medicine upon the diet of lactating Haitian women. 'The data indicates that practices
stemming from this belief system have an even more serious limiting impact upon rural
dietary behaviour than the economic, technological, and environmental factors, and
must, therefore, be considered in any nutritional intervention program for Haitians
either in Haiti or abroad'.

Politics and Government

574 **Political handbook of the world: 1992; governments and intergovernmental organizations as of July 1, 1992 (with major political developments noted through September 1, 1992).**
Edited by Arthur S. Banks. Binghamton, New York: CSA Publications, 1975- . annual.

The section entitled 'Haiti' (p. 319-24) is a succinct summary of Haiti's political history, concentrating on recent developments. Haiti's active political parties and their leaders are identified, the structure of the government is described and members of the administration in power are listed.

575 **Up by the roots.**
Greg Chamberlain. *NACLA Report on the Americas*, vol. 21, no. 3 (May/June 1987), p. 15-23.

Reports on Haiti during the summer of 1987, when what Chamberlain describes as 'a bloody national deadlock' was taking place prior to the national elections scheduled for November. Chamberlain provides the background for the fall of the Duvalier régime in 1986 and describes the contending forces – both old and new – completing for power during the interregnum which was headed by General Henri Namphy.

576 **Religion and politics in Haiti: two essays.**
Harold Courlander, Rémy Bastien, with a preface by Richard P. Schaedel. Washington, DC: Institute for Cross-Cultural Research, 1966. 81p. maps. bibliog. (ICRS Studies, 1).

In his preface, Schaedel characterizes the two essays that make up this book as 'an imaginative approach to understanding the complexity of Haitian culture and politics'. Courlander and Bastien, two writers from entirely distinct backgrounds and with clearly different socio-political orientations attempt to show how Voodoo has been, since before the birth of the Haitian nation, inextricably associated with the adventures of the state, and underline the significant role that it is playing under the government of François Duvalier. Harold Coulander's 'Vodoun in Haitian culture' focuses on the social and political significance of the Voodoo cult, while Rëmy Bastien's 'Vodoun and politics in Haiti' traces the role Voodoo has filled as the political situation in Haiti has varied over the years. Of special interest is Bastien's discussion of François Duvalier and Voodoo – Duvalier having been one of Bastien's assistants in the Haitian Bureau of Ethnology in 1942. The book also contains a critically annotated bibliography of books on Voodoo.

577   **A reporter at large: beyond the mountains – I.**
Mark Danner.   *The New Yorker*, vol. 65 (27 Nov. 1989), p. 55ff. maps.

A journalist's account of the *dechoukaj* (uprooting) of Duvalierism in 1987-88 Haiti. Danner describes the 1987 presidential campaign, the massacres perpetrated during the November 1987 ballot, and the election in January 1988 of Leslie Manigat.

578   **A reporter at large: beyond the mountains – II.**
Mark Danner.   *The New Yorker*, vol. 65 (4 Dec. 1989), p. 68ff. maps.

Danner supplies historical background on Haitian politics, from the era of slavery to the transition from François Duvalier's régime to that of his son, Jean-Claude.

579   **A reporter at large: beyond the mountains – III.**
Mark Danner.   *The New Yorker*, vol. 65 (11 Dec. 1989), p. 100ff. map.

Describes Haitian politics 1971-89: the Jean-Claude Duvalier régime and its collapse; the Manigat government and its overthrow; the return of General Henri Namphy and his removal by General Prosper Avril.

580   **Armée et politique en Haiti.** (The army and politics in Haiti.)
Kern Delince.   Paris: L'Harmattan, 1979. 271p. bibliog.

Haiti's military plays a major role in its politics. Delince's work is a study of the Haitian army's political involvement from the end of the American occupation through the 1970s.

581   **Voodoo and politics in Haiti.**
Michel S. Laguerre.   New York: St. Martin's Press, 1989. 152p. bibliog.

An exegesis of the central role that the Voodoo faith has played in Haitian politics from colonial days to today's post-Duvalier era. Among the topics investigated are the evolution of colonial Voodoo, the practice of Voodoo among the maroons, Voodoo in the Haitian Revolution, the Bizango secret society, the shrine of Saut D'Eau, Voodoo in the Duvalier régime, and the military symbolism of Voodoo.

582   **Contemporary political developments in Haiti.**
Gerard R. Latortue.   In: *Politics and economics in the Caribbean.* Edited by T. G. Mathews, F. M. Andric. Rio Piedras, Puerto Rico: Institute of Caribbean Science, University of Puerto Rico, 1972, rev. ed. p. 51-72 (Special Study, no. 8).

Latortue states that his purpose in this essay is 'to analyse the political situation at the fall of General Paul E. Magloire's government and the reasons why Dr. François

Politics and Government

Duvalier has been elected; to review the methods of government used by Dr. Duvalier to maintain himself in power; to make a brief appraisal of Dr. Duvalier's régime; and finally to discuss the programs of the different opposition groups to his administration'. Latortue sees Haiti as being involved in a tragic crisis, not as a direct result of the Duvalier régime, but through the relationship of the three political groups in Haitian society: the mulattoes, the educated blacks, and the black masses.

583   **The European lands.**
Gerard R. Latortue.   In: *The United States and the Caribbean.* Edited
by Tad Szulc.   Englewood Cliffs, New Jersey: Prentice-Hall, 1971,
p. 173-90. (A Spectrum Book). (Reprinted, Ann Arbor,
Michigan: Books on Demand, 1991).

A Haitian scholar's analysis of politics during the 1960s in those nations of the West Indies – Haiti included – where continental European influences have outweighed British or American. Latortue's discussion of political trends and social and economic life under François Duvalier is largely – but not entirely – negative.

584   **Haiti: problems of a transition to democracy in an authoritarian soft
state.**
Anthony P. Maingot.   *Journal of Interamerican Studies and World
Affairs,* vol. 28, no. 4 (winter 1986-87), p. 75-102. bibliog.

In this 'think peace', a social scientist offers a fresh and perceptive analysis of the kleptocractic operation of Jean-Claude Duvalier's régime – essentially, a rule by thieves – indicating the means by which the younger Duvalier modernized and institutionalized corruption in order to drain state-owned enterprises and amass a personal fortune. Maingot discusses six problems facing Haiti in its transition from authoritarian rule, and lists the parties and presidential candidates running for election in 1987.

585   **Haiti of the sixties, object of international concern; a tentative global
analysis of the potentially explosive situation of a crisis country in the
Caribbean.**
Leslie F. Manigat.   Washington, DC: Washington Center of Foreign
Policy Research, 1964. 104p. bibliog.

An analysis of the early Duvalier régime, originally presented in a series of lectures given at several American universities in 1964. Manigat, a distinguished academic, was elected President of Haiti in January, 1988, but ousted from office by an army coup in June of that same year.

586   **Embryo-politics in Haiti.**
David Nicholls.   *Government and Opposition,* vol. 6, no. 1 (winter
1971), p. 75-85.

Defines the François Duvalier government in Haiti as a constitutional dictatorship, a traditional despotism where the régime's main concern is to retain power. It is not totalitarian as it lacks an overriding ideological position. At the same time, it is not entirely without ideology. Three ideological viewpoints can be detected in Duvalier's administration: negritude, technology, and fascism.

587 From Dessalines to Duvalier: race, colour and national independence in
Haiti.
David Nicholls. Cambridge, England; New York: Cambridge
University Press, 1979. 357p. map. bibliog. (Cambridge Latin
American Studies, no. 34).
From the author's preface: 'The present volume is the result of ten years' work on
Haitian history and politics. It deals with the role played by ideas of race and colour in
the period of national independence. . . . It has been central to my thesis that divisions
closely connected with colour have been one of the principal reasons why Haiti has
failed to maintain an effective independence. It is not the only reason, but I hope I
have shown in the body of the book that colour has played a major role in Haitian
politics from Dessalines to Duvalier'. The contents comprise 'Introduction'; 'Fathers of
national independence (1804-1825)'; 'Pride and prejudice (1820-1867)'; 'Liberals and
nationals (1867-1910)'; 'Occupied Haiti (1911-1934)'; 'Literature and dogma (1930-
1945)'; 'Authentics and their adversaries (1946-1957)'; 'Culture and tyranny (1957-
1971)'; and a conclusion.

588 Politics and religion in Haiti.
David Nicholls. *Canadian Journal of Political Science*, vol. 3, no. 3
(Sept. 1970), p. 400-14.
The author, a political scientist, examines the role played by Roman Catholicism in the
politics of Haiti, both in the past and under the François Duvalier régime. The major
part of the article scrutinizes the 1960-66 conflict between the Haitian government and
the Church. In Nicholls's view, the relationship between politics and religion in
Duvalier's Haiti must be analysed in the light of nationalist ideas that developed in
Haiti in reaction to the US occupation, 1915-34. Readers will find this factual and
detailed essay a valuable contribution to an understanding of Haitian politics.

589 Haiti's despotism: from father to son to . . .
William Paley. *Caribbean Review*, vol. 13, no. 1 (winter 1984),
p. 13-15ff.
A succinct presentation of the Haitian political situation that made possible the smooth
succession of Jean-Claude Duvalier to the Presidential office on the death of his father,
François Duvalier, in 1971. Paley notes how, in 1984, Jean-Claude's political support
has shifted from the black middle class – his father's political base – to the Haitian
élite. He emphasizes the vulnerability of Jean-Claude's position, which ultimately
depended on the United States, and makes an astute guess as to the future of his
régime.

590 The Haitians: class and color politics.
Lyonel Paquin. Brooklyn, New York: Multi-type, 1983. 271p. bibliog.
Presents a political history by an outspoken Haitian exile in the United States who
writes on the history of his country in a colloquial style. The reader will be most
interested in Paquin's depiction of the events of the 1946-58 period, during which he
was a friend and confidant of three rival political leaders: Louis Dejoie, Daniel Fignole
and Clement Jumelle. While in exile, Paquin participated in opposition to François
Duvalier during 1958-60.

591 The Duvalier phenomenon.
Anselme Remy. *Caribbean Studies*, vol. 14, no. 2 (July 1974),
p. 38-65.

An interesting analysis of François Duvalier's political ideology, 'Duvalierism', as a nationalistic phenomenon. After setting the Duvalier phenomenon in its historical context, Remy analyses Duvalier's ideology as it appears in his writings. He then examines the cultural, economic and political manifestations of Duvalierism in action, in order to demonstrate how it exemplifies both the power and the limitations of nationalism.

592 Haiti: the politics of squalor.
Robert I. Rotberg, with Christopher K. Clague. Boston,
Massachusetts: Houghton Mifflin, 1971. 456p. map. bibliog.
(A Twentieth-Century Fund Study).

The report of a research project directed by Rotberg that studied Haitian political and economic development. Rotberg begins by presenting his theory of Haitian 'national' psychology (the result, in his view, of Haitian child-rearing practices), then provides a critique of conditions in Haiti during the Duvalier era. In what was a generally favourable review of his book ('A scientific study of Papa Doc', *Government and Opposition*, vol. 8, no. 3 [summer 1973], p. 385ff.), David Nicholls comments that he feels Rotberg makes a mistake in attempting 'to explain political events with reference to the ill-digested fragments of psychological theories', and 'to understand Duvalier himself in terms of individual psychological abnormality'.

593 Haiti's past mortgages its future.
Robert I. Rotberg. *Foreign Affairs*, vol. 67, no. 1 (fall 1988),
p. 93-109.

Writing in the summer of 1988, at the time of the Namphy junta, Rotberg offers a sketch of Haiti's political history and a look towards the country's future.

594 Haiti: the Duvaliers and beyond.
Aaron Segal. In: *The Caribbean after Grenada: revolution, conflict, and democracy*. Edited by Scott B. MacDonald, Harald M. Sandstrom, Paul B. Goodwin, Jr. New York: Praeger, 1988, p. 139-51.

Summarizes the impact of Duvalier rule on Haiti. Segal, a political scientist, considers the Duvalier régime to have imposed 'immiseration' – a gradually falling standard of living – on Haiti. The Duvaliers ran the government as a 'kleptocracy' (rule by thieves) and were primarily concerned with channeling public funds to themselves and their collaborators. Identifying the major problems of the post-Duvalier era as population increase and soil erosion, Segal is pessimistic about Haiti's future, and states that 'authoritarianism with effective constraints' is the realistic solution to the nation's distress.

595 **Haiti: state against nation; the origins and legacy of Duvalierism.**
Michel-Rolph Trouillot.   New York: Monthly Review Press, 1990.
282p. map. bibliog.
Analyses the two Duvalier dictatorships (1957-86) in the context of Haiti's historical
evolution. Trouillot states that 'the main arguement of [his] book is that the Duvalierist
state emerged as the result of a long-term process that was marked by an increasing
disjuncture between political and civil society'. The first part of the volume discusses
Haiti's historical legacy; the second, Duvalier's 'totalitarian solution'. Trouillot is a
practicing anthropologist whose knowledge of Haiti's history, politics and economics is
illuminated by cultural insights. Readers of this book will be rewarded with many acute
observations on Haiti's crisis-ridden politics.

596 **Haiti: the failure of politics.**
Brian Weinstein, Aaron Segal.   New York: Praeger, 1992. 203p. map.
bibilog.
This examination of political corruption in Haiti concentrates on the Duvalier era.
Weinstein and Segal are also the co-authors of an earlier study of Haiti's politics, *Haiti;
political failure, cultural successes* (New York: Praeger, 1984).

Constitution and Legal System

597 **Les 150 [i.e. cent cinquante] ans du régime du code civil dans le contexte social Haitien, 1826-1976.** (One hundred and fifty years of the administration of the civil code in the Haitian social context, 1826-1976.)
Ferdinand Delatour.   Port-au-Prince: Les Editions Fardin, 1977. 301p.
bibliog.
A history of civil law in Haiti, viewed in relation to social conditions.

598 **Constitution de la République d'Haïti, 29 mars 1987.** (Constitution of the Republic of Haiti, 29 March 1987.)
Assemblée Nationale Constituante.   Port-au-Prince: République d'Haiti, 1987. 85p.
This is the Constitution now in force in Haiti, ratified by a plebiscite on March 29, 1987. Reflecting its recognition of Haitian Creole as an official language of Haiti, the Constitution was also issued in that language: *Konstitisyon Repiblik Ayiti* (Port-au-Prince: Ministe Enfomasyon ak Kowadinasyon, 1987). For an English translation of Haiti's present Constitution see *Constitutions of the countries of the world: a series of updated texts, constitutional chronologies and annotated bibliographies*, edited by Albert P. Blaustein and Gisbert H. Flanz (Dobbs Ferry, New York: Oceana Publications, 1971- .)

599 **Les constitutions d'Haïti (1801-85).** (The constitutions of Haiti [1801-85].)
Louis Joseph Janvier.   Paris: Marpon & Flammarion, 1886. 624p.
map. (Reprinted, Port-au-Prince: Editions Fardin, 1977).
An important source for the constitutional history of Haiti, this volume contains texts and analyses of Haiti's nineteenth-century constitutions.

148

600 **Paper laws, steel bayonets: breakdown of the rule of law in Haiti.**
Lawyers Committee for Human Rights. New York: Lawyers
Committee for Human Rights, 1990. 215p.

Investigates the breakdown of the Haitian legal system in the years following the toppling of the Jean-Claude Duvalier government. The authors find that with the collapse of the Haitian judiciary, power has concentrated in the hands of the military and human rights abuses are common.

601 **Rural code of Haiti, in French and English, with a prefatory letter to
the Right Hon. the Earl Bathurst.**
Haiti (Republic). London: J. Ridgway, 1827. 100p. (Reprinted,
Westport, Connecticut: Negro Universities Press, 1970). (West Indian
Slavery. Selected Pamphlets, no. 8).

Presents agricultural laws passed by the Boyer administration. French and English texts are provided in parallel columns.

Human Rights

602 **Haiti: human rights under hereditary dictatorship.**
Americas Watch Committee. New York; Washington, DC:
Americas Watch, in conjunction with the National Coalition for Haitian
Refugees, 1985. 33p. (An Americas Watch Report).
Relates the findings of a mission to Haiti undertaken in late July 1985, by Michael
Hooper of the National Coalition for Haitian Refugees and Aryeh Neier of Americas
Watch. The aim of the mission was to discover the facts on the human rights situation
in Haiti with regard to elections, political parties and the treatment of critics of Jean-
Claude Duvalier's government.

603 **Return to the darkest days: human rights in Haiti since the coup.**
Anne Fuller, Amy Wilentz. New York: Americas Watch [with] the
National Coalition for Haitian Refugees [and] Physicians for Human
Rights, 1991. 20p.
In this report dated December 1991, the authors document political persecution in
Haiti occurring after the coup of September 29 1991, that deposed President Jean-
Bertrand Aristide.

604 **In the Army's hands: human rights in Haiti on the eve of the elections.**
New York: Americas Watch [with] the National Coalition for Haitian
Refugees [and] Caribbean Rights, 1990. 71p.
Reports on the corrupt election practices in Haiti, compiled in December 1990, as the
country prepared for the December 16th presidential elections. Americas Watch also
documented election violations in an earlier report, *Haiti: terror and the 1987 elections*
(New York: Americas Watch [with] the National Coalition for Haitian Refugees,
1987).

150

605 **Haiti.**
US State Department. In: *Country reports on human rights practices for 1991: report submitted to the Committee of Foreign Affairs, US House of Representatives, and the Committee on Foreign Relations, US Senate.* Washington, DC: Government Printing Office, 1992, p. 633-42.

Country reports on human rights practices is compiled annually by the US State Department as required by the Foreign Assistance Act of 1961. The report for 1991 covers the dismal state of human rights in Haiti both during and after President Jean-Bertrand Aristide's truncated term of office (February 7 to September 29 1991). According to the report, the Aristide government 'repeatedly attempted to interfere with the judical process or usurp it through "mob justice"'.

Administration and Local Government

606 The Haitian *chef de section*.
J. L. Comhaire. *American Anthropologist*, vol. 57, no. 3, pt. 1 (June 1955), p. 620-24. bibliog.

An article examining the role of the local police chief, the real power and often the only representative of the government in rural areas of Haiti. It is based on field-work conducted from 1937-41 and in 1951 and 1952.

607 La administration publica en Haiti. (Public administration in Haiti.)
Jean-Claude Garcia Zamor, introduction by Richard M. Morse. Guatemala City: Editorial Landivar, 1966. 186p. bibliog.

Written in 1960 as the author's MA thesis at the Graduate School of Public Administration of the University of Puerto Rico, this book – which has not been translated – is one of the few studies of public administration in Haiti. After providing background information, Garcia Zamor covers governmental organization, public finances, public services and planning and development in Haiti.

608 The *chef de section*: structure and functions of Haiti's basic administrative institution.
Pnina Lahav. In: *Working papers in Haitian society and culture*. Edited by Sidney W. Mintz. New Haven, Connecticut: Yale University, Antilles Research Program, 1975, p. 51-83. (Occasional Papers, no. 4).

The most recent study of Haiti's powerful local police chiefs.

609   **Research problems and perspectives of the Haitian civil service.**
Serge Vieux.   In: *The Haitian potential; research and resources of Haiti.* Edited by Vera Rubin, Richard P. Schaedel.   New York: Teachers College Press, 1975, p. 240-72. (Publications of the Center for Education in Latin America).

One of the few studies of public administration in Haiti. Vieux discusses the problems involved in the organization of an administrative apparatus for Haiti.

Foreign Relations

General

610 **Dantès Bellegarde and Pan-Africanism.**
Patrick D. Bellegarde-Smith. *Phylon*, vol. 42, no. 3 (Sept. 1981), p. 233-44.
Dantès Bellegarde (1877-1966) was Haiti's leading ideologue and premier diplomat in the early to mid-twentieth century. This article, written by Bellegarde's grandson, details his international diplomatic career, emphasizing his defence of the rights of African and colonial peoples.

611 **Haiti: perspectives of foreign policy: an essay on the international relations of a small state.**
Patrick Bellegarde-Smith. *Caribbean Quarterly*, vol. 20, nos. 3 & 4 (Sept.-Dec. 1974), p. 21-38.
Bellegarde-Smith states that his intention in this work is to analyse 'the contemporary trends and past diplomatic history of Haiti in the hope of isolating and defining the salient factors and variables of Haitian foreign policy within the context of small power politics, through its international relations'. He traces the diplomatic history of Haiti from its early ostracism by white powers – who feared an independent black country – through the regularization of Haiti's relations with Great Britain, France, the Holy See and finally, the United States. He covers Haiti's interference in Latin America, the shock of the American occupation of the country, and more recently, Haiti's attempts to reassert its connection with Africa.

612 **La vraie dimension de la politique extérieure des premiers gouvernements d'Haïti (1804-1843).** (An accurate perspective on the foreign policy of Haiti's first governments [1804-1843].)
Eddy V. Etienne. Sherbrooke, Quebec: Editions Naaman, 1982. 188p. bibliog. map. (Collection Thèses ou Recherches, no. 14).
A lucid summary of Haiti's diplomatic history from the country's declaration of independence in 1804 to the fall of the Boyer régime in 1843. The issue around which

154

the foreign policy of this era centred was Haiti's quest for diplomatic recognition by the other countries of the world, particularly France and the United States. Etienne traces this problem through the reigns and administrations of Dessalines, Henry Christophe, Pétion, and Boyer.

613 **Foreign policy behavior of Caribbean states: Guyana, Haiti, and Jamaica.**
Georges A. Fauriol.   Lanham, Maryland: University Press of America, 1984. 338p. bibliog.

A revision of its author's doctoral thesis, this book makes an important contribution to the small amount of material available on contemporary foreign policy in Haiti. Fauriol analyses the dynamics of foreign policy formation in Haiti in the context of its lack of development and repressive political atmosphere, and in comparison with two other less-developed states of the Caribbean area.

614 **Haiti and the Caribbean community: profile of an applicant and the problematique of widening the integration movement.**
Mirlande Hippolyte-Manigat, translated from the French by Keith Q. Warner.   Kingston, Jamaica: Institute of Social and Economic Research, University of the West Indies, 1980. 256p. bibliog.

Written by a political scientist, this work analyses Haiti's economic relations with the English-speaking countries of the Caribbean Community.

615 **Boundaries, possession, and conflicts in Central and North America and the Caribbean.**
Gordon Ireland.   Cambridge, Massachusetts: Harvard University Press, 1941. 432p. maps.

This older work remains a useful summary of pre-1940 Haitian foreign relations. The section on Haiti, (p. 53-68), lists the highlights of the Republic's first constitutions (1801-1935), then surveys Haitian-Dominican Republic boundary disputes and adjustments. A map of the border between the two countries is provided. The settlement of the conflict initiated by the Dominican massacre of Haitian migrant workers in October 1937, is also described. On p. 331 of the volume, the conflicting claims of Haiti and the United States to Navassa Island are outlined.

616 **Haiti and the Great Powers, 1902-1915.**
Brenda Gayle Plummer.   Baton Rouge: Louisiana State University Press, 1988. 255p.

Provides a thorough investigation of Haiti's foreign relations with those Western nations – France, Germany, Great Britain and the United States – that were globally dominant prior to the First World War and which squabbled amongst themselves for control, influence and advantages in the Caribbean area. Plummer discusses this competition as it affected Haiti, detailing the nation's struggle to maintain its sovereignty in spite of increasing international pressures. In her analysis of this period, Plummer covers trade and diplomacy, Haiti's peculiar place in the world community, the arrival of finance capitalism in Haiti and the characteristics and policies of Haiti's 1911-14 American occupation.

With the United States

617 **A black diplomat in Haiti: the diplomatic correspondence of US Minister Frederick Douglass from Haiti, 1889-1891.**
Frederick Douglass, edited and introduced by Norma Brown.
Salisbury, North Carolina: Documentary Publishers, 1977. 2 vols.
The noted black American Frederick Douglass served as Minister Resident and Consul-General in Haiti for nearly two years. During his tenure, he made an unsuccessful attempt to secure Môle St. Nicholas as a US naval base.

618 **The Duvaliers and Haiti.**
Georges Fauriol. *Orbis: a Journal of World Affairs*, vol. 32, no. 4 (fall 1988), p. 587-607.
This case study deals with the rise, rule, and final crisis of the Duvalier dynasty and 'the roles played and not played by the US government' during the Duvalier régime and at its close. Fauriol takes a clear-eyed look at America's problems with 'friendly tyrants' (i.e. friendly to the United States), as illustrated by American responses to the two dictatorial Duvalier governments. The elements that Fauriol highlights as playing a major role in determining recent American policy towards Haiti are ethnic and racial elements, humanitarian concerns and the character of Jean-Claude Duvalier. In the final crisis of the régime, events spiraled out of the control of the US State Department, which was unprepared for the collapse of the Duvalier government.

619 **Nineteenth century black thought in the United States: some influences of the Santo Domingo revolution.**
Monroe Fordham. *Journal of Black Studies*, vol. 6, no. 2 (Dec. 1975), p. 115-26. bibliog.
Fordham notes and discusses some of the ways in which the Haitian Revolution and the establishment of a black-ruled republic influenced American blacks in their thinking and actions in pre-Civil America. Haiti was both psychologically and symbolically significant as an inspiration for armed insurrections, as a counter to arguments of black inferiority, and as as symbol for black achievement.

620 **Gunboat diplomacy in the Wilson era: the U.S. Navy in Haiti, 1915-1916.**
David F. Healy. Madison, Wisconsin: University of Wisconsin Press, 1976. 268p. bibliog.
This study of US policy in the Caribbean during the Wilson administration focuses on the critical first year of US intervention in Haiti, when the country, to all intents and purposes, was ruled by Rear Admiral William B. Caperton, USN. Healy stresses the *ad hoc* nature of the United States practice at the start of this 'colonial' venture, and details how Wilsonian policy shifted from its high-minded beginnings, so that 'within a year Wilsonian intervention had become indistinguishable from previous kinds, and the remnants of the Haitian political system inadequately concealed the primacy of a US military autocracy.'

621   **Haiti's influence on antebellum America: slumbering volcano in the Caribbean.**
Alfred N. Hunt.   Baton Rouge, Louisiana: Louisiana State University Press, 1988. 196p.

An enlightening, well-researched presentation of American relations and attitudes towards Haiti in the pre-Civil War era, when the island's history of anti-white revolt and black rule provided a troubling challenge to Americans. Hunt traces the influence that Haitian immigrants to the United States – both white and black – had on American culture, and discusses the Black Republic, both as it actually existed and as it appeared as a symbol for opposing pro- and anti-slavery forces. The work is documented from primary archival sources.

622   **The diplomatic relations of the United States with Haiti, 1776-1891.**
Rayford W. Logan.   Chapel Hill, North Carolina: University of North Carolina Press, 1941. 516p. bibliog. (Reprinted, New York: Kraus, 1969).

Based on documentary materials, many of which were made available for the first time, this is the definitive study for the period in question. Logan discusses Haitian-American relations from the newborn American republic's early trade with the French colony of Saint-Domingue, through to the nineteenth century, to the eve of the Spanish-American War and America's emergence as a world power.

623   **The substitution of American for French preponderance in Haiti: the situation in 1910-1911.**
Leslie Manigat, translated from the French and edited with an introduction by Birgit Sonesson.   In: *Diplomatic claims: Latin American historians view the United States*. Edited by Warren Dean (et al.). Lanham, Massachusetts: University Press of America, 1985, p. 120-56.

In this important article, Manigat examines a crucial turning-point in Haiti's international relations, the key years 1909-11, when the United States was 'drawing under its influence weak peripheral states in the Western Hemisphere'. Manigat presents a case study of how Haiti was brought under American dominance, drawing on the diplomatic archives of several countries to construct a step-by-step account of the manoeuvres that accomplished this end. At the beginning of the twentieth century, German, French, British and American foreign offices were all concerned with the Haitian question, as all viewed Haiti as being in a strategic geographical location and as poised on the verge of economic development. In 1908 French influence predominated in Haiti, but the Americans rapidly gained an advantage through location, cheap exports, investments, and a cultural model that found favour with Haitian intellectuals. At the same time, the Germans were pressing hard for trade and for an expansion of their already considerable economic connection with the island. When a banking crisis developed, all tried to exploit the opportunity, but the United States outmanoeuvred the rest. Manigat's careful exposition of this period is required reading for those seeking to understand how economic and political interests coalesced in the American occupation of Haiti. This article was originally published in French in the *Revue d'histoire moderne et contemporaine*, vol. 14 (Oct.-Dec. 1967), p. 321-55.

624 **Haiti and the United States, 1714-1938.**
Ludwell Lee Montague, with a foreword to the reprint by J. Fred
Rippy. Durham, North Carolina: Duke University Press, 1940. 308p.
bibliog. (Reprinted, New York: Russell & Russell, 1966). (Duke
University Publications).

This standard source for the history of United States-Haitian diplomatic relations
covers a longer period of time than Rayford W. Logan's *Diplomatic relations of the
United States with Haiti, 1714-1938* (see entry no. 622) and is best used in conjunction
with this work.

625 **Intervention and dollar diplomacy in the Caribbean, 1900-1921.**
Dana G. Munro. Princeton, New Jersey: Princeton University Press,
1964. 553p. Reprinted, Westport, Connecticut: Greenwood Press,
1980.

Contains an excellent one-chapter presentation of the occupation and pacification of
Haiti, 1915-21, written from an American point of view.

626 **The United States and the Caribbean Republics, 1921-1933.**
Dana G. Munro. Princeton, New Jersey: Princeton University Press,
1974. 394p. bibliog.

Munro was US High Commissioner in Haiti, 1930-34. This book on US foreign policy
in the Caribbean region includes an authoritative treatment of the rationale for US
intervention in Haiti.

627 **Diplomats to Haiti and their diplomacy.**
James A. Padgett. *Journal of Negro History*, Vol. 25, no. 3 (July
1940), p. 265-330.

A lengthy article about the Americans who represented the US government in Haiti
from 1862 – when Haiti was accorded diplomatic recognition by the United States –
through the 1930s. Padgett provides biographical information on each US chief
minister in Haiti, describing the problems each faced and how they were resolved. The
article is based on research in government documents and printed biographical sources.

628 **Haiti and the CBI: a time of change and opportunity.**
Ernest H. Preeg. Coral Gables, Florida: Institute of Interamerican
Studies, University of Miami, 1985. 69p. (University of Miami Institute
of Interamerican Studies, 1985-1).

Discusses the benefits that Haiti stands to gain from the economic policy of the United
States as expressed in President Ronald Reagan's Caribbean Basin Initiative.

629 **Frederick Douglass: letters from the Haitian legation.**
Benjamin Quarles. *Caribbean Quarterly*, vol. 4, no. 1 (Jan. 1955),
p. 75-81.

Presents and discusses thirteen personal letters written by Douglass from Port-au-
Prince to his daughter, Rosetta Douglass Sprague, in Washington, DC.

630   **Frederick Douglass and the mission to Haiti, 1889-1891.**
Louis Martin Sears.   *The Hispanic American Historical Review*,
vol. 21, no. 2 (May 1941), p. 22-38.
Frederick Douglass was appointed by President Benjamin Harrison as Minister
Resident and Consul General to Haiti during the heyday of American imperialism.
The aim of his 1889-91 diplomatic mission was to facilitate American naval expansion
by the lease of Haiti's Môle St. Nicolas as a US naval depot. In this article, Sears traces
the progress of the mission, discussing possible reasons for its failure. The article is
based on US State Department documents.

631   **The United States and Santo Domingo, 1789-1866.**
Mary Treudley.   *The Journal of Race Development*, vol. 7, no. 1 (July
1916), p. 88-145.
The first part of Treudley's chronicle of 'the interrelations between the histories of the
United States and Santo Domingo, 1789-1866' covers 1789 to 1809, focusing largely on
Saint-Domingue. Treudley covers early trade relations, the consequences of the French
Revolution, the Saint-Domingue refugees in the United States, American relations
with Toussaint Louverture, and how Napoleon's colonial policy towards the island
affected American-Haitian relations.

632   **The United States and Santo Domingo, 1789-1866.**
Mary Treudley.   *The Journal of Race Development*, vol. 7, no. 2 (Oct.
1916), p. 220-74. bibliog.
The second part of Treudley's study (see previous item for first part) concentrates on
American relations with the Dominican Republic, but also covers independent Haiti's
pursuit of recognition by the United States, a request not granted until 1862. Treudley
concludes her article with a valuable bibliographical essay in which she comments on
both printed and archival materials dealing with the 1789-1866 period which can be
found in American libraries and depositories. Treudley's exploration of Haitian-
American relations is a pioneer study, but it is limited by its being restricted to largely
American sources.

With the Dominican Republic

633   **Documentos del conflicto dominico-haitiano de 1937: recopilacion y
notos.** (Documents of the Dominican-Haitian conflict of 1937:
compilation and notes.)
Jose Israel Cuello H.   Santo Domingo, Dominican Republic: Taller,
1985. 606p. bibliog. (Biblioteca Taller, no. 175).
A primary source for the study of the Dominican-Haitian conflict of 1937, this book
reproduces documents from the Cancilleria Dominicana in Santo Domingo, Dominican
Republic. The volume also contains a lengthy bibliography listing Spanish, French,
English and Creole works on Haiti.

634 **The United States and inter-American security, 1889-1960.**
John Lloyd Mecham.   Austin, Texas: University of Texas Press, 1961.
514p. map. bibliog.
On p. 485-89 of this book, Mecham describes the 1937 Dominican massacre of Haitian
braceros and the controversy ignited by the outrage. For the terms of the conciliatory
settlement by inter-American peace procedures, see 'Settlement of the Dominican
Republic-Haitian Controversy', in *Pan American Union Bulletin*, vol. 72 (March 1938),
p. 288-304.

635 **Haiti and Santo Domingo, 1790-c. 1870.**
Frank Moya Pons, translated from the Spanish by Richard Boulind.
In: *The Cambridge History of Latin American. Vol. 3: From
independence to c. 1870.*   Edited by Leslie Bethell.   Cambridge,
England: Cambridge University Press, 1885, p. 237-75. maps. bibliog.
The best presentation in English of the early relations between revolutionary and
independent Haiti and its eastern neighbour on the island of Hispaniola, Santo
Domingo. During the period covered, Haitian policy centred around aggressive
attempts to unify the island under Haitian rule. In a bibliographical essay (p. 860-65),
Moya Pons comments on pertinent historical and interpretative sources for the history
of this period. His bibliography is especially valuable for its listing of Spanish works on
Haitian-Dominican relations.

636 **La République d'Haïti et la République Dominicaine: les aspects divers
d'un problème de géographie et d'ethnologie, depuis les origines du
peuplement de L île Antileenne en 1492 jusqu'à l'évolution des deux
Etats qui en partagent la souveraineté en 1953.** (The Republic of Haiti
and the Dominican Republic: various aspects of a historical,
geographical and ethnological problem from the beginnings of
settlement on the Antillean island in 1492 to the evolution of the two
states who share its sovereignty in 1953.)
Jean Price-Mars.   Port-au-Prince: 1953. 2 vols. (Collection du
tricinquantenaire de l'independence d'Haïti).
A thoughtful work by a leading Haitian intellectual. The major work on Haitian-
Dominican relations from the Dominican viewpoint is Manuel Pena Batlle's multi-
volume *Historia de la cuestion fronteriza dominicano-haitiano* (Ciudad Trujillo,
Dominican Republic: Editoria L. Sanchez Andujar, 1946).

637 **The Haitian-Dominican Republic controversy of 1963 and the OAS.**
Robert D. Tomasek.   *Orbis*, vol. 12, no. 1 (spring 1968), p. 294-313.
In the late spring of 1963, a crisis occurred between two members of the Organization
of American States, Haiti and the Dominican Republic. After a series of provocations,
culminating in Haitian police breaking into the Dominican Embassy in Port-au-Prince
to search for Haitians seeking asylum there, the Dominican Republic threatened to
invade her western neighbour. Tomasek's article is a perceptive and objective analysis
of how this crisis developed and how it was resolved: 'the first part of [the] article
develops the events of this dispute in some detail in the belief that the effectiveness of
the Organization can be more accurately evaluated by relating its actions to problems

as they arose. The second section analyses the causes of the controversy in an attempt to ascertain the most significant. The last part appraises the effectiveness of the Organization through a critique of its strategy, goals, and ability to influence various parties.'

638 **The Dominican Republic and Haiti.**
Larman C. Wilson. In: *Latin American foreign policies: an analysis.*
Edited by Harold E. Davis, Larman C. Wilson. Baltimore, Maryland:
John Hopkins University Press, 1975, p. 198-218. bibliog.

An essay on the foreign policy problems of the two neighbouring republics, whose relations with other countries and with each other have been marked by episodes of foreign control, economic dependency and mutual distrust. The section on Dominican-Haitian relations discusses the long-standing border dispute between the two neighbours, with Wilson stressing the racial dimension of the problem. A valuable bibliographical note attached to the essay mentions the paucity of works on Dominican-Haitian relations and lists those available.

Economy

General

639   **Haiti in the world economy: class, race, and underdevelopment since 1700.**
Alex Dupuy.   Boulder, Colorado: Westerview Press, 1989. 245p.
bibliog. (Latin American Perspective Series, no. 4).

Against a firm theoretical background, Dupuy presents an empirical survey of Haiti's economic development from French colonial times to the post-Duvalier era. In his view, the economy of Haiti for its entire history has 'remained extroverted and unintegrated [with Haiti] never developing its own capital and consumer goods sectors'. Thus, Haiti was ultimately incorporated into the world economy as a peripheral economy, and such it has remained.

640   **Spanish colonialism and the origin of underdevelopment in Haiti.**
Alex Dupuy.   *Latin American Perspectives*, vol. 3, no. 2, iss. 9 (spring 1976), p. 5-29.

A Marxist analysis of the origin and history of underdevelopment in Haiti. Dupuy concludes that Haiti plays the same dependent role in the international division of labour now in its national period as it did under Spanish and French colonial rule.

641   **Political economy in Haiti: the drama of survival.**
Simon M. Fass.   New Brunswick, New Jersey: Transaction Books, 1988. 369p. map. bibliog.

A sophisticated examination of the economic life of the ordinary Haitian, set against the political background of present day Haiti. After an introductory overview of Haiti's political and economic history, 1492 to 1986, Fass concentrates on post-Duvalier Haiti, exploring, 'the productive meaning to ordinary people of six simple things [employment, food, water, shelter, schooling, and credit] that individuals and organizations of the political class sometimes call "basic needs", of the complexity of interactions between various components of the political class and the same things, and through these last, of the often hopeless and sometimes hopeful connections between the two classes'. The data upon which Fass bases his study were collected over a ten-year period in St. Martin, a neighbourhood in downtown Port-au-Prince. This highly interesting book contains a wealth of detail that enables its reader to comprehend the reality of the economic lives of the people of St. Martin. The volume's bibliography is especially useful for its listing of unpublished studies on economic development in Haiti.

642 **Some problems of a colonial economy: a study of economic dualism in Haiti.**
Giles A. Hubert. *Inter-American Economic Affairs*, vol. 3, no. 4 (spring 1950), p. 3-29.

Hubert defines economic dualism as the system that results when the economy of a less-advanced country of a colonial or semi-colonial nature comes into contact with the capitalist system of a more advanced country that is trying to aid the lesser-developed state by exporting capital and technical knowledge to it. In this article, Hubert develops the hypothesis that Haiti's economy in 1950 contains elements of economic dualism, then discusses the problem of economic development in Haiti from this perspective.

643 **The market system of Part-au-Prince.**
Uli Locher. In: *Working papers in Haitian society and culture.* Edited by Sidney W. Mintz. New Haven, Connecticut: Yale University, Antilles Research Program, 1975, p. 127-82. (Occasional Papers, no. 4).

Locher provides a good contribution to the study of Haiti's marketing system.

644 **The Haitian economy: man, land and markets.**
Mats Lundahl. New York: St Martin's Press, 1983. 290p. bibliog.

Presents a selection of Lundahl's articles on rural economic conditions in Haiti, originally published in scholarly journals.

645 **Peasants and poverty: a study of Haiti.**
Mats Lundahl. New York: St. Martin's Press, 1979. 699p. bibliog.

This weighty tome is the most complete study of Haiti's contemporary agricultural economy available. Lundahl states that his book 'analyzes the Haitian peasant economy and its problems mainly from the early 1950s to the early 1970s, but often the time perspective has been extended backwards since full comprehension of today's problems requires thorough acquaintance with events that took place during the 19th century and in certain instances during the colonial period'. The work is interdisciplinary since 'it is not possible to understand Haiti's plight fully without venturing outside the scope of economics proper. Account must be taken of a number of political and social factors as well. . . .' Chapters deal with the peasant economy, rural income, poverty and the market, soil erosion, land reform, the passive government, Haitian public finance, malnutrition and disease, education, rural credit, and resistance to innovation. The book contains an excellent bibliographical essay on post-1935 literature on the Haitian peasant economy.

646 **Politics or markets? Essays on Haitian underdevelopment.**
Mats Lundahl. London; New York: Routledge, 1992. 519p.
A collection of essays on the Haitian economy in relation to the economic policies
adopted by successive Haitian governments. The essays were originally published
between 1984 and 1992.

647 **The employment of capital by market womem in Haiti.**
Sidney W. Mintz. In: *Capital, saving, and credit in peasant societies.*
Edited by Raymond Firth, Basil S. Yamey. Chicago: Aldine, 1964,
p. 256-86.
Examines the way in which Haitian female entrepreneurs came to manipulate the
market system.

648 **Peasant markets.**
Sidney W. Mintz. *Scientific American*, vol. 203, no. 2 (Aug. 1960),
p. 112-22.
Studies the market system in Haiti, where it is the central economic institution, in
order to show how trading activities express the interests of the competing elements in
society.

649 **Haiti: its stagnant society and shackled economy: a survey.**
O. Ernest Moore. New York: Exposition, 1972. 281p. bibliog.
(Exposition University Book).
Moore, an economist who was closely involved with monetary and fiscal planning in
Haiti in the 1950s, traces the history of economic and social development in the
country since 1804, then criticizes conditions under the François Duvalier régime.

650 **L'Economie Haïtienne.** (The Haitian economy.)
Paul Moral. Port-au-Prince: Imprimerie de l'Etat, 1959. 190p. maps.
An important scholarly study, highly recommended by a reviewer in the *Handbook of
Latin American Studies*, who writes: 'The growing literature on Haiti is definitely
enriched by [Moral's] volume which is . . . thorough and well-documented. . . . The
book is descriptive and informative; the opinions it contains are balanced and well
reasoned.' (*HLAS* 23, 1836).

651 **Economic problems of the Black Republic: a critical bibliography.**
David Nicholls. In: *Haiti in Caribbean context: ethnicity, economy and
revolt.* New York: Macmillan, 1985, p. 130-34.
A bibliographical essay that lists and evaluates scholarly works on the economic life of
Haiti from independence to the present.

652 **Haitian peasant economy.**
George E. Simpson. *Journal of Negro History*, vol. 25, no. 4
(Oct. 1940), p. 498-519.
One of the first studies of Haiti's peasant economy, based on field-work completed in
1936-37 in the commune of Plaisance in northern Haiti. The sections examine:

economic life and Haitian social structure; peasant habitations and plantations; specialization of labour; cultivation of land; coumbites (loosely-organized work groups of neighbours and friends); garden magic; land ownership; markets; exports; coffee; planes of living; foods consumed by the peasants; incentives to work; overpopulation and migration; the future of Haitian agriculture; and the élite and social change.

653 **The marketing system in peasant Haiti.**
Frances W. Underwood. In: *Papers in Caribbean anthropology.*
Edited by Sidney W. Mintz. New Haven, Connecticut: Yale
University, Department of Anthropology, 1960, p. 3-33. bibliog. (Yale
University Publications in Anthropology, nos. 57-64). (Reprinted, New
Haven, Connecticut: HRAF Press, 1970).
In publication no. 60 of this collection, Underwood combines her own ethnographic data, gathered from field-work in Beaumont, Haiti, in 1944, with information drawn from published accounts in Herskovit's *Life in a Haitian valley,* (see item no. 510), Simpson's 'Haitian peasant economy' (q.v.) and Metraux's *Making a living in the Marbial Valley* (see item no. 512) and constructs a synthetic model of the Haitian internal marketing system. She concludes her article with a list of twelve characteristics that form the keynotes of the system.

Development projects

654 **Politics, projects, and people: institutional development in Haiti.**
Edited by Derick W. Brinkerhoff, Jean-Claude Garcia-Zamor. New
York: Praeger, 1986. 288p.
In this collection of articles on the development of institutions in Haiti, theoretical commentary is integrated with studies of particular organizations funded by foreign donors and designed to intervene in Haiti to further the country's socio-economic progress. The articles and their authors are: 'Resource transfers and institutional sustainability: HACHO and Haiti's Northwest' (Derick W. Brinkerhoff); 'Seeing the forest while planting the trees; an anthropological approach to agroforestry in rural Haiti' (Gerald F. Murray); 'The St. Martin Project: a decade of pain and progress in the evolution of an urban development institution' (Simon M. Fass); 'Obstacles to institutional development in Haiti' (Jean-Claude Garcia-Zamor); 'Peasants' councils and the politics of community' (Glen R. Smucker); and 'The rural health delivery system project: initiative and inertia in the Ministry of Health' (Jon E. Rohde).

655 **Canadian development assistance to Haiti: an independent study.**
E. Philip English. Ottawa, Canada: North-South Institute, 1984.
167p. map. bibliog.
A study of Canada's economic assistance programme to Haiti.

656 **Development planning in Haiti: a critique of the U.N. report.**
John R. P. Friedman. *Economic Development and Cultural Change*,
vol. 4, no. 1 (Nov. 1955), p. 39-54.
This is a valuable analysis of the report of the 1949 United Nations Mission to Haiti
(see item no. 660). Through his critique of the report that resulted from the UN
Haitian project, Friedman probes some fundamental issues in planning for economic
development, and he concludes his criticism by highlighting five important omissions
from the report. The article is well-documented and draws on Friedman's personal
contacts with UN development personnel based in Haiti and with Haitian officials in
1953.

657 **Bottom-up development in Haiti/Desarrollo desde las bases en Haiti.**
Robert Maguire, translated into the Spanish by Virginia Schofield.
Rosslyn, Virginia: Inter-American Foundation, 1981. 2nd ed. 46p.;
50p. bibliog.
This book is a double publication: the English section, numbered p. 1-46, has been
translated into a corresponding Spanish section, numbered p. 1-50. Following a general
presentation of Haiti's underdevelopment, Maguire summarizes development agency
operations in the country since the 1960s, describing two projects in particular, one
undertaken by the US Agency for International Development (USAID), the other by
the Haitian-American Community Help Organization (HACHO). The focus of the
book is on a project sponsored by IDEA (Institut d'Education des Adultes) in Le
Borgne parish on the north coast of Haiti, a programme aimed at stimulating grass
roots development through the involvement of the area's rural population in
programme planning.

658 **United Nations technical assistance programs in Haiti.**
Marian Neal. *International Conciliation*, no. 468 (Feb. 1951),
p. 81-118.
In this most informative article, Neal describes in detail the programme undertaken in
Haiti by the United Nations and specialized agencies in 1948-50. She summarizes the
findings and recommendations of the United Nations report *Mission to Haiti* (q.v.),
describes the work of A. J. Wakefield, an expert on economic development assigned as
the UN's Permanent Representative in Haiti, discusses the UNESCO Fundamental
Education Pilot Project in Marbial, and details the WHO-UNICEF Yaws Eradication
Campaign. Her article is especially valuable because Neal is frank in her coverage of
the defeats suffered as well as the victories won in these efforts.

659 **Haiti: mission d'assistance technique integrée.** (Haiti: mission of
integrated technical assistance.)
Organization of American States. Office of Regional Development.
Washington, DC: General Secretariat, Organization of American
States, 1972. 656p. maps. bibliog.
A study of Haiti's natural resources and development policies undertaken by the Office
of Regional Development of the Organization of American States in collaboration with
Haiti's National Council of Development and Planning, CONADEP (Conseil National
de Developpement et de Planification). The text of the report is in French, with
English summaries.

660   **Mission to Haiti: report.**
       United Nations. Mission of Technical Assistance to Haiti.   Lake
       Success, New York: United Nations, 1949. 327p. (United Nations
       Publication, 1942. IIB.2).
The report of the results of a comprehensive survey of Haiti's agriculture, fisheries,
industrial development, finance, education, and public health, conducted by the
United Nations in 1948 at the request of the Estimé administration. Haiti was the first
member of the United Nations to request this type of assistance. A United Nations
team of twelve experts spent two months in Haiti. Their report examines problems,
formulates proposals and appraises Haiti's needs.

Investment, Finance and Banking

661 **La Banque Nationale: son histoire, ses problèmes.** (The National Bank: its history, its problems.)
Joseph Chatelain.   Lausanne, Switzerland: Imprimerie Held, 1954. 330p. bibliog. (Collection du Tricinquantenaire de l'Independance d'Haïti).

Chatelain's volume remains the only book available on the Banque Nationale de la République d'Haïti, Haiti's central bank and bank of issue, established in 1880.

662 **Histoire monetaire de Saint-Domingue et de la République d'Haïti jusqu'en 1874.** (Monetary history of Saint-Domingue and Haiti to 1874.)
Robert Lacombe, preface de Robert Goetz-Girey.   Paris: Editions Larose, 1958.

Presents the history of Haiti's money during the colonial era and in independent Haiti to the end of the administration of Nissage Saget.

663 **Monetary-fiscal policy and economic development in Haiti.**
O. Ernest Moore.   *Public Finance*, no. 3 (1954), p. 23-53.

A valuable article by a financial expert. Moore first presents the 20th century financial history of Haiti in two sections: monetary and debt history, 1910-1919; and the period of economic stability, 1919-1950; then describes the country's money, banking and fiscal system in 1950. He next discusses the economic reforms, development initiatives, and banking and monetary system reorganizations proposed in 1951 by the Magloire administration. Moore is optimistic about Haiti's future if plans for economic reorientation can be implemented.

168

664 **The assembly industries in Haiti: causes and effects, 1967-1973.**
Monique P. Garrity. *Review of Black Political Economy*, vol. 11,
no. 2 (winter 1981), p. 203-15.
Reviews Haitian manufacturing industries which assemble American-made components for re-export to the United States.

665 **The multi-national corporation in extractive industries: a case study of Reynolds Haitian Mines, Inc.**
Monique P. Garrity. In: *Working papers in Haitian society and culture.* Edited by Sidney W. Mintz. New Haven, Connecticut: Yale University, Antilles Research Program, 1975, p. 183-290. (Occasional Papers, no. 4).
An in-depth case study of the bauxite mining industry in Haiti.

666 **Le commerce du café en Haïti: habitants, speculateurs et exportateurs.**
(The coffee trade in Haiti: producers, agents and exporters.)
Christian A. Girault, preface by Paul Moral. Paris: Editions du Centre National de la Recherche Scientifique, 1981. 293p. bibliog.
(Mémoire du Centre d'études de géographie tropicale).
The first major study of coffee marketing in Haiti, where coffee is the primary export, comprising twenty to thirty-five percent of the country's GNP (Gross National Product). Based on extensive field-work in Haiti, Girault's investigation highlights the inequality and dependent position of Haiti's commerce in world markets. The French text is accompanied by English and Spanish summaries.

667 **Identity and experience in Haitian Voodoo shows.**
Alan Goldberg. *Annals of Tourist Research*, vol. 10, no. 4 (1983),
p. 479-95. bibliog.
Goldberg, an anthropologist, delineates 'the process by which tourist settings are constructed' in this article which discusses the tourist Voodoo performance in Haiti as an example of 'staged authenticity'. Focusing on a show regularly performed for tourists in Port-au-Prince, Goldberg identifies and discusses the identities assumed by tourists, hosts and performers in this type of tourist interaction, presenting a 'Voodoo' event from a perspective from which it is not often studied. After describing a staged show, he compares it with a non-touristic Voodoo ceremony.

668 **Play and ritual in Haitian Voodoo shows for tourists.**
Alan Goldberg. In: *The paradoxes of play: proceedings of the 69th annual meeting of the Association for the Anthropological Study of Play.* Edited by John Loy. West Point, New York: Leisure Press, 1982,
p. 42-49. bibliog.
In writing this article, Goldberg has drawn on his doctoral dissertation, *Commercial folklore and Voodoo in Haiti* (PhD thesis, Indiana University, Bloomington, Indiana, 1981). Goldberg analyses a Voodoo show at the pseudonymous Haitian nightclub 'La Tonnelle' as an example of 'staged authenticity', entertainment calculated to provide an emotionally vivid 'Voodoo' experience for visitors to Haiti. Goldberg explores how

'play' and 'ritual' frames interact in these performances. He then evaluates the theoretical paradigms constructed by social scientists to explain such 'authentic' tourist events, focusing in particular on the ideas of Don Handelman.

669 **Foreign assembly in Haiti.**
Joseph Grunwald, Leslie Delatour, Karl Voltaire. In: *The global factory: foreign assembly in international trade*. Edited by Joseph Grunwald, Kenneth Flamm. Washington, DC: Brookings Institution, 1985, p. 180-205.

Provides an informative summary of the most dynamic element in the Haitian economy, the assembly production industry, whose Haitian workers assemble sporting goods, textile items, stuffed toys and dolls, and electric and electronic products, all for export. The authors describe the assembly industry's firms, wages, labour force, and the linkages between assembly activities and the rest of the Haitian economy.

670 **Made in Haiti.**
Robert Heuer. *Americans*, vol. 42, no. 2 (1990), p. 22.

A sidebar in a general article on Latin American baseball. Heuer notes that 'Every major league baseball used in the last 20 years has been handstitched by a Haitian factory worker'. The Rawlings Sporting Goods Company of St. Louis, Missouri, the official supplier of baseballs to the game, employs approximately 1,000 Haitians to do the demanding hand work of drawing 88 inches of waxed thread through 108 stitches for each ball. Information about the baseball-stitchers' wages and working conditions is a closely-guarded secret.

671 **Case study of a 'least developed country' successfully exporting manufactures: Haiti.**
Thomas K. Morrison. *Inter-American Economic Affairs*, vol. 29, no. 1 (summer 1975), p. 21-31.

An article by an economist on the success of light manufacturing and export industries in Haiti since the late 1960s. Morrison examines Haiti's performance in exporting light manufactures in relation to the performances of other developing countries and explains the factors contributing to Haiti's success: proximity to the United States, low labour costs, favourable government policies, and convenient United States tariff provisions for offshore assembly of manufactured goods. Tables of Haitian exports to the United States are also included.

672 **The metropolitan connection: foreign and semiforeign elites in Haiti, 1900-1915.**
Brenda G. Plummer. *Latin American Research Review*, vol. 19, no. 1 (1984), p. 119-42.

Plummer discusses Haiti as a classic example of how 'commerce, rather than plantation enterprise or extensive capital investment, could foster socioeconomic decline', and amply demonstrates how 'trade relations, conducted by elites that were culturally and socially wedded to the values and institutions of the metropolitan powers, created a pattern of economic dependency and cultural limitation in Haiti that has persisted into the contemporary period'. Little has been written on this theme, and Plummer makes a valuable contribution by tracing the interrelationship between the Haitian bourgeois élite with foreign merchants and entrepreneurs in the establishment of Haiti's unequal commerce and disadvantageous trading patterns. The American occupation neutralized French and German competitive power, but perpetuated the élite status of foreign and semi-foreign groups of trading élites.

673 **Doing business with Haiti.**
Libby Colen Roper. Washington, DC: US Dept. of Commerce, International Trade Administration, 1985. 15p. (Overseas Business Reports, OBR 85-11).
A pamphlet prepared with the assistance of the US Embassy in Port-au-Prince as a guide to American exporters.

674 **Prospects and potential for mineral development in Haiti.**
K. Voltaire, L. Delatour. *Mining Engineering*, vol. 31, no. 3 (March 1979), p. 277-79.
Following a thumbnail sketch of the history of geological exploration and mining in Haiti, the authors describe post-1970 initiatives to identify commercially viable mineral deposits in the country. They then present various legal and economic aspects of exploration for mineral resources in Haiti, summarizing the nation's first mining law (1976).

Manpower, Labour and Employment

675 **The role of Haitian *braceros* in Dominican sugar production.**
Arismendi Diaz Santana. *Latin American Perspectives*, vol. 3, no. 1,
iss. 8 (winter 1976), p. 120-32.
This article, by a Dominican author in a special issue of Latin America Perspectives
entitled 'Imperialism and the working class in Latin America', analyses the reasons
behind the Dominican Republic's dependence on imported Haitian labourers in the
sugar industry. Diaz Santana noted that Haitian migration is encouraged by the
Dominican Republic's mill owners – despite a high unemployment rate among their
own labour force. He concludes that profit in the sugar industry requires cheap labour
and that the Haitian will accept lower wages than the Dominican.

676 **Notes sur le developpement du mouvement syndical en Haïti.** (Notes
on the development of the labour movement in Haiti.)
Jean-Jacques Doubout, Ulrich Joly. [n.p.]: Imprimerie Abece, 1974.
112p.
François Duvalier destroyed Haiti's trade unions in 1964. Doubout and Joly summarize
the history of Haiti's labour movement up to that time.

677 **Reflections on the Haitian labor force.**
Francois Latortue. In: *The Haitian potential; research and resources of
Haiti.* Edited by Vera Rubin, Richard P. Schaedel. New York:
Teachers College Press, 1975, p. 221-39. (Publications of the Center for
Education in Latin America).
Characterizes the Haitian manpower situation in 1950 – age, education, employment,
unemployment, working conditions – and compares it to the Haitian labour force of
1960.

678 **Quelques aspects des problèmes de la main-d'oeuvre Haïtienne.** (Some
aspects of Haitian manpower problems.)
L. Paret-Limardo de Vela. *Journal of Inter-American Studies*, vol. 4,
no. 1 (Jan. 1962), p. 121-44.

The first part of this article covers employment patterns in Haiti itself, emphasizing the
nation's endemic unemployment and under-employment. The second part deals with
emigration – the routine solution for Haiti's excess manpower. The movement of
Haitian labourers to the Dominican Republic, Cuba, South America, Central
America, North America and the West Indies in the early 1960s is considered largely in
terms of the constraints placed upon it.

Agriculture and Rural Conditions

679   **Land tenure in the Marbial region of Haiti.**
       Suzanne Comhaire-Sylvain.   In: *Acculturation in the Americas; proceedings and selected papers of the 29th International Congress of Americanists, New York, 1949.* Edited by Sol Tax, with an introduction by Melville J. Herskovits.   Chicago: University of Chicago Press, 1952, p. 180-84. (Reprinted, New York: Cooper Square Publishers, 1967).

This short, factual report, derived from materials gathered in connection with the UNESCO Marbial Valley Project, covers the tenure of agriculture land in Haiti: landowners; forms of landownership; the acquisition of land; the amount of land owned; the acquisition of the right to use land; sharecropping; and land management.

680   **Man and land in the Haitian economy.**
       Maurice De Young.   Gainesville, Florida: University of Florida Press, 1958. 73p. (Latin American Monographs, no. 3).

De Young takes exception to foreign experts' analyses of problems in Haitian agriculture and questions plans to reorganize the country's agricultural economy. In *Geographical Review*, vol. 50, no. 2 (April 1960), p. 276-78, John P. Augelli describes De Young's book as 'a competent exposé of some of the typical misconceptions that may plague the unwary planner in underdeveloped regions'.

681   **Swine fever ironies: the slaughter of the Haitian black pig.**
       Bernard Diederich.   *Caribbean Review*, vol. 14, no. 1 (winter 1985), p. 16ff.

Discusses the economic and social repercussions of the eradication of the species of black pig in Haiti after an outbreak of African swine fever in the Artibonite Valley in 1979. The United States government has provided money to restock the farm animal, but Diederich explains why the new breed of pig may not be able to replace the now-extinct *cochon-planche* in the life of the Haitian peasant.

682 **Reboisement et lutte contre l'érosion, Haiti: le charbon de bois, combustible renouvelable.** (Reforestation and the fight against erosion in Haiti: charcoal as a renewable resource.)
Derek E. Earl. Rome: FAO, UN Development Programme, 1976. (Rapport Technique, vol. 1).

Soil erosion is the paramount problem of Haitian agriculture, traceable to the radical deforestation of the country. This report proposes a solution in the management of charcoal production. See also Gerald F. Murray's 'The wood tree as a cash crop: an anthropological strategy for the domestication of energy', in *Haiti – today and tomorrow: an interdisciplinary study* (see item no. 5) P. 141-160, and Winthrop P. Carty's 'The regreening of Haiti: is tree cropping the answer?' in *Americas*, vol. 35, no. 5 (Sept. 10, 1983), p. 5-7ff.

683 **Agriculture change in Haiti: patterns of resistance and acceptance.**
Charles John Erasmus. *Human Organization*, vol. 11, no. 4 (winter 1952), p. 20-26.

A paper by a field ethnologist involved in the Artibonite Valley Project. Erasmus briefly describes the patterns of resistance and acceptance demonstrated by Haitian farmers towards attempts to change their agricultural practices. The article ends with an account of how the plough was successfully introduced to farmers at St. Michel and St. Raphael.

684 **Agriculture in Haiti, with emphasis on irrigation.**
Megh R. Goyal. In: *Agricultural mechanization in Asia, Africa and Latin America*, vol. 18, no. 4 (autumn 1987), p. 54-56. map. bibliog.

A brief note on agricultural development projects in Haiti.

685 **The Societe Congo of the Île à Gonâve.**
Robert Burnett Hall. *American Anthropologist*, n.s., vol. 31, no. 4 (Oct.-Dec 1929), p. 685-700. map.

Société Congo is the general name for a type of co-operative agricultural association found in Haiti that is probably of African origin. A *Société Congo* is organized around the peasant's need to share farm work, but it also exercises economic, social, protective and benevolent functions. In this article, the author studies the *Model de Paris*, a *Société Congo* of the Île à Gonâve, as it existed in 1926. He describes its membership, its officers, the responsibilities of membership in the *Société*, how its co-operative work groups operate, and how it exercises control over its members. The article is illustrated with photographs.

686 **Agriculture in Haiti, with special reference to rural economy and agricultural education.**
Marc Aurele Holly. New York: Vantage Press, 1955. 313p. (Sesquicentennial Collection).

This book by an agronomist was poorly received by critics when first published in 1955.

Agriculture and Rural Conditions

687   **Haiti: a brief survey of its past and present agricultural problems.**
Elmire M. Loback.   *Journal of Geography*, vol. 53, no. 7 (Oct. 1954),
p. 277-90. map.
After viewing the problems of Haitian agriculture in the early 1950s against the background of Haiti's turbulent history, Loback describes several agricultural development projects, including the Artibonite Valley Project irrigation scheme.

688   **Etude sur l'agriculture paysanne dans une vallée Haïtienne.** (A study of peasant agriculture in a Haitian valley.)
Alfred Metraux.   *Acta Americana*, vol. 4, nos. 3-4 (July-Dec. 1948),
p. 173-91.
Writing in French, Metraux summarizes the results pertaining to agriculture obtained from the anthropological investigation that preceded the UNESCO Marbial Valley Project near Jacmel. He discusses the importance of land ownership for the Haitian peasant; the system of land proprietorship; the qualities of the soil in the Marbial Valley; the agricultural cycle in the region; tools; work methods; soil conservation; and manpower. After evaluating the positive and negative elements of Haitian agriculture, he concludes with a list of eight recommendations for its improvement.

689   **Le paysan Haitien: étude sur la vie rurale en Haïti.** (The Haitian peasant: a study of rural life in Haiti.)
Paul Moral.   Paris: Maisonneuve & Larose, 1961. 375p. maps. bibliog.
(Reprinted, Port-au-Prince: Editions Fardin, 1978).
This important work by a French geographer remains a classic. The work emphasizes economic geography, but matters of sociological interest are also treated. Of note is Moral's explanation for the decline of the traditional lakou system among the peasants. The lakou was the traditional form of family organization, an extended family that lived together in a cluster of homes.

690   **Haitian bean circuits: cropping and trading manoeuvers among cash-oriented peasantry.**
Gerard F. Murray, Maria D. Alvarez.   In: *Working papers in Haitian society and culture*. Edited by Sidney W. Mintz.   New Haven, Connecticut: Yale University, Antilles Research Program, 1975,
p. 85-126. (Occasional Papers, no. 4).
In this paper Murray and Alvarez closely examine one aspect of the economic life of Haiti's rural population.

Business, Trade and Industry

691 Population pressure, land tenure, and Voodoo: the economics of Haitian peasant ritual.
Gerald F. Murray.   In: *Beyond the myth of culture: essays in cultural materialism*. Edited by Eric B. Ross.   New York: Academic Press, 1980, p. 295-321.
Voodoo is considered from a unique perspective in this essay as Murray examines its economic effect in preserving land rights in rural Haiti.

692 The role of agriculture in the economy of Haiti: perspectives for a better development.
Raymond Myrthil.   Flushing, New York: The Haitian Book Center, 1979. 93p. bibliog.
Myrthil divides his study into two parts: the first section of the book is a general survey of Haiti's social and economic structure, with particular attention paid to the Haitian system of land tenure and the characteristics of Haiti's prospects for future development as an exporter of agricultural products.

693 An annotated bibliography of agricultural development in Haiti.
Clarence Zuvekas, Jr., with the editorial and secretarial assistance of Suzanne Cooper.   Washington, DC: Rural Development Division, Bureau for Latin America, Agency for International Development, 1977. 106p. (Working Document Series: General Working Document, no. 1).
Provides citations to material on the economic aspects of Haiti's agriculture and rural development.

Business, Trade and Industry

694 **Land tenure and its policy implications: a survey of the literature.**
Clarence Zuvekas, Jr. *Social and Economic Studies*, vol. 28, no. 4
(Dec. 1979), p. 1-30. bibliog.

Drawing on a survey of relevant published and unpublished materials, Zuvekas explains the pattern of land holding in rural Haiti, where a majority of farmers describe themselves as landowners, although most do not have a clear title. Zuvekas speculates as to whether the Haitian farmer's insecurity in regard to land tenure is an obstacle to development. Also discussed in the article are Haiti's landless labourers and the Haitian land distribution system. The fifty-four items reviewed for the study are listed in its bibliography. This article is derived from Zuvekas's *Land tenure, income, and employment in rural Haiti: a survey* (1978) (q.v.).

695 **Land tenure, income, and employment in rural Haiti: a survey.**
Clarence Zuvekas, Jr., with the secretarial assistance of Mary T.
Carter, Maria E. Reed. Washington, DC: Rural Development
Division, Bureau for Latin America, Agency for International
Development, 1978. Rev. ed. 123p. (Working Document Series: Haiti:
General Working Document, 2).

A study of rural conditions in Haiti by an economist that provides valuable material on land tenure, income distribution, and labour supply. Zuvekas is also the author of *Agricultural development in Haiti: an assessment of sector problems, policies, and prospects under conditions of severe soil erosion* (Washington, DC: 1978).

Transport

696 **Haiti upgrades transport links.**
Engineering News-Record, vol. 204, no. 8 (Feb. 1980), p. 30-31.
Describes highway, road and port projects which recently had either been completed,
or were under construction, or in the planning stages as of 1980. Facilities at the Port-
au-Prince international airport are also scheduled for expansion.

697 **Railways of Central America and the West Indies.**
W. Rodney Long.   Washington, DC: GPO, 1925. 376p. maps. (US
Bureau of Foreign and Domestic Commerce. Trade Promotion Series,
no. 5).
The section entitled 'Haiti', on pages 283-94 of this US government publication, is a
detailed report on existing and projected rail systems in Haiti as of 1925, prepared by
W. Rodney Long of the Transportation Division of the US Bureau of Commerce.
Long traces the operation of the Compagnie Nationale des Chemins de Fer d'Haiti
(National Railway Company of Haiti) from 1904 until it entered receivership in June
1920. He describes the various divisions of the railroad, and provides information on
traffic statistics, right of way and rolling stock, as well as the receiver's balance sheet as
of December 31 1921. The article includes a map indicating completed and proposed
routes for the railway.

Statistics

698 **Caribbean economic handbook.**
Edited by Peter D. Fraser.   London: Euromonitor Publications, 1985.
241p. maps.
The global and regional economic overviews in this work as well as a final chapter
entitled 'Outlook', are written by Peter D. Fraser. Chapter 7, 'Haiti', (p. 107-14), is
the work of Paul Hackett. He provides short interpretative paragraphs on Haiti's
domestic economy, industry and trade, accompanied by tables showing vital statistics,
main economic indicators, GDP sector growth, coffee production and exports,
agricultural production, and balance of trade. In 'Fact File', (p. 211-35), Haiti is
included in tables of comparative regional statistics.

699 **The statesman's year-book; statistical and historical annual of the states
of the world for the year 1992-1993.**
Edited by Brian Hunter.   New York [etc.]: St. Martin's Press [etc.],
1864- . 129th ed. annual.
'Haiti', (p. 669-73) presents facts and statistics on the country's area and population,
climate, elections, agriculture, trade, education and health. A short bibliography
follows the text.

Education

700 **Instruction publique en Haïti, 1492-1945.** (Public education in Haiti, 1492-1945.)
Edner Brutus.   Port-au-Prince: Imprimerie de l'Etat, 1948. 533p. bibliog.
A well-regarded history of Haitian education, covering the leading educators and important events of over 400 years.

701 **Education in the Republic of Haiti.**
George Allen Dale.   Washington, DC: US Department of Health, Education, and Welfare, 1959. 180p. map. (US Office of Education Bulletin 1959, no. 20).
A detailed and comprehensive report on the Haitian educational system, its problems and its institutions, as of the late 1950s.

702 **Education in Haiti.**
Rayford W. Logan.   *Journal of Negro History*, vol. 15, no. 4 (Oct. 1930), p. 401-60.
This often-cited article traces the history of education in Haiti from 1804 to the 1920s.

703 **America's policy-making in Haitian education, 1915-1934.**
Leon D. Pamphile.   *Journal of Negro Education*, vol. 54, no. 1 (winter 1985), p. 99-108.
Based on research in US State Department archives, this study evaluates the impact of American involvement in Haitian education that began with the American occupation of the country. Despite Haitian protests, the Americans insisted on directly controlling Haiti's public schools, and undertook to eliminate Haiti's traditional classical curriculum and impose a system of vocational education on the country. This plan was viewed as high-handed and condescending by the Haitians, with the result that educational reform stalled and educational development for the Haitian masses stagnated.

704 **Education and development: the case of Haiti.**
Bernard Salome. Paris: Organisation for Economic Co-operation and
Development, 1984. 136p. bibliog. (Development Centre Papers).
Emphasizes the link between economic conditions and educational planning in Haiti.

705 **Haiti: a study of the educational system of Haiti and a guide to the
academic placement of students in educational institutions in the United
States.**
Ruth J. Simmons. Washington, DC: International Education
Activities Group of the American Association of Collegiate Admissions
Officers, 1985. 119p. bibliog. (World Education Series).
Simmons provides information on the management and organization of Haiti's school
system and interprets Haitian academic degrees and school credits as an aid for
American educational administrators.

706 **Primary education in Haiti.**
Kleber Vielot. In: *The Haitian potential: research and resources of
Haiti.* Edited by Vera Rubin, Richard P. Schaedel. New York:
Teachers College Press, 1975, p. 114-43. (Publications of the Center for
Education in Latin American).
Provides an excellent overview of the history of the entire Haitian educational system
since colonial times, as well as a diagnosis of the ills of Haiti's elementary education
programmes.

Language

General

707 **La langue française et le créole haïtien.** (The French language and
Haitian Creole.)
Dantes Bellegarde. *Conjonction*, vol. 19 (Feb. 1949), p. 39-43.
Bellegarde presents his reasons for his stand against the use of Creole as a literary
language.

708 **French and Creole patois in Haiti.**
Edith Efron. *Caribbean Quarterly*, vol. 3, no. 4 (1954), p. 199-213.
Writing in the 1950s, Efron describes the nature of the language conflict in Haiti
between French and Creole, explaining the sociological and political implications of
the two tongues. She also makes a good case for the acceptance of Creole as Haiti's
language.

709 **Diglossia in Haiti: a comparison with Paraguayan bilingualism.**
Gerard A. Ferere. *Caribbean Studies*, vol. 23, no. 1 (March 1977),
p. 50-60. bibliog.
Gives the results of a questionnaire asking bilingual Haitians to choose whether they
would speak French or Creole in fifty-eight domestic and social situations. Their
responses indicate that French receives a higher social rating than Haitian Creole.

710 **The language situation in Haiti.**
Albert Valdman. In: *The Haitian potential: research and resources of
Haiti*. Edited by Vera Rubin, Richard P. Schaedel. New York:
Teachers College Press, 1975, p. 61-82. (Publications of the Center for
Education in Latin America).
Presents valuable information on the bilingual situation in contemporary Haiti.
Valdman reviews works on language in Haiti and identifies areas where further
research is needed.

French

711 **La langue française en Haiti.** (The French language in Haiti.)
Pradel Pompilus. Paris: Institut des Hautes Etudes de l'Amérique
Latine, 1961. 278p. bibliog. (Travaux et Mémoires de l'Institut des
Hautes Etudes de L'Amérique Latine, 7).

An authoritative description of the standard French spoken in Haiti by the urban
upper classes. Major sections cover phonology, grammar and vocabulary; in the latter,
Pompilus lists and discusses borrowings into Haitian French from Haitian Creole and
American English, and remaining traces of French classicisms found in the language of
francophone Haitians.

712 **American speech and Haitian French.**
William Leonard Schwartz. *American Speech*, vol. 24, no. 4 (Dec.
1949), p. 282-85.

A brief article, based on its author's observations in 1948 of the variety of French
spoken and written in Haiti and on the American English element found in Haitian
Creole. Schwartz comments on such words and expressions as 'bye-bye' and 'parloir
funèbre'.

Haitian Creole

713 **Literacy and the question of Creole.**
Paul Berry. In: *The Haitian potential; research and resources of Haiti.*
Edited by Vera Rubin, Richard P. Schaedel. New York: Teachers
College Press, 1975, p. 83-113. bibliog. (Publications of the Center for
Education in Latin America).

Although his focus is on the illiteracy problem in contemporary Haiti, Berry includes
an excellent historical survey of attempts to write Haitian Creole. He provides a short
bibliography of printed works in the Creole language.

714 **Teaching English to Speakers of ESD, ESL and EFL.**
Sheilah Ann Bobo, Pearl Monica Thompson. Lanham, Maryland:
University Press of America, 1990. 200p. bibliog.

This is a methodological textbook, aimed at those teaching English to foreign-born or
inner-city students whose first language is Haitian Creole or Jamaican Creole. The
authors describe the grammatical systems of these Creole languages, indicate the types
of problems students may experience in learning standard English because of language
interference, and offer techniques for teaching English to Creole speakers. Although
designed for pedagogical use, others besides teachers will find this book useful for its
clear presentation of the linguistic system of Haitian Creole, illuminated by the
contrast made between Haitian Creole and English.

715 **Toward a bibliography of works dealing with the Creole languages of the Caribbean area, Louisiana, and the Guianas.**
J. L. Dillard. *Caribbean Studies*, vol. 3, no. 1 (April 1963), p. 84-95.

Dillard adds to Joan Rubin's earlier list (see item no. 720) of published materials on West Indians Creoles, including Haitian Creole.

716 **Philologie créole.** (Creole philology.)
Jules Faine. Port-au-Prince: Imprimerie de l'Etat, 1936. 303p.

The pioneer grammatical work on Haitian Creole, reasonably complete and accurate, although lacking a general phonetic frame of reference.

717 **Haitian Creole: grammar, texts, vocabulary.**
Robert A. Hall, Suzanne Comhaire-Sylvain, H. Ormonde McConnell, Alfred Metraux. Philadelphia: American Folklore Society, 1953. 309p. (Reprinted, New York: Kraus Reprint, 1970). (Memoirs of the American Folklore Society, vol. 43).

The first genuinely modern and comprehensive Haitian Creole grammar, based on a linguistic survey made in 1949 as part of the UNESCO Fundamental Education Pilot Project in the Marbial Valley. The Haitian texts are presented with English translations and include an autobiography, folklore, a Voodoo text, 215 proverbs, and 124 riddles.

718 **Kreyòl lessons for English speaking people.**
Ernst Mirville. Port-au-Prince: Enstiti Lengistik Aplike Pòtoprens, 1982. 1st ed. 120p. map. (Collection Coucouille).

A Creole textbook published by the Institut de linguistique appliquée de Port-au-Prince. Another textbook designed to teach Haitian Creole to English speakers is Marie Jocelyne T. Levy's *Liv pratik Kreyòl-Anglé = Creole-English handbook* (Port-au-Prince: Haitian Educational Services, Inc., 1982).

719 **La littérature Haïtienne d'expression créole: son avenir.** (Haitian literature in Creole: its future.)
Felix Morisseau-Leroy. *Presence Africaine*, vol. 17 (Dec. 1957-Jan. 1958), p. 46-59.

Morisseau-Leroy wrote *Antigone en créole* in 1947 to prove that the Haitian language was an adequate vehicle for classical themes. Here, he writes in favour of encouraging its use as a literary language, marshals convincing arguments as to why Haitians should write in it, and foresees a bright future for Haitian Creole literature. A two-page précis in English follows the French text.

720 **A bibliography of Caribbean Creole languages.**
Joan Rubin. *Caribbean Studies*, vol. 2, no. 4 (Jan. 1963), p. 51-61.

After an introductory paragraph summarizing the theoretical problems involved in the study of Caribbean Creole languages, the main body of Rubin's article is a bibliographical listing of items pertaining to Creole linguistics, with brief descriptive annotations. Materials on Haitian Creole are included. This bibliography is of value to those wishing to track down older work in this field.

721   **Cric? Crac! Fables de La Fontaine racontée par un montagnard
      haïtien et transcrites en vers créoles.** (Cric? Crac! Fables of La
      Fontaine told by a Haitian peasant and transcribed in Creole verse.)
      Georges Sylvain.   Port-au-Prince, En vente chez Mme. Georges
      Sylvain, 1929. 163p. (Reprinted, Nendeln, Liechlenstein: Kraus
      Reprint, 1971).

Originally published in 1901 (Paris: Ateliers Haïtiens), this was an early effort in
writing literature in Haitian Creole. Sylvain utilizes the persona of a Haitian peasant to
retell the fables of La Fontaine. A study of this work, 'Cric? Crac! Fables of La
Fontaine in Haitian Creole: a literary ethno-socio-linguistic curiosity' by Douglas
Parmee can be found in *Nottingham French Studies*, vol. 15, no. 2 (1976), p. 12-26.

722   **Ann pale kreyòl: an introductory course in Haitian Creole.** (Let's speak
      Creole: an introductory course in Haitian Creole.)
      Albert Valdman, in collaboration with Renote Rosemond.
      Bloomington, Indiana: Creole Institute, Indiana University, 1988.
      264p. bibliog.

A course designed to impart a working command of Haitian Creole, with an emphasis
on the spoken language, to beginning and intermediate learners through twenty-five
chapters of dialogues, grammar sections, practice drills, and reading selections.
Illustrations by Pierre-Henri Philippe add a cultural component to the text. Twelve
hour-long audio-cassette tapes accompany the lessons, making the course suitable for
self-instruction.

723   **Basic course in Haitian Creole.**
      Albert Valdman.   Bloomington, Indiana: Research Center for
      Language Sciences, Indiana University, 1970. 345p. (Indiana University
      Publications: Language Science Monographs, vol. 5).

Aimed at the beginner, this well-organized course covers the fundamentals of Haitian
Creole phonology, grammar, and vocabulary in twenty-four units. Seventeen audio-
cassettes that accompany the text supply more than fifteen hours of listening and
speaking practice.

Dictionaries

724   **Ti diksyonne kreyòl-franse. Dictionnaire elementaire créole haïtien-
      français.** (Elementary Haitian Creole-French dictionary.)
      Pierre Nougayrol (et al.).   Port-au-Prince: Editions Caraïbes, 1976.
      511p.

A Haitian Creole-French dictionary prepared under the direction of Alain Bentolila,
based on the Creole spoken in the St. Marc district of central Haiti.

725 **Haitian Creole-English-French dictionary.**
Albert Valdman (et al.).   Bloomington, Indiana: Indiana University
Creole Institute 1981. 2 vols. bibliog.

This dictionary is the first work of its kind, and will serve as a valuable reference tool in libraries. Volume one (582p.) glosses more than 10,000 Haitian Creole words in English and French, illustrating usage in sentences. Volume two (298p.) provides French-Creole and English-Creole indexes.

Cultural and Intellectual Life

726 **Modern Haitian thought.**
Stéphen Alexis. *Books Abroad*, vol. 30 (summer 1956), p. 261-65.
The period that began with the American occupation of Haiti was an important one for the gestation of a living Haitian literature. In this brief article, Alexis outlines Haitian intellectual, cultural and literary development in the decades that followed *le choc* (as the occupation was termed by writer Leon Laleau). He discusses the work of the *groupe indigène* of the 1920s, the influence of Jean Price-Mars's ethnographic landmark *Ainsi parla l'oncle* (1928) (q.v.), the cultural import of the group known as *Les Griots* in the 1930s, and the avant-garde movement of the 1930s and 1940s spearheaded by the *La Relève* group. Alexis also provides much informative detail about Haitian fiction, drama and historical writing during this period.

727 **Jean Price-Mars and Haiti.**
Jacques C. Antoine, with a preface by Jean Brierre. Washington, DC: Three Continents Press, 1981. 224p. bibliog.
The first book-length biography in English of the noted Haitian, a central force in Haiti's intellectual life for more than half a century. The author narrates the events of Price-Mars' life and discusses the ideas he expressed in his writings within the context of Haitian politics and society.

728 **The role of the intellectual in Haitian plural society.**
Rémy Bastien. *Annals of the New York Academy of Sciences*, vol. 83, art. 5 (Jan. 1960), p. 843-49.
In this paper, Rémy Bastien considers the intellectual as a social scientist whose task it is to point a new direction to his society. Latin American intellectuals face a multitude of difficulties, as illustrated by Bastien's country, Haiti. Bastien traces the history of Haitian intellectual life from the late 19th century. His discussion of the effects of the ideas of Jean Price-Mars and James G. Leyburn, as expressed in their books *Ainsi parla l'oncle* (q.v.) and *The Haitian people* (q.v.), on Haitian political life is especially interesting.

729 **Haitian social thought in the nineteenth century: class formation and Westernization.**
Patrick Bellegarde-Smith. *Caribbean Studies*, vol. 20, no. 1 (March 1980), p. 5-33.

A lucid presentation of the development and course of European ideologies and ideas in 19th-century Haiti. Bellegarde-Smith studies the reshaping of European philosophical systems to fit the Haitian political scene, tracing such transformations from the revolutionary ideologies of the late 18th century through Liberalism-Romanticism, Positivism, and Bergsonianism. His article is enlightening on the men who first wrote the history of Haiti: he describes the perspectives from which these 19th-century intellectuals viewed themselves and their nation, and explains their viewpoint with reference to the politics of their time.

730 **In the shadow of the powers: Dantès Bellegarde in Haitian social thought.**
Patrick Bellegarde-Smith. Atlantic Highlands, New Jersey: Humanities Press, International, 1985. 244p. bibliog. (AIMS Historical Series, no. 11).

Dantès Bellegarde espoused Westernization, political liberalism, capitalism and assimilation to French culture for Haiti. In this book, Bellegarde's political and social views are discussed in the context of Haiti's intellectual history.

731 **Price-Mars: the father of Haitianism.**
Leon G. Damas. In: *Negritude: essays and studies.* Edited by Albert H. Berrian, Richard A. Long. Hampton, Virginia: Hampton Institute Press, 1967, p. 24-38.

The poet who, along with Aimé Césaire and Léopold Sédar Senghor (of Senegal), launched the cultural movement known as Negritude, discusses Price-Mars' contribution to black-orientated culture in Haiti.

732 **Vibrancy, or the weight of inertia: a testimonial to Haitian original creative expression across endogenous or exogenous constraints.**
Jean Leopold Dominque. Tokyo: United Nations University, 1982, 14p.

Remarks on Haiti's impressive intellectual creativity.

733 **The 'New Movement' in Haiti.**
Edith Efron. *Caribbean Quarterly*, vol. 4, no. 1 (Jan. 1955), p. 14-31.

Discusses the changes in Haitian letters and in the intellectual and cultural life of Haiti that were inaugurated by the publication of Jean Price-Mars's *Ainsi parla l'oncle* (q.v.) in 1928. Writing from the viewpoint of a partisan of the 'New Movement', Efron discusses the writers who followed Price-Mars's lead in reasserting the African roots of Haitian culture.

Cultural and Intellectual Life

734 **Phylon profile, XX: Dantès Bellegarde – miracle of Haiti.**
Edward Allen Jones. *Phylon*, vol. 11, no. 1 (first quarter 1950),
p. 16-22.

A panegyrical sketch of the internationally known Haitian who was a proponent of
French culture and Christianity for Haiti. The article emphasizes his achievement as
diplomat, educator and writer.

735 **When horses talk: reflections on Zora Neale Hurston's Haitian
anthropology.**
Gwendolyn Mikell. *Phylon*, vol. 43, no. 3 (Sept. 1982), p. 218-30.

Analyses Hurston's approach to Haitian culture in *Tell my horse* (see item no. 452),
which, Mikell believes, was methodologically both unique and ahead of its time.
Drawing simultaneously on her personal background as a southern American black
and on her professional anthropological training directed by Franz Boas and Ruth
Benedict, Hurston was able to sustain a double vision of Haitian culture both as an
'insider' – personalized and subjective – and an 'outsider' – scholarly and analytical.
Her expression of this perspective has earned her a special place in the field of
anthropology.

736 **Biology and politics in Haiti.**
David Nicholls. *Race*, vol. 13, no. 2 (Oct. 1971), p. 203-14.

A discussion of the theoretical views on race held by several Haitian writers and
intellectuals. Nicholls focuses primarily on the ideas in respect to the connection
between biology and politics of François Duvalier and the group with whom he was
associated. Nicholls then relates these ideas to the 19th-century racial theories of
Arhur de Gobineau.

737 **Idéologie et mouvements politiques en Haïti, 1915-1946.** (Ideology and
political movements in Haiti, 1915-1946.)
David Nicholls, translated from the English by Ch. Carlier. *Annales,
Economies, Sociétés, Civilisations*, vol. 30, no. 4 (July-Aug. 1975),
p. 654-79.

Nicholls focuses on the role played by ideology in this study of the origins and
development of three Haitian political movements: nationalism, noirisme, and
socialism. He points out that nationalism and noirisme were inspired by the
ethnological movement that began with Jean Price-Mars's publication of *Ainsi parla
l'oncle* in 1928. The socialist political movement, which succeeded nationalism in the
1930s, had two supportive ideologies: Marxist-Communist and non-Marxist-tech-
nocratic. Nicholls ends his article with an explanation of how the ideologies of the
preceding decades influenced the political events of 1946.

738 **Ideology and political protest in Haiti, 1930-46.**
David Nicholls. *Journal of Contemporary History*, vol. 9, no. 4 (Oct.
1974), p. 3-26.

Discusses the three protest movements active in Haiti in the 1930s: noirisme, marxism,
and technocratic socialism. Nicholls details the ideological underpinnings of these
movements, and indicates how they influenced the crucial 1946 elections. This article

190

was later translated into French and incorporated into Nicholls's 'Idéologie et mouvements politiques en Haiti, 1915-1946', (q.v.).

739 **The widsom of Salomon: myth or reality?.**
David Nicholls. *Journal of Interamerican Studies and World Affairs*, vol. 20, no. 4 (Nov. 1978), p. 377-92.

Challenges the assertion that Louis Etienne Lysius Félicité Salomon, President of Haiti, 1879-1888, advocated Africanism for his country.

740 **A work of combat: mulatto historians and the Haitian past, 1847-1867.**
David Nicholls. *Journal of Interamerican Studies and World Affairs*, vol. 16, no. 1 (Feb. 1974), p. 15-38. bibliog.

Nicholls states that the subject of his article is 'the way in which a group of mulatto historians in the mid-nineteenth century developed an elaborate legend of the past which was calculated to strengthen the position of the [mid-19th-century mulatto] ruling class and to legitimate its ascendancy'. This 'mulatto version of the past' was in large part the work of Beaubrun Ardouin and Joseph St. Rémy. In their historical writings, these authors enlisted history in the service of ideology. Emphasizing the necessity for all Haitians to unite under the leadership of the mulatto élite, they portrayed the *affranchis* (the free mulattoes or the free coloured people of Haiti) as the true leaders of the Haitian Revolution and extolled the government of Alexandre Pétion.

Literature

General history and criticism

741 **Bibliography of women writers from the Caribbean (1831-1986).**
Brenda F. Berrian, Aart Broek.   Washington, DC: Three Continents
Press 1989. 360p.
While this is primarily a bibliography of creative work – novels, short stories, poetry,
folklore, autobiographies, biographies and children's literature – critical works and
book reviews are also included. The volume is organized in four parts: works by forty-
seven Haitian women writers are listed on p. 167-225 in the 'French Caribbean and
Guyane' section. The unannotated entries are grouped by literary type.

742 **Histoire de la littérature Haïtienne: illustrée par les textes.** (History of
Haitian literature: illustrated by texts.)
Raphael Berrou, Pradel Pompilus.   Port-au-Prince: Editions Caraïbes,
1975-1977. 3 vols. bibliog.
A substantial multi-volume work in French. Each writer discussed is represented by
extensive selections from his work, making this set as much an anthology as a literary
history. Volume one covers the period 1804-1898; volume two, 1898-1927; and volume
three, 1927 to the present.

743 **Toward literary freedom: a study of contemporary Haitian literature.**
H. P. Bostick.   *Phylon*, vol. 17, no. 3 (1956), p. 250-56.
Bostick divides Haitian literature into three periods: the first, 1804-60, he terms the
patriotic period of 'La période Dessalinienne'; the second, 1860-1915, the period of
'Haitian Romanticism' and the last, 1915 to the present (i.e. 1956), the period of 'La
Littérature engagée'. His article concentrates on the latter, which began with the US
occupation of Haiti and is characterized by Haitian reassertion of black-racial and
African-cultural identiy. The works of Jacques Roumain and Jean Price-Mars
exemplify the literature of this period.

744 **Voodoo myths in Haitian literature.**
Asselin Charles. *Comparative Literature Studies*, vol. 17, no. 4 (Dec. 1980), p. 391-98.
Charles considers Voodoo to be the mythic foundation of Haitian literature and interprets the increasing prominence of Voodoo mythology in Haitian literary works as 'a vector tracing the evolution of written Haitian literature from its status as a footnote to French letters to its present stage of independence'. Charles remarks on the appearance of references to Voodoo myths in the poetry of Oswald Durand and René Depestre, and the novels of Jacques Roumain, Jacques Stéphen Alexis, and Franketienne.

745 **Rejection of European culture as a theme in Caribbean literature.**
G. R. Coulthard. *Caribbean Quarterly*, vol. 5, no. 4 (June 1959), p. 231-44.
Provides examples from works by Haitian writers which are among those chosen to support the author's discussion of four reasons for the rejection of European culture in the Caribbean.

746 **Trends in recent Haitian literature.**
Mercer Cook. *Journal of Negro History*, vol. 32, no. 2 (April 1947), p. 220-31.
In this paper, which was read at the 1946 annual meeting of the Association for the Study of Negro Life and History, Cook surveys the difficulties of writing in Haiti, points out the achievements of contemporary Haitian literature, and discusses the work of Jacques Roumain and other poets and novelists. The article includes translations of Roumain's poem to Langston Hughes and Roussan Camille's 'Nedje'.

747 **Haiti and the United States: national stereotypes and the literary imagination.**
J. Michael Dash. New York: St. Martin's Press, 1988. 152p.
A perceptive analysis of literary representation as it reflects history and politics. Dash examines fictional works and travel narratives by both Haitians and Americans 'to show how polarizing stereotypes in imaginative literature are developed which make historical and political realities intelligible'. The work covers 19th-century racial stereotypes, then discusses literature stemming from the American occupation, works promoting racial solidarity, writings that appeared in the post-occupation years, and literary productions of the Duvalier era.

748 **Literature and ideology in Haiti, 1915-1961.**
J. Michael Dash. New York: Barnes & Noble, 1981. 214p. bibliog.
A welcome book for the English-speaking reader: Dash clarifies the relationship between literature and political ideas in 20th-century Haiti, tracing the interconnections between the two from the years of the American occupation to the advent of the François Duvalier régime in the 1950s.

193

749 **Writers of the Caribbean and Central America: a bibliography.**
M. J. Fenwick.   New York: Garland, 1992. 2 vols. (Garland
Reference Library of the Humanities, vol. 1244).
The 'Haiti' section, on p. 610-61 of Volume 1 of this bibliography, lists Haitian writers
alphabetically with dates of birth and death and a reference to the genre in which they
specialized. Poets, dramatists and novelists are included. Each author's original works
are listed in chronological order (with date of publication but no other bibliographical
information given), followed by a listing of magazines and anthologies in which the
writer's work appeared.

750 **Ideyoloji ak reyalite nan literati ayisyen.** (Ideology and reality in
Haitian literature.)
Ulrich Fleischmann, translated from the German by Jeannot Hilaire.
Geneva: Koleksion, 1981. 355p. bibliog.
A critical literary history that emphasizes the interaction of literature and society in
Haiti. This book was first published in German as *Ideologie und Wirklichkeit in der
Literatur Haitis* (Berlin: Colloquium-Verlag, 1969).

751 **The renaissance of Haitian poetry.**
Naomi M. Garret.   Paris: Présence Africaine, 1963. 257p. bibliog.
(Enquêtes et études).
Provides both history and analysis in English of the directions taken by Haitian poetry
beginning in 1925. Garret explores the causes of the literary effervescence that took
place in Haiti in the twentieth century, then discusses the themes and techniques of
Haiti's most important poets, including Normil Sylvain, Philippe Thoby-Marcelin,
Jacques Roumain, Carl Brouard, Emile Roumer, Léon Laleau, Jean Brierre, Robert
Lataillade, Roland Chassagne, Roussan Camile, Rene Belance, Clement-Magloire
Saint-Aude, René Depestre and Roland Dorcely.

752 **Images of the American literature during the occupation.**
Yvette Gindine.   *Caribbean Studies*, vol. 14, no. 3 (Oct. 1974),
p. 37-52.
Gindine adds her comments on the literary depiction of the American in Haitian
literature, a topic discussed by Leon-François Hoffmann in 'The US and Americans in
Haitian letters', in his *Essays on Haitian literature* (see next item) and J. Michael Dash
in his *Haiti and the United States: national stereotypes and the literary imagination* (see
item no. 747).

753 **Essays on Haitian literature.**
Léon-François Hoffmann.   Washington, DC: Three Continents, 1984.
1st ed. 184. bibliog.
This collection of Hoffmann's critical essays on Haitian literature provides the reader
with interesting discussions of a number of literary topics. The essays included are:
'Haitian literature: an overview'; 'The linguistic situation in Haiti'; 'Slavery and race in
Haitian letters'; 'The U.S. and Americans in Haitian letters'; 'The image of woman in
Haitian poetry'; and 'The first Haitian novel: Emeric Bergeaud's *Stella*'. A valuable
'Bibliography of critical studies on Haitian literature', (p. 123-68) lists bibliographies,
histories of Haitian literature, anthologies, general studies, works on the Haitian

novel, drama, poetry, and critical studies of nearly one hundred individual Haitian authors, citing books and articles in French, English, Spanish and German.

754 **Etat présent des études littéraires Haïtiennes.** (The present state of Haitian literary studies.)
Léon-François Hoffmann. *French Review*, vol. 49, no. 5 (April 1976), p. 750-58. bibliog.
A bibliography of criticism of Haitian literature. Among its useful features is a list of older literary and critical works that have been reprinted by Kraus Reprints. This bibliography is updated by 'A bibliography of critical studies on Haitian literature', p. 123-68, in Hoffmann's *Essays on Haitian literature* (q.v.).

755 **The originality of the Haitian novel.**
Léon-François Hoffmann. *Caribbean Reivew*, vol. 8, no. 1 (Jan.-March 1979), p. 44-50.
In Hoffmann's view, Haitian society is unique, and the Haitian novelist attempts to capture in his work his country's 'profound (and not uniformly attractive) originality'. With his readership split between the Haitian élite and the French-reading public, a novelists must be able 'to speak simultaneously to two very different audiences', a situation that has an impact on his work. Hoffmann examines the themes and characteristics of the Haitian novel, discussing works by Frédéric Marcelin, Justin Lhérisson, Fernand Hibbert, and the writers of the Indigenist movement.

756 **Slavery and race in Haitian letters.**
Léon-François Hoffmann. *Caribbean Review*, vol. 9, no. 2 (spring 1980), p. 28-32.
Discusses how racial issues have been expressed by Haiti's poets and novelists. This article is reprinted in Hoffmann's *Essays on Haitian literature* (q.v.).

757 **Haitian writers in exile: a survey of North America.**
Jean Jonassaint, translated by J. M. Dash. *Caribbean Quarterly*, vol. 27, no. 4 (Dec. 1981), p. 13-20. bibliog.
A short presentation of writers of Haitian origin who in the 1970s published their works in the United States or Canada. While not an extended discussion, this article is useful as an introduction to Haitian authors not published in their own country.

758 **Haiti.**
Maximilien Laroche. In: *Handbook of Latin American literature*. Edited by David William Foster. London; New York: Garland Publishing, 1992, 2nd ed., p. 333-45. bibliog.
A skilful summary of Haiti's literary history that centres on the dual nature of Haitian literature: written in two languages (French and Haitian Creole), by authors in two different situations (within Haiti and in exile), Haitian literature comprises two literary corpora of texts. Laroche discusses Haiti's diglossic language situation and outlines the work of the nation's major writers from an ideological perspective.

759 **L'image comme écho: essais sur la littérature et la culture Haïtiennes.**
(Image as echo: essays on Haitian literature and culture.)
Maximilien Laroche. Montreal: Editions Nouvelle Optique, 1978.
240p. (Collection Materiaux).

Essays by a Haitian literary scholar. The theme of this collection is the double culture –
African and French – of the Haitian, with Laroche focusing on the African element.
Among the subjects treated are Aimé Césaire's *Tragedy of King Christophe* (see item
no. 808), the Negritude movement, the Haitian poet Clement-Magloire Saint-Aude,
and the myth of the zombie. Laroche handles his material with considerable finesse,
providing valuable insights into the motifs of Haitian culture.

760 **Haitian writers and the American occupation: literary responses to a
political crisis.**
Renée Larrier. *CLA Journal*, vol. 33, no. 2 (Dec. 1989), p. 203-14.

Analyses literary works composed by Haitian during the 1915-34 period which can be
categorized as direct responses to the American occupation. During this time poets
expressed sadness, resignation and outrage or composed panegyrics on those who
resisted foreign rule (e.g. Charlemagne Peralte) or earlier heroes; playwrights
dramatized and satirized the conflicts of the time or recreated the signal events of
Haiti's past as an oblique commentary on its present; novelists wrote fiction that either
centred on the occupation or alluded to it. Larrier summarizes that, during the
occupation, 'what these [creative writers] had in common was their nationalist fervor'.

761 **A bibliography of Haitian literature, 1900-1972.**
Wilma Primus. *Black Images: a Critical Quarterly on Black Culture*,
vol. 1, no. 1 (spring 1973), p. 44-59.

A bibliography of 900 unannotated entries, classified in six sections: bibliographies;
relevant studies on black literature and culture; background studies on Haitian history
and society; general works and articles; anthologies; and literary works. The
last section lists novels, plays, short stories and poems by 187 Haitian writers, and also cites
critical reviews and English and Spanish translations.

Criticism of individual writers

762 **French Romanticism in a Haitian setting: the poetry of Oswald Durand.**
Martha K. Cobb. *CLA Journal*, vol. 16, no. 3 (March 1973),
p. 302-11.

Oswald Durand (1842-1906) is considered as one of Haiti's major nineteenth-century
poets, a writer who introduced aspects of French Romantic verse into Haitian poetry
while at the same time infusing his work with race consciousness and racial pride. Cobb
examines several of Durand's poems as illustrative of his combination of French
influence and Haitian elements. While most of Durand's work is in French, he
composed his well-known poem *Choucoune* in Haitian Creole.

763 **Harlem, Haiti, and Havana: a comparative critical study of Langston Hughes, Jacques Roumain, and Nicolás Guillén.**
Martha K. Cobb.   Washington, DC: Three Continents Press, 1978. 250p. bibliog.
A scholarly study that compares the work of the Haitian writer Jacques Roumain with that of Langston Hughes of the United States and Nicolás Guillén of Cuba.

764 **Five French negro authors.**
Mercer Cook.   Washington, DC: The Associated Publishers, Inc. 1943. 164p.
Provides both a literary history and biographical information on five black men who wrote in French, two of whom had connections with Haiti: Julien Raymond, whom Cook terms 'the Father of French Negro Authors', a wealthy Saint-Domingue mulatto who wrote *Mémoire sur les causes des troubles et desastres de la colonie de St.-Domingue* (Paris: 1793), and Alexandre Dumas, père, author of *The Count of Monte Cristo* and *The Three Musketeers*, who was the son of a Haitian mulatto.

765 **The Haitian novel.**
Mercer Cook.   *French Review*, vol. 19, no. 6 (May 1946), p. 406-12.
Discusses five novels published 1939-45: Pétion Savain's *La case de Damballah* (1939); the Marcelin brothers' *Canapé-vert* (1944); Jacques Roumain's *Gouverneurs de la rosée* (1944); J. B. Cineas's *Heritage sacré* (1945); and Marc Verne's *Marie Villarceaux* (1945).

766 **Jacques Stéphen Alexis.**
J. Michael Dash.   Toronto: Black Images, 1975. 62p.
A commentary on the work of Jacques Stéphen Alexis, author of the novel *Compère General Soleil* (Paris: Gallimard, 1955). For further criticism of Alexis, see the essays collected in issue no. 501 of the *Revue Europe* ('Jacques S. Alexis et la littérature d'Haïti') (Paris: 1971, 252p). The issue also contains a work by Alexis entitled 'La belle amour humaine'.

767 **The Marxist counterpoint – Jacques Roumain: 1930's to 1940's.**
J. Michael Dash.   *Black Images*, vol. 2, no. 1 (spring 1973), p. 25-29.
Marxism played a central role in Jacques Roumain's political and intellectual life: he founded the Haitian Communist Party in 1934 and wrote the first Marxist analysis of the Haitian situation, his *Analyse schematique* (1934). In this article, Dash examines Roumain's relationship to Marxism, discussing how Roumain's commitment to the ideology influenced both his intellectual formation and his literary work, particularly his novel *Gouverneurs de la rosée* (Masters of the dew) (see item no. 794). Dash concludes that 'in Haiti [Marxism] provided Roumain and those that he influenced with a level of objectivity that would resist the much more tempting and much more disastrous myth of racial authenticity'.

Literature. Criticism of individual writers

768 A knot in the thread; the life and work of Jacques Roumain.

Carolyn Fowler. Washington, DC: Howard University Press, 1980. 383p. bibliog.

The only full-length study in English of the work of Jacques Roumain, poet, novelists, ethnologist, political figure and diplomat, whose *Gouverneurs de la rosée* (Masters of the dew) (see item no. 794) is a key book in twentieth-century Haitian literature. Fowler's volume is organized chronologically, discussing Roumain's literary work in a biographical context. Quotations from Roumain's writings are given in French in the text, but translated into English in an appendix. The bibliography lists Roumain's publications in all genres, criticism of his work, and a selection of books and articles about Haiti and Haitian literature.

769 Satire and the birth of Haitian faction (1901-1905).

Yvette Gindine. *Caribbean Quarterly*, vol. 21, no. 3 (Sept. 1975), p. 30-40.

Summarizes and provides a criticism of three satirical novels published within a four-year period, 1901-05, which caustically depict the corruption and demagoguery that characterized Haitian political life. The novels and their authors are *Thémistocle Epaminodas Labasterre* by Frédéric Marcelin, *La Famille de Pititie-Caille* by Justin Lhérisson, and *Séna* by Fernand Hibbert. Gindine comments that 'by deliberately holding up a mocking mirror to vexatious Haitian realities [these writers] became the founding fathers of modern Haitian fiction'.

770 Comrade Eros: the erotic vein in the writing of René Depestre.

Bridget Jones. *Caribbean Quarterly*, vol. 27, no. 4 (Dec. 1981), p. 21-30. bibliog.

René Depestre is better-known for his anti-imperialistic writings than for his love poetry, thus, Jones adopts a new approach to his work by analysing the erotic aspect of his work, focusing on two specific problems in regard to Depestre's expression of his sensuality: 'the potential conflict between revolutionary discipline and the anarchistic face of love, and the vulnerability of a machismo, however revolutionary, to criticism from a feminist view point'. In order to explore these issues, Jones traces Depestre's poetic development chronologically, linking his literary work with his personal and political autobiography.

771 Cultural identity, negritude, and decolonization: the Haitian situation in the light of the Socialist Humanism of Jacques Roumain and René Depestre.

Guy Viet Levilain. New York: American Institute for Marxist Studies, 1978. 59p. (Occasional Papers; Marxist Studies, no. 29).

Supplies a Marxist perspective on two politically-conscious Haitian writers.

772 Jean F. Brierre and his work.

Maurice A. Lubin, translated from the French by Martha K. Cobb. *Black World*, vol. 22, no. 3 (Jan. 1973), p. 36-48.

One of the few studies in English on this important Haitian poet. Lubin discusses Jean Brierre's themes, his part in the Negritude movement, and his vision of man. The article includes English versions of Brierre's 'Me revoici Harlem' ('Here I am again,

Harlem'), 'Black soul', and 'Et tombent les murailles de Chine' ('And the walls of Chinal fall down').

773 **The Haitian novel of social protest.**
Murdo J. MacLeod. *Journal of Inter-Amercan Studies*, vol. 4, no. 2 (April 1962), p. 207-21.
Provides an unsympathetic criticism of the novels of Jacques Roumain and the Marcelin brothers.

774 **An introduction to the French Caribbean novel.**
Beverley Ormerod. London: Heinemann Educational Books, 1985. 152p. bibliog. (Studies in Caribbean Literature).
This is not a general survey but a critical work that closely examines the major novels of six French Caribbean writers. The novels chosen for analysis in the two chapters devoted to Haitian writers are Jacques Roumain's *Masters of the Dew* and Jacques Stéphen Alexis's *Compère General Soleil*. Ormerod considers these works to be centred around the themes of 'a fall from Paradise' and 'a return to the Promised Land', biblical themes that these writers transposed to a secular plane.

775 **Four poets of the Greater Antilles.**
Eric Williams. *Caribbean Quarterly*, vol. 2, no. 4 (1952), p. 8-15.
Jacques Roumain and Jean Brierre are among the poets dealt with in this article. Williams emphasizes their concern with achieving racial equality for blacks, and stresses the attraction that Communist ideology held for them.

776 **The Marcelins – novelists of Haiti.**
Edmund Wilson. *The Nation*, vol. 171, no. 16 (Oct. 1950), p. 341-44.
An eminent American critic records his favourable reaction to the novels of the Marcelin brothers, whose work reminds him of that of the Italian, Ignazio Silone.

Selected works by individual writers

777 **Stella.**
Emeric Bergeaud. Paris: E. Dentu, 1887. 330.
Written in French and originally publlished in 1857, *Stella* is the first novel written by a Haitian. Léon-François Hoffmann summarizes and analyses the book's allegorical plot in an essay. 'The first Haitian novel: Emeric Bergeaud's "Stella"' in his *Essays on Haitian Literature* (see item no. 753).

Literature. Selected works by individual writers

778 **Black poets in French.**
Compiled and edited by Marie Collins. New York: Scribner, 1972.
165p.
Poetry in French with English translations and commentary. Haitians included:
Jacques Roumain, Jean Brierre, René Depestre and Anthony Phelps.

779 **Caribbean literature: an anthology.**
Edited and translated by G. R. Coulthard. London: University of
London Press, 1966. 128p.
This anthology includes an English translation of Jacques Roumain's 'Guinée'.

780 **The festival of the greasy pole.**
René Depestre, translated from the French and with an introduction by
Carrol F. Coates. Charlottesville, Virginia: University Press of
Virginia, 1990. 142p. (CARAF Books).
A translation of *Le mât de cocagne* (Paris: Gallimard, 1979). Depestre's first novel is
set in François Duvalier's Haiti.

781 **A rainbow for the Christian West.**
René Depestre, translated from the French by Joan Dayan. Amherst,
Massachusetts: University of Massachusetts Press, 1977. 258p. bibliog.
A translation of Depestre's *Un arc-en-ciel pour l'occident chrétien*. The Voodoo
religion is the source of much of the imagery in this surrealistic poem.

782 **Anthology of contemporary Latin-American poetry.**
Edited by Dudley Fitts. Norfolk, Connecticut: New Directions, 1947.
677p. bibliog. Reprinted, New York: Greenwood Press, 1976.
A bilingual edition, with English and original text on facing pages. Haitians included:
Jacques Roumain, *Quand bat le tam-tam, Guinée*; Emile Roumer, *Declaration
paysanne*; and Duracine Vaval, *Les mangoes*. Biographical and bibliographical
information on these three poets by H. R. Hayes is provided on p. 589-641.

783 **Dézafi; roman.**
Frankétienne. Port-au-Prince: Fardin, 1795. 312p.
This work, which is the first full-length novel written in Haitian Creole, presents a
sinsister picture of a revolt in a zombie colony. Readers may also see its author's name
spelt elsewhere as Franck Etienne.

784 **From the green Antilles: writings of the Caribbean.**
Edited by Barbara Howes. London: Souvenir Press, 1967; New York:
Macmillan, 1966. 368p. map.
This anthology includes two prose selections by Haitian writers: Clement-Magloire
Saint-Aude's *The wake*, and Philippe Thoby-Marcelin's *The submarine*.

785 **The poetry of the Negro, 1746-1970: an anthology.**
Edited by Langston Hughes, Arna Bontemps. Garden City, New
York: Doubleday, 1970. Rev. and updated ed. 645p.

Includes English translations of the work of a broad selection of Haitian poets: Oswald
Durand, Isaac Toussaint Louverture, Louis Morpeau, Ignace Nau, Luc Grimard,
Philippe Thoby-Marcelin, Christian Werleigh, Normil Sylvain, Duracine Vaval, Emile
Roumer, Charles F. Pressoir, Jacques Roumain, Roussan Camille and Jean Brierre.

786 **Voices of Negritude: the expression of Black experience in the poetry of
Senghor, Césaire, and Damas.**
Edward Allen Jones. Valley Forge, Pennsylvania: Judson Press, 1971.
125p. bibliog. (Reprinted, Ann Arbor, Michigan: Books on Demand
[n.d.]).

Although this book is a literary study of the three poets named in its title, it also
contains a chapter 'Other poets of the Negritude school', which includes two poems by
Jean Brierre (*Me revoici Harlem* and *Black soul*) and one work by Jacques Roumain
(*Nouveau sermon nègre*). The poems are presented in French with an English
translation on the facing page.

787 **The negritude poets; an anthology of translations from the French.**
Edited and with an introduction by Ellen Conroy Kennedy, foreword
by Maya Angelou. New York: Thunder's Mouth Press, 1989. 284p.
bibliog.

Originally published by Viking Press in 1975, this is a reprint of a collection of English
translations of selections from the work of twenty-seven French-speaking poets
representative of the Negritude movement. Seven Haitians are included: Oswald
Durand, Massilon Coicou, Léon Laleau, Jacques Roumain, Emile Roumer, Charles F.
Pressoir, and René Depestre. Each writer's selection is preceded by introductory
biographical and critical information. The book also includes material on the Negritude
movement, a chronology of the movement in relation to social and political events, and
a bibliography.

788 **Camourade: selected poems.**
Paul Laraque, translated from the French by Rosemary Manno.
Willimantic, Connecticut: Curbstone Press, 1988. 124p.

A bilingual edition of Laraque's poems, with French and English on facing pages.

789 **Three thousand years of black poetry: an anthology.**
Edited by Alan Lomax, Raoul Abdul. New York: Dodd-Mead, 1970.
261p. (Reprinted, Greenwich, Connecticut: Fawcett Publications, 1971.
255p). (Fawcett Premier Book, M538).

This collection includes English translations of poems by Isaac Toussaint Louverture,
Emile Roumer, Oswald Durand, Jacques Roumain, Jean Brierre and Roussan
Camille. Brief biographical information is provided for each poet.

790 **Latin American revolutionary poetry. Poesia revolucionaria latinoamericano. A bilingual anthology.**
Edited and with an introduction by Robert Marquez.   New York: Monthly Review Press, 1974. 505p.

The editor selects René Depestre's *Mineral noir* (Black ore) and *Confession* to represent Haitian writing in this anthology of the poetry of the Latin American left. A biographical-bibliographical note (p. 288-89), informs readers about Depestre's life and politics.

791 **Ebony rhythm: an anthology of contemporary Negro verse.**
Edited by Beatrice M. Murphy.   New York: Exposition Press, 1948. 162p. (Reprinted, Freeport, New York: Books for Libraries Press, 1968). (Granger Index Reprint Series). (Reprinted, Salem, New Hampshire: Ayer, 1988).

Includes English versions of three poems by Jean Brierre: *Areytos*, *Harlem*, and *To Paul Robeson.*

792 **Poetisas de America. Antologia.** (Women poets of America. Anthology.)
Edited and translated by Helen Wohl Patterson.   Washington, DC: Mitchell Press, 1960. 219p.

A bilingual edition that includes the poetry of three Haitian women: Marie-Therèse Colimon, Emmeline Carries Lemaire, and Virginie Sempeur.

793 **Ebony wood. Bois-d'ébène. Poems.**
Jacques Roumain, translated from the French by Sidney Shapiro.
New York: Interworld Press, 1972. 45p.

Accompanied by an English translation, this is the French text of Roumain's *Ebony wood*, *Love and death*, *New negro sermon*, and *Sales nègres.*

794 **Masters of the dew.**
Jacques Roumain, translated from the French by Langston Hughes, Mercer Cook, introduction by J. Michael Dash.   London: Heinemann, 1978. 192p. (Caribbean Writers Series, 12).

A reissue of the translation of Roumain's *Gouverneurs de la rosée* that originally appeared in 1947, with a new introduction by J. Michael Dash. The book is Roumain's most successful novel, lyrical, but with a social message. The work was first published in Port-au-Prince in 1944.

795 **Black poetry of the Americas (a bilingual anthology).**
Compiled by Hortensia Ruiz del Vizo.   Miami, Florida: Ediciones Universal, 1972. 176p. (Coleccion Antologias).

Among the selections in this volume are the original French texts accompanied by Spanish and English translations of three poems by Haitian poets: Jacques Roumain's *Quand bat le tam-tam*, Duracine Vaval's *Les mangoes*, and Emile Roumer's *Declaration paysanne*. The editor states that the anthology is aimed at students, and thus is 'more concerned with making literal translations than with making poetical translations'.

796 **Panorama de la poésie haïtienne.** (Panorama of Haitian poetry.)
Edited by Carlos Saint-Louis, Maurice A. Lubin. Port-au-Prince:
Editions Henri Deschamps, 1950. 635p. map. bibliog. (Reprinted,
Nendeln, Liechtenstein: Kraus Reprint, 1970). (Collection Haitiana).

An anthology that presents the work of approximately 150 Haitian poets writing in
French (two lyrics in Creole are included: *Choucoune* and *Souvenir d'Haïti* [*Haiti
chérie*]). The poems are grouped chronologically into four periods: patriotic poetry;
Haitian romanticism; generation of 1915 or of the occupation; and revolutionary
poetry. The editors provide a short introduction and a 'Biographie et Bibliographie'
section that identifies each poet; also included is an interesting map, Carte de la poésie
Haïtienne, which links poets to Haitian locations.

797 **Negritude: black poetry from Africa and the Caribbean.**
Edited and translated from the French by Norman R. Shapiro, with an
introduction by Wilfred Cartey. New York: October House, 1970.
247p. bibliog.

Each poem is printed in its original French, accompanied by an English translation on
the opposite page. Haiti is represented by selections from the work of eleven poets:
Léon Laleau, Carl Brouard, Jean Brierre, Rodolphe Moise, Roussan Camille, René
Depestre, Louis Neptune, Paul-E. Najac, Anthony Phelps, René Philoctete and Frantz
Leroy. The editor provides detailed biographical and bibliographical notes on each
poet at the end of the volume.

798 **Negro poets of the French Caribbean: a sampler.**
Norman R. Shapiro. *Antioch Review*, vol. 27, no. 2 (summer 1967),
p. 211-28.

After a general discussion of the black poets of the Antilles and their reaffirmation of
their African heritage in the Negritude movement, the author chooses works by Léon
Laleau and René Depestre to represent Haitian poetry. The article includes French
texts and English translations of Laleau's *Silhouette* and Depestre's *Mon ami, voici ta
Noel* and *Confession*.

799 **All men are mad.**
Philippe Thoby-Marcelin, Pierre Marcelin, translated from the French
by Eva Thoby-Marcelin, with an introduction by Edmund Wilson.
New York: Farrar, Straus & Giroux, 1970. 179p.

A translation of *Tous les hommes sont fous*. A young French priest, newly arrived in
Haiti, courts disaster when he pits himself against the forces of Voodoo in a small
Haitian town.

800 **The beast of the Haitian hills.**
Philippe Thoby-Marcelin, Pierre Marcelin, translated from the French
by Peter C. Rhodes with a afterword by Philippe Thoby-Marcelin.
San Francisco: City Lights Books, 1986. 179p.

A new edition of the translation of *La bête du Musseau* originally published in 1946.
The protagonist of this tragic narrative is city-dweller Morin Dutilleul, whose dream of
becoming a planter in the country village of Musseau is destroyed by his encounter
with the occult.

801 Canapé-Vert.

Philippe Thoby-Marcelin, Pierre Marcelin, translated from the French by Edward LaRocque Tinker. New York: Farrar & Rinehart, 1944. 225p.

Winner of the second Latin American fiction prize offered by Farrar & Rinehart, this was the author's first novel, and introduced Haitian fiction to the American public. Canapé-Vert is the name of the country village in which this tragic tale unfolds.

802 The pencil of God.

Philippe Thoby-Marcelin, Pierre Marcelin, translated from the French by Leonard Thomas, with an introduction by Edmund Wilson.

Boston, Massachusetts: Houghton Mifflin, 1951. 204p.

A translation of *Le crayon de Dieu*. A small town in Haiti serves as the backdrop for the tragi-comic adventures of a Haitian philanderer.

803 The poets of Haiti, 1782-1934.

Edited and translated by Edna Worthley Underwood.   Portland, Maine: Mosher Press, 1934. 159p. (Reprinted, New York: Gordon Press, 1977).

This volume is still the only anthology of Haitian poetry in English translation. Poets included: MacDonald Alexander, Fernand Ambroise, Louis Borno, Jean Brierre, Carl Brouard, Frederic Burr-Reynaud, Adrian Carrenard, Maurice Casseus, Pascal Casseus, Roland Chassagne, Arsène Chevry, Massilon Coicou, Louis-Henri Durand, Luc Grimard, Tertullian Guilbaud, Dominique Hippolyte, Edmund La Forest, Léon Laleau, Robert Lataillade, George Lescouflair, Paul Lochard, Léon Louhis, Clement Magloire-Fils, Victor Mangones, Constantin Mayard, Pierre Maynard, Charles Moravia, Louis Morpeau, Ignace Nau, Edgard Numa, Timothee Paret, Charles F. Pressoir, Christian Regulies, Justinien Ricot, Volvick Ricourt, Milo Rigaud, Jacques Roumain, Emile Roumer, George Sylvain, Normil Sylvain, Philippe Thoby-Marcelin, Isaac Toussaint Louverture, Duracine Vaval, Damocles Vieux, Etzer Vilaire, Jean-Joseph Vilaire and Christian Werleigh.

804 Black poetry of the French Antilles: Haiti, Martinique, Guadeloupe, Guiana.

Translated by Seth L. Wolit.   Berkeley, California: Fybate Lecture Notes, 1968. 37p.

Poems by Jean Brierre, Roussan Camille and Jacques Roumain are among the selections chosen for this pamphlet.

Works about Haiti by foreign writers

805 Continental drift.

Russell Banks.   New York: Harper & Row, 1985. 366p.

A novel in which a Haitian refugee in the United States and an American worker are united in their pursuit of the American dream.

806 **Popo and Fifina: children of Haiti.**
Arna Bontemps, Langston Hughes, illustrations by E. Simms
Campbell. New York: Macmillan, 1932. 100p. (Reprinted with an
introduction and afterword by Arnold Rampersad, New York: Oxford
University Press, 1993. 120p). (The Opie Library.).
Two major writers of the Harlem Renaissance collaborated in the creation of this tale
of life in Haiti. It has since become a children's classic.

807 **The kingdom of this world.**
Alejó Carpentier, translated from the Spanish by Harriet de Onis.
New York: Knopf, 1957. 150p. (Reprinted, New York: Farrar, Straus
& Giroux, 1989). (Noonday).
A translation of *El reino de este mundo*. This novel by an important Cuban writer takes
place during the Haitian Revolution and the reign of Henry Christophe.

808 **The tragedy of King Christophe; a play.**
Aimé Césaire, translated from the French by Ralph Manheim. New
York: Grove Press, 1969. 96p. (Everygreen Original, E-547).
A translation of Césaire's *La tragedie du roi Christophe*, a drama based on the life of
the King of Haiti, Henry Christophe, by Martinique's leading writer.

809 **The Bordeaux narrative.**
Harold Courlander. Albuquerque, New Mexico: University of New
Mexico Press, 1990. 192p.
Courlander, best known for his scholarly studies of Haitian folklore, turns to fiction in
this tale of Dosu Bordeaux's journey to rescue his brother, said to have been turned
into a zombie. Courlander puts his anthropological knowledge to good use in depicting
the cultural setting of nineteenth-century Haiti, and the Voodoo spirits and demons
who help or hinder Dosu's quest.

810 **Monsieur Toussaint.**
Edouard Glissant, translated from the French by Joseph G. Foster,
Barbara A. Franklin, introduction and notes by Juris Silenieks.
Washington, DC: Three Continents Press, 1982. 131p. maps. bibliog.
Glissant, a Martiniquais writer, has composed a tragedy in which Toussaint Louverture
looks back over his life from the confines of his prison cell in Fort Joux. This is a study
edition of the drama, with an introduction, maps, chronology, glossary, bibliography
and a prose outline of Toussaint's life and the events of the Haitian Revolution.

811 **The Comedians.**
Graham Greene. New York: Viking Press, 1965, 309p. (Reprinted,
New York: Viking Press, 1981.354p).
The British novelist depicts solemn adultery against a background of tropical politics in
François Duvalier's Haiti.

812 **Toussaint L'ouverture, a dramatic history.**
Leslie Pinckney Hill. Boston, Massachusetts: Christopher Publishing
House, 1928. 137p.

This lengthy play is the most important work of Harlem Renaissance writer Lesley Pinckney Hill, who uses the historical figure of Toussaint Louverture to illustrate black achievement. In 'Lesley Pinckney Hill's "Toussaint L'Ouverture"' (*Phylon*, vol. 48, no. 3 [fall 1987], p. 190-95), Edward O. Ako emphasizes Hill's reinterpretation of the events of the Haitian Revolution, undertaken in order to fulfill the emotional needs of his Afro-American audience.

813 **Bug-Jargal.**
Victor Hugo, translated from the French by Eugenia de B.
Philadelphia G. Barrie, 1894. 304p. (The novels Complete and
Unabridged of Victor Hugo).

Victor Hugo began his career as a novelist with this tale of the 1791 slave revolt in Saint-Domingue, which was first serialized in *Le Conservateur Littéraire*. An English translation entitled *The slave king* was published in Philadelphia in 1833. The most accessible modern edition in French of this work can be found in *Oeuvres complètes de Victor Hugo*, edited by Jean-Louis Cornuz (Paris: Editions Rencontre, 1966-1968), vol. 7: *Bug-Jargal. Le dernier jour d'un condamné. Claude Gueux.*

814 **Toussaint Louverture; poeme dramatique.**
Alphonse de Lamartine. Paris: Michel Lévy Frères, 1850. 302p.

A five-act verse play by the French romantic poet which was presented in Paris at the Théâtre de la Porte-Saint-Martin on April 6, 1850. The most accessible edition of the play can be found in *Oeuvres poétiques complètes de Lamartine*, edited by Marius-François Guyard (Paris: Gallimard, 1963), p. 1265-1401. (Bibliothèque de la Pléiade, vol. 165).

815 **Lydia Bailey.**
Kenneth Roberts. Garden City, New York: Doubleday & Co., 1947.
488p.

The hero of this romantic best-seller, an American, Albion Hamilton, begins his search for his beloved Lydia Bailey in the tumultuous period of the Haitian Revolution. Toussaint Louverture is one of the fictionalized historical characters who plays a role in Hamilton's adventurous quest.

816 **Murder in Haiti.**
John W. Vandercook. New York: Macmillan, 1956. 193p. (Cock
Robin Mystery).

British intelligence agent Bertram Lynch joins a search for German gold off the coast of Haiti. This books was also issued as a paperback with the title *Out for a killing* (New York: Avon, 1956).

Visual Arts

General

817 **The art of Haiti.**
Eleanor Ingalls Christensen.   Philadelphia: Art Alliance Press, 1975.
76p. bibliog.
Nine short chapters sketch Haitian art from the pre-Columbian period through the
1960s, with emphasis placed on DeWitt Peters and his Centre d'Art, Port-au-Prince.
Two useful appendices, 'Chronology of the Centre d'Art, May 1944-May 1972', and
'Brief biographies of more than one hundred twentieth-century Haitian artists', are
also included. The book has forty-eight pages of illustrations.

818 **Divine horsepower.**
Donald Cosentino.   *African Arts*, vol. 21 no. 3 (May 1988), p. 39-42.
A unique article on the art that embellishes Haiti's 'tap-taps' – the passenger vans that
ply their trade at Port-au-Prince's Boulevard Jean-Jacques Dessalines (the 'Grande
Rue'). These vans are much more than urban transportation, with their extravagantly
painted exteriors and lavishly cluttered dashboards they combine the qualities of art
gallery, nightclub and Voodoo shrine. Cosentino discusses the iconography of tap-tap
art, exploring how the Haitian popular artist merges the sacred with the profane, the
African gods with the saints of the Roman Catholic Church. The article is illustrated
with colour photographs of this exuberant popular art form.

819 **Where art is joy: forty years of Haitian art.**
Selden Rodman, Candice Russel, foreword by Karen Valdes.   Fort
Lauderdale, Florida: Museum of Art, 1989. 15p.
This catalogue to an exhibition of the work of Haitian artists, held March 10 to May 28
1989, at the Fort Lauderdale (Florida) Museum of Art, includes essays by the show's
curators, Selden Rodman and Candice Russell. Other recent exhibition catalogues of
Haitian art are *Under the spell: the art of Haiti* (Chicago: Chicago Council on Fine
Arts, 1983) and *Master painters of Haiti in the collection of Siri von Reis* (Rochester,
Michigan: Meadow Brook Art Gallery, Oakland University 1984).

820 **Haitian art.**
Edited by Ute Stebich. New York: Brooklyn Museum, 1978. 176p.
bibliog.

This catalogue, compiled for an exhibition of Haitian art held in three American
museums, 1978-79, is a comprehensive survey, covering history, criticism and
interpretation. Ute Stebich's contributions, 'History in painting', 'Voodoo and art',
and 'Everyday and festive life', constitute the main part of the volume, and are
illustrated with reproductions. Other sections are of equal interest: essays by Gerla
Nordland, ('Haitian art; a western view'); Irving Rouse, ('Roots: Pre-Columbian');
and Robert Farris Thompson, ('The Flash of the spirit: Haiti's africanizing Vodun
art'); a chronology of Haitian art, 1807-1976; a biographical sketch of DeWitt Peters; a
list of selected exhibition of or including twentieth-century Haitian art; brief
biographies of Haitian artist; and a bibliography of books, periodical articles, and
exhibition catalogues concerned with Haitian art.

Painting and sculpture

821 **Religion in the art of Haiti.**
L. Chalom. New York: Maple Press, 1968. 43p.

This is a catalogue of paintings chosen for an exhibition on the iconography of Voodoo
held at the Student Center Art Gallery, Seton Hall University, South Orange, New
Jersey, in 1968. The volume is quite informative on the Voodoo religion itself. It is
illustrated with black-and-white reproductions of the pieces exhibited.

822 **Myth and mystery: the art of Haiti.**
Richard R. Doornek. *School Arts*, vol. 90, no. 2 (Oct. 1990),
p. 31-34. bibliog.

A pedagogically-orientated introduction to Haitian art, this article is of most interest
for its full-colour centrefold illustration of Serge Jolimeau's joyful cut metal sculpture,
Demon.

823 **Haiti: art naïf, art vaudou.** (Haiti: naive art, Voodoo art.)
Jean-Marie Drot. Paris: Galeries Nationales du Grand Palais; Rome:
Edizioni Carte Segrete, 1988. 276. map.

This is the catalogue to an exhibition of Haitian art held at the Galeries Nationales du
Grand Palais in Paris in 1988. Three generations of Haitian artists displayed their
paintings and sculptures in the exhibit, works which are splendidly reproduced in full
colour in this catalogue.

824 **The naïve tradition: Haiti; the Flagg Tanning Corporation Collection.**
Milwaukee Art Center, foreword by Tracy Atkinson. Milwaukee,
Wisconsin: Milwaukee Art Center, 1974. 116p.

A catalogue of selected paintings by Haitian artists from the collection assembled by
Richard Flagg, president of the Flagg Tanning Corporation, for display at the

Milwaukee Art Center. The book also includes an introductory essay, 'Haitian art: birth of a new world', by Selden Rodman on Haitian naïve painting from the 1940s through to the 1960s, and an alphabetical list of sixty-six Haitian painters, giving biographical information and descriptions of those of their works included in the Flagg Collection.

825 **Haitian painting: art and kitsch.**
Eva Pataki.   Jamaica Estates, New York: The author, 1986. 161p.
bibliog.
Provides an informative overview of Haitian painting. Pataki states in her introduction that her study is intended 'to show Haitian painting as it existed in the past, where it stands today, and how significant both primitive and modern artists are in the context of Haitian painting'. Chapters cover painting in Haiti before 1944; the founding of the Centre d'Art in Port-au-Prince by Dewitt Peters; artists Hector Hyppolite and Philomé Obin; styles and subjects; Haiti's murals; applied art; art reproductions; and art education in Haiti. Chapter twelve is a list of 1,264 Haitian painters. The ninety-three-page text is followed by sixty-seven pages of black-and-white illustrations.

826 **Haitian painting: the naïves and the moderns, a traveling exhibition for the New York City schools, 1987/88.**
Eva Pataki.   New York: School of Education, Queens College, City University of New York, 1987. 71p.
The catalogue to an exhibition organized to introduce schoolchildren to the art of Haiti. The volume consists chiefly of illustrations.

827 **Peintures haïtiennes: photographiées de Warren E. Leon, Jr.** (Haitian paintings: photographed by Warren E. Leon, Jr.)
Boulogne, France. Delroisse, 1978. 143p. bibliog.
For the most part, this volume reproduces paintings created by the artists associated with DeWitt Peters' Centre d'Art in Port-au-Prince, works which are now in the collections of the Musée d'Art Haïtien du College Saint-Pierre. Pierre Monosiet, Curator-Director of the Museum, has written an introduction to the book. The main body of the volume is an alphabetical presentation of the painters and their work: one or more paintings are reproduced for each artist, accompanied by a biographical-critical note.

828 **Cutting fantastic figures: figments of the Master's imagination.**
Selden Rodman.   *Americas*, vol. 40, no. 1 (Jan.-Feb. 1988), p. 26-30.
Discusses the life and work of Georges Liautaud, the 'first great artist of cut-out iron sculptures in Haiti'. Liautaud, a blacksmith in Croix des Bouquets, shapes and cuts steel into lively and complex figures which now grace the world's most prestigious museums. The article is illustrated with photographs of Liautaud's creations.

829 **The miracle of Haitian art.**
Selden Rodman.   Garden City, New York: Doubleday, 1974. 95p.
This short survey of twentieth-century Haitian art focuses on the painters connected with DeWitt Peters' Centre d'Art in Port-au-Prince. The book is illustrated with photographs of the artists at work and reproductions of their paintings.

830 **A mural by Wilson Bigaud.**
Selden Rodman. *Magazine of Art*, vol. 44, no. 6 (Oct. 1951), p. 238-42.

A sound article on Wilson Bigaud and his masterpiece, the mural *Miracle of Cana*, which the Haitian artist painted on the wall of the south transept of the Protestant Episcopal Cathedral in Port-au-Prince in 1950-51. Rodman discribes Bigaud's painting techniques in some details and discusses the mural. The piece is illustrated with black-and-white photographs.

831 **Renaissance in Haiti: popular painters in the Black republic.**
Selden Rodman. New York: Pellegrini & Cudahy, 1948. 134p. map.

This is the work that introduced Haitian naïve painting to the world. Rodman tells the history of the first four years of the Centre d'Art of Port-au-Prince, founded in 1944 by an American, DeWitt Peters, with the aim of encouraging and promoting the artists that he had discovered in Haiti. Rodman emphasizes the work of Philomé Obin, Hector Hyppolite, Rigaud Benoit and Wilson Bigaud, although works by many other painters are included, all amply illustrated in photographs and plates.

832 **Cutting fantistic figures: fanciful images of iron.**
A. R. Williams. *Americas*, vol. 40, no. 1 (Jan.-Feb. 1988), p. 31-37.

Discusses the work of Haitian metal sculptors Murat Brierre, Serge Jolimeau and Gabriel Bien-Aimé, commenting on the sophistication of the first artist, the fantasy of the second, and the humour of the third. The article is illustrated with photographs, and provides information on where these exuberant and expressive sculptures can be viewed and purchased in Haiti.

Architecture

833 **Haiti's majestic monuments.**
Randa Bishops. *Americas*, vol. 39, no. 1 (Jan.-Feb. 1987), p. 2-7;
64-65.

Bishop takes her readers on a tour of Henry Christophe's remarkable edifices, the Citadelle Laferrière and the Sans Souci Palace, and describes preservation projects underway and plans for future restoration. She states that the architect of the massive Citadelle was probably Etienne Barre.

834 **Cockpit at Haiti.**
Notes and photographs by David Pleydell Bouverie. *Architectural Review*, vol. 107, no. 642 (June 1950), p. 417-18.

Accompanied by photographs, this is a description of the Cockfighting Arena at the International Exhibition in Haiti in 1950. The white pine, royal palm, and bamboo structure was constructed on-site without drawn plans by Haitian architect Albert Mangonès.

835 **The cathedral at Cape Haytien, St. Domingo, as restored by Messrs. Cummings and Sears, architects, Boston.**
American Architect and Building News, vol. 4, no. 154 (Dec. 1878),
p. 189.

A short unsigned note that relates the history of the successive church buildings constructed on the site of the Cap Haïtien cathedral, beginning with the first primitive structure in 1680. The writer describes the progress of restoration work undertaken in 1878 on the most recent edifice by the Boston firm of Cummings and Sears, and concludes his article with a sketch of Cap Haïtien in 1878.

836 **King Christophe's citadel.**
Michael Crowder. *History Today*, vol. 31 (June 1981), p. 55-57. map.
bibliog.
Crowder describes Henry Christophe's Citadelle, whose imposing walls and prow-like
shape give it the appearance of a great ship beached on the summit of Pic Laferrière.
The article includes both colour and black-and-white photographs of the fortress, as
well as plans and elevations. Crowder says that the massive building was the work of a
Haitian engineer, Henry Barre, about whom nothing is known.

837 **A little-known marvel of the Western hemisphere: Christophe's citadel,
a monument to the tyranny and genius of Haiti's king of slaves.**
G. H. Osterhout. *National Geographic Magazine*, vol. 38, no. 6 (Dec.
1920), p. 469-82.
This article is of interest for its detailed description and photographs of Henry
Christophe's fortress, Citadelle Laferrière, and his palace, Sans Souci, as they
appeared in 1920 when visited by the author, a major in the US Marine Corps.

838 **Haiti's endangered gingerbread.**
Anghelen Phillips. *Américas*, vol. 35, no. 1 (Jan.-Feb. 1983),
p. 27-31.
In this article, which is illustrated with meticulous pen and ink drawings, Phillips briefly
describes the charming gingerbread houses of Port-au-Prince and gives a little
information on their creators. A full-page colour photograph of the Villa Miramar, a
striking example of this ornate architecture, can be found inside the magazine's front
cover.

839 **Concerning the creation of a museum in a historic monument.**
Georges Henri Rivière. *Museum*, vol. 32, no. 3 (1980), p. 103-05.
A brief note on the Haitian government's plans to preserve the Citadelle de la Ferrière
and the Sans-Souci Palace, historical edifices currently in a serious state of disrepair.

840 **Letter from Haiti.**
Selden Rodman. *Architecture Plus*, vol. 2, no. 4 (July-Aug. 1974),
p. 10ff.
Examines those buildings in Haiti which have been constructed in Victorian Gothic
'Haitian Gingerbread' style. Rodman lists and describes the colourful and charming
mansions whose fantastic minarets, towers and verandas grace the streets of Cap
Haïtien, Jacmel and Port-au-Prince. He also comments on the possible origins of this
indigenous style and adds some information on Haiti's builders and designers.
Photographs of many of the buildings accompany the text. The end of the article
strikes a sad note when Rodman describes the deterioration of several of the most
striking examples of this architecture.

841 **Caribbean style.**
Suzanne Slesin, Stafford Cliff, Jack Berthelot, Martine Gaume, Daniel
Rozensztroch, foreword by Jan Morris, photographs by Gilles de
Chabaneix.   New York: Clackson N. Potter, 1985. 290p. map.
A splendid presentation of Caribbean architecture, with over 600 full-colour
photographs. The book is organized according to type of architecture rather than
island: Haiti's eclectic architectural style is dealt with in several sections. Illustrated
and discussed are both urban buildings and the humble but delightful rural *case*.
Among the examples featured are the 1912 home of Bernard Sejourné, the 1898 home
of Nicholas Roude, and the Hotel Oloffson in Port-au-Prince and the Alexandra Hotel
in Jacmel.

Theatre and Film

842 **Material para una pre-historia del cine haitiano.** (Material for a
prehistory of the Haitian cinema.)
Arnold Antonin. Caracas, Venezuela: Foncine [n.d.] 175p.

A collection of photographs and facsimiles of press reports on cinema in Haiti. The
text is in both French and Spanish.

843 **Ex-iles: essays on Caribbean cinema.**
Edited by Mbye B. Cham. Trenton, New Jersey: Africa World Press,
1992. 415p.

This volume, the first collection of essays to be published on Caribbean cinema,
contains three useful articles on motion pictures in Haiti. Michaëlle Lafontant-Médard
contributes 'Cinema in Haiti 1899 to 1982' (p. 59-97), and 'A thematic analysis of
Rassoul Labuchin's *Anita*' (p. 134-54), the former tracing the history of Haitian film
and the latter analysing a Haitian poet's first cinematic production. John Stewart's
'Culture, heroism, and the Haitian documentary' (p. 117-33), is a discussion of non-
feature films produced in Haiti.

844 **Le théâtre Haïtien des origines à nos jours.** (The Haitian theatre from
its origins to today.)
Robert Cornevin. Montreal: Lemeac, 1973. 300p. bibliog. (Collection
Caraïbes).

Available only in French, this useful handbook presentation of the history of the
Haitian theatre begins with the theatre in colonial Saint-Domingue and continues
through to contemporary Haitian dramatic productions, including 'théâtre créole' and
the theatre of the Haitian diaspora in Paris and New York. A nine-page chart lists
authors and plays of the Haitian theatre, 1791-1969.

845 **Le théâtre à Saint-Domingue.** (The theatre in Saint-Domingue.)
     Jean Fouchard.   Port-au-Prince: Imprimerie de l'Etat, 1955. 353p.
Provides a complete account of the theatre in Haiti during the colonial period.

846 **La crise de possession et la possession dramatique.** (The possession crisis
     and drama.)
     Antonio Louis-Jean.   Montreal: Lemeac, 1970. 173p. bibliog.
     (Collection Caraïbes).
The author, a Haitian critic, compares Voodoo experiences with theatrical presentations. The work is illustrated with photographs of Haitian dramatic productions.

Libraries and Archives

Within Haiti

847 Creation of a research and documentation center for Hait.
Ernst T. Brea.   In: *The Haitian potential; research and resources of Haiti.* Edited by Vera Rubin, Richard P. Schaedel.   New York: Teachers College Press, 1975, p. xv-xxi. (Publications of the Center for Education in Latin America).
Discusses the creation of a Haitian Centre for Documentation and Information that would function as an aid to the country's economic and social development.

848 Checklists for archives and private collections in Haiti.
Maurice De Young.   In: *Handbook of Latin American Studies 23.* Edited by Nathan A. Haverstock, Earl J. Pariseau.   Gainesville, Florida: University of Florida Press, 1961, p. 406-08.
This annotated bibliography of nineteen catalogues and lists of holdings of libraries and archives of Haitian materials in Haiti and the United States is a valuable aid to research. In a note preceding the list, De Young describes the University of Florida-Rockefellar Foundation Mission to Haiti Project to microfilm a Haitian newspaper collection.

849 Research guide to Central America and the Caribbean.
Editor-in-chief Kenneth J. Grieb, associated editors, Ralph Lee Woodward, Jr., Graeme S. Mount, Thomas G. Mathews.   Madison, Wisconsin: University of Wisconsin Press, 1985. 431p.
A useful reference tool that identifies archival resources available to those doing research on Caribbean topics. For students of Haiti, the work describes depositories located both within and outside of the country. In a short sketch ('Haiti' p. 311-12), Henock Trouillot outlines the resources of Haiti's National Archives, libraries and museums. In his article 'The Haitian Revolution' (p. 278-84), Tadeusz Lepkowski discusses the historiography of the Haitian Revolution, noting topics that deserve

further study and indicating archives that are relatively unexploited – British, Spanish, provincial and private French – and which should provide abundant documentary materials relevant to this tremendous event. Lepkowski notes that 'Cuban, Dominican, French, British, Dutch, Brazilian, Spanish, Mexican, Venezuelan, and many more archives' hold important material for the study of 'the influence of the [Haitian] revolution upon the emancipation process of slaves and of blacks in general'. Many references of interest to those studying Haiti can also be found in other articles in this guide.

850 **Latin American archivology, 1948-1949.**
Roscoe R. Hill. *Hispanic American Historical Review*, vol. 30, no. 1 (Feb. 1950), p. 115-39. bibliog.

On p. 130-31 of this survey, Hill notes work accomplished 1948-49 in Haiti's Archives Nationales, summarizing records received and processed and progress made in sorting and classifying archivalia. He mentions that 'forty-four dossiers containing interesting autographic documents' were compiled in the Section Historique.

851 **The national archives of Latin America.**
Edited by Roscoe R. Hill. Cambridge, Massachusetts: Harvard University Press, 1945. 169p. (Joint Committee on Latin American Studies of the National Research Council of Learned Societies, and the Social Science Research Council. Miscellaneous Publication, no. 3).

In the section on Haiti (p. 105-06), the editor comments that 'the unsettled conditions which have obtained so often (in Haiti) have not been conducive to the preservation of the records of its history'. He then briefly describes the collection at the National Archives, Port-au-Prince, as it existed in the early 1940s: 'the bulk of the material consists of records of the various ministries . . . the archive . . . has a very complete collection of (Haiti's) civil laws. Little material dating from the time of the colony is extant'.

852 **Catalogue de la bibliothèque Haïtienne des Frères de l'Instruction Chrétienne.** (The catalogue of the Haitian library of the Brothers of Christian Instruction.)
Lucien Jean Legendre. Port-au-Prince: The author, 1958. 533 leaves.

Classified by subject, this is a list of approximately 5,000 books indexed both by author and by title. The library of the Brothers of Christian Instruction has been called the most complete and best organized in Haiti. Its collection is particularly strong in material relating to the religious history of Haiti. The Edmond Mangonès collection of letters, papers, and historical documents (see next item) also forms part of the library.

853 **Catalogue de la collection Mangonès, Pétionville, Haiti.** (Catalogue of the Mangonès collection, Pétionville, Haiti.)
Edited by Ira P. Lowenthal, Drexel G. Woodson. New Haven, Connecticut: Antilles Research Program, Yale University, 1974. 377p. (ARP Occasional Papers, 2).

A catalogue of the library of Edmond Mangonès, a Haitian scholar. The volume is a companion to *La Collection Mangonès*, a set of twenty-three microfilm reels of the books, manuscripts, and serials collected by Mangonès. This work is now part of the library of the Brothers of Christian Instruction (see preceding item for information).

854 **Les archives nationales d'Haiti hier, aujourd'hui et demain.** (The National Archives of Haiti, yesterday, today and tomorrow.) Laurore St.-Juste. *Caribbean Studies*, vol. 1, no. 2 (July 1961), p. 12-15.
A note on Haiti's archives as they were in 1961.

Outside of Haiti

855 **The Caribbean collections at the University of Florida: a brief description.** David Geggus. Gainesville, Florida: University of Florida Libraries, 1985. 26p. bibliog.
A valuable guide for scholars. The University of Florida libraries at Gainesville house the largest collection of Caribbean materials in the United States, a collection comprising approximately 50,000 printed works and 12,000 reels of microfilm. In this pamplet, Geggus describes the University's manuscript microfilm and newspaper holdings. Among the items of particular interest to Haitianists in the manuscript collection are the Rochambeau Papers, the Jérémie Papers, the Haitian Registry Papers, the Haitian Papers, the Haitiana Collections, and the Frank Crumbie Papers. In the microfilm collection the Saint-Domingue Collection of the Archives Nationales in Paris, the British Consular Papers from the British Foreign Office, the [Edmond] Mangonés Collection, the US State Department Papers to 1906, and the Beaunay Papers, from the Archives départmentales de la Sarthe, France, may all be found. The non-current newspaper collection also contains microfilmed copies of *Le Moniteur*, 1847-1968; *Le Nouvelliste*, 1899-1979; the *Exposé Général de la Situation d'Haiti*, 1881-1933 (incomplete); and *Le Télégraphe*, 1836-38.

856 **Material on Latin America in the United States Marine Corps archives.** Neill Macaulay. *Hispanic American Historical Review*, vol. 46, no. 2 (May 1966), p. 179-81.
Briefly mentions several printed sources and special subject files pertaining to, or resulting from, Marine Corpos operations in Haiti which are now held in the Marine Corps Historical Archives in Arlington, Virginia.

857 **Libraries and special collections on Latin America and the Caribbean: a directory of European resources.**
Roger Macdonald, Carole Travis.   London; Atlantic Highlands, New Jersey: Published for the Institute of Latin American Studies, University of London, [by] the Athlone Press, 1988. 2nd ed. 339p. (Institute of Latin Studies, 14).

This is a revised edition of the *Directory of libraries and special collections on Latin America and the West Indies* compiled by Bernard Naylor, Laurence Hallewell and Colin Steele (London: Institute of Latin American Studies, Athlone Press, 1975). It has been updated and expanded to included resources in continental Europe as well as Great Britain.

858 **Guida delle fonti per la storia dell'America Latina: negil archivi della Santa Sede e negli archivi eccelesiastici d'Italia.** (Guide to sources for the history of Latin America in the archives of the Holy See and in Italian eccelesiastical archives.)
Edited by Lajos Pásztor.   Vatican City State: Archivo Vaticano, 1970. 665p. (Collectanea Archivi Vaticani, 2).

A UNESCO-sponsored guide to materials preserved in the Vatican, both in the Archivo Segreto Vaticano and in other Vatican archives, and in the archives of religious orders in Italy. Depositories containing materials on Haiti can be located by means of the index. This is an important resource for the history of the Roman Catholic Church in Haiti.

859 **Catalog of the Latin American collection, University of Florida libraries.**
University of Florida Libraries.   Boston: G. K. Hall, 1973. 13 volumes. *First supplement*, 1980. 7 vols.

Photographic reproduction of 201,000 card entries for approximately 120,000 books, pamphlets, periodicals and government documents. The libraries of the University of Florida at Gainesville house the most extensive collection of Caribbean materials of any university library, with particularly strong holdings in Haitian materials. The main catalogue is also available on microfilm (26 reels). The *First supplement* adds another 91,400 card entries. (See also entry no. 855.)

Guide des sources de l'histoire de l'Amérique latine et des Antilles dans les archives françaises.
See item no. 135.

Guide des sources de l'histoire d'Amérique latine conservées en Belgique.
See item no. 139.

Documentos para la historia de Haiti en el Archivo Nacional [de Cuba].
See item no. 141.

Libraries and Archives. Outside of Haiti

Unexploited sources for the history of the Haitian revolution.
See item no. 198.

A calendar of Rochambeau papers at the University of Florida Libraries.
See item no. 206.

Mass Media

General

860   **Bibliographic guide to Caribbean mass communication.**
John A. Lent.   Westport, Connecticut: Greenwood Press, 1992. 301p.
(Bibliographies and Indexes in Mass Media and Communications,
no. 5).
In a chapter entitled 'Haiti' (p. 205-241), Lent gives an introductory overview of the
mass communication situation in Haiti, emphasizing how press freedom has always
been problematic. The bibliographical entries that follow are unannotated and are
classified in six sections covering bibliography, general studies, broadcasting, freedom
of the press, history of media, and print media. Books, journal articles, theses,
pamphlets and unpublished materials are listed.

861   **Mass communications in the Caribbean.**
John A. Lent.   Ames, Iowa: Iowa State University Press, 1990. 398p.
bibliog.
Chapter fifteen of this book, 'Haitian mass media', provides both a background to, and
current information on, Haiti's mass communications. The chapter covers the history
of Haiti's press – largely the struggle of Haitian journalists against government
suppression from 1764 to today – and the history of radio and television broadcasting
in Haiti, which began with Radio HHK in 1926 and Télé Haiti in 1959. Lent describes
the attacks on the press during the Duvalier era, and the state of journalism under
General Henri Namphy and President Leslie Manigat. Other chapters of Lent's book
treat topics of interest to students of communications in the region, including a review
of research in Caribbean media.

Printing, publishing and journalism

862 **Cabon's history of Haiti journalism.**
Adolphe Cabon, with an introduction and notes by Clarence S.
Brigham. Worcester, Massachusetts: American Antiquarian Society,
1940. 87p.

A scholarly history of early Haitian journalism that begins with the *Gazette de St.-Domingue*, Haiti's first newspaper, in 1764 and continues to 1792. The text of the edition cited here is in French (in spite of its English title), with notes and introduction in English, and is the third publication of this material, which first appeared as a series of articles in the *Petite Revue Hebdomadaire*, Port-au-Prince, 12 April-14 November 1919. It was then reprinted with the title 'Un siècle et demi de journalisme en Haïti', in the *Proceedings of the American Antiquarian Society*, n.s., vol. 49, p. 121-205.

863 **A poor king without a crown: a review of the Haitian press during the Manigat months.**
Bernard Diederich. *Caribbean Review*, vol. 16, no. 2 (winter 1988),
p. 10-12; 35.

Reports on the state of Haiti's press during the truncated term of office of President Leslie Manigat (January to June 1988).

864 **L'imprimerie royale d'Haïti (1817-1819): a little known royal press of the Western hemisphere.**
Ralph T. Esterquest. *Papers of the Bibliographical Society of America*, vol. 34 (1940), p. 171-84.

Discusses the two royal presses established by Henry Christophe: the first at Cap Henri, where between 1811 and 1816 books were issued bearing the imprint Chez P. Roux, Imprimeur du Roi; and the second at Sans Souci, where the Imprimerie Royale printed a small number of works, 1817-19. The article includes bibliographies of the books issued by these presses.

865 **Idylles et chansons ou, éssais de poésie créole.** (Idylls and songs *or* essays on Creole poetry.)
Un Habitant d'Haiti. Philadelphia: Edwards, 1811. 22p.

This item has been identified as the first example of a book printed in Haitian Creole. A facsimile edition was published in the *Proceedings of the American Antiquarian Society*, vol. 67, pt. 1 (April 1957), p. 49-76, under the title *Gombo comes to Philadelphia*, edited by Edward Larocque Tinker. The facsimile was also published as a separate thirty-two page booklet by the University Press of Virginia, Charlottesville, Virginia.

866 **The press in Haiti.**
The Nation, vol. 125, no. 3241 (Aug. 17, 1927), p. 166-68.

Contains excerpts from an address made by a Haitian, Carlos Martins, at the Congress against Colonial Oppression and Imperialism in Brussels, detailing the curtailment of press freedom and the arbitrary imprisonment of Haitian journalists and editors in Haiti during the American occupation.

Newspaper, Magazines and Periodicals

Published in Haiti

867 **Bulletin d'Information.** (Information Bulletin.)
Port-au-Prince: Association des Archivistes, Bibliothècaires,
Documentalistes Francophone de la Carïbe, Section Haïti, 1980- .
quarterly.

A publication carrying news of the activities of Haitian libraries, archives and
documentation centres.

868 **Bulletin du Bureau National d'Ethnologie.** (Bulletin of the National
Bureau of Ethnology.)
Port-au-Prince: Bureau National d'Ethnologie, n.s. 1958- .
semi-annual.

A scholarly anthropological journal, successor to the original *Bulletin du Bureau
d'Ethnologie* founded in 1942 by Jacques Roumain, the Bureau's first director.
Publication of the journal was suspended between September 1965, and October 1974.

869 **Bulletin Trimestriel de Statistique.** (Quarterly Bulletin of Statistics.)
Port-au-Prince: Institut Haïtien de Statistique, 1951- . quarterly.

Provides the main source for the reporting of government statistics on the Haitian
population. Publication is often irregular.

870 **Cahiers du Centre Haïtien d'Investigations en Sciences Sociales.**
Port-au-Prince: Centre Haïtien d'Investigations en Sciences Sociales,
1970- . semi-annual.

CHISS Cahiers publishes scholarly articles dealing with all areas of the social sciences.

Newspaper, Magazines and Periodicals. Published in Haiti

871 **Conjonction: Revue Franco-Haïtienne.** (Conjunction: French-Haitian Review.)
Port-au-Prince: Institut Français d'Haïti, 1946- . bi-monthly.
The journal of the Institut Français d'Haïti publishes articles of general intellectual interest, often in history or the social sciences. Book reviews are a regular feature. Since 1974, *Conjonction* has filled the role of Haiti's current national bibliography, the record of the country's book production – probably less than one hundred books a year – appears in the periodical, compiled by the librarian of the Institut Français d'Haïti.

872 **La Conviction.**
Port-au-Prince: Parti Démocrat Chrétien Haïtien, 1980- . semimonthly.
The magazine of the Haitian Christian Democratic Party, founded by Rev. Silvio Claude, a Protestant minister.

873 **Fraternité** (Fraternity.)
Port-au-Prince: Parti Social Chrétien d'Haïti, 198?- . biweekly.
This is the organ of the Social Christian Party founded by Grégoire Eugene. Its circulation is estimated at 5,000.

874 **Les Griots.**
Port-au-Prince: Impr. de l'Etat, July, 1938- March, 1940.
A *griot* is an African storyteller. *Les Griots* was founded in 1938 by Lorimer Denis, along with François Duvalier, Carl Brouard, Kléber George Jacob, and Clement Magloire, as the magazine of a cultural movement that stressed the Africanism of Haitian culture. Although the periodical lasted only five issues, the movement has far-reading cultural and political implications for Haiti.

875 **Haiti-Journal.**
Port-au-Prince, 1930- . daily.
A government organ, distributed gratis in Port-au-Prince. The *Haiti-Journal's* founder, Sténio Vincent was president of Hait, 1930-1941. Circulation is 2,000.

876 **Haiti Libérée.** (Free Haiti.)
Port-au-Prince, 1958- . daily.
Formerly *Le Nouveau Monde* (renamed in 1986), *Haiti Libérée* is a government paper, which prints official statements. Circulation is 7,000.

877 **Le Jour.** (Day.)
Port-au-Prince, 1939- . daily.
A government newspaper with a circulation of 700 copies.

878 **Le Matin.** (Morning.)
Port-au-Prince, 1906- . daily.
An independent morning paper, founded by Clement Magloire. Estimates of its circulation vary from 5,000-10,000 copies. Back issues of *Le Matin* beginning with

1968 are available on microfilm from University Microfilms International, Ann Arbor, Michigan.

879 **Le Moniteur.** (The monitor.)
Port-au-Prince, 1945- . twice-weekly.

The official gazette of the Haitian government. This paper publishes texts of laws, decrees, treaties and international contracts, as well as the Budget and official statistics. From 1821 to 1845, documents issued by the Haitian government were printed in the weekly *Le Télégraphe*. Back files of *Le Moniteur*, 1949 to 1968, can be purchased on microfilm (26 reels) from Kraus Microfilms, Millwood, New York. An index to laws published in *Le Moniteur* 1944-1978 is available: *Index thématique des lois haïtiennes: référence de toutes les lois publiées au journal officiel 'Le Moniteur' de 1944 à 1978* (Port-au-Prince: Editions Fardin, 1986, 503p).

880 **Le Nouvelliste.**
Port-au-Prince, 1896- . daily.

The evening paper of Port-au-Prince, and the most politically independent daily, *Le Nouvelliste* was founded in 1896 by Cheraquil and Henry Chauvet and is still owned by the Chauvet family. Aimed at the more literate Haitians, it has a circulation of 6,000. Back issues of the newspaper from 1899 to 1950 are available on microfilm from University Microfilm International, Ann Arbor, Michigan.

881 **Panorama.**
Port-au-Prince, 1956- .daily.

A respected independent newspaper with a circulation of approximately 2,000.

882 **Le petit samedi soir: la revue indépendante de actualité culturelle haïtienne.** (Saturday evening: the independent review of Haitian cultural news.)
Port-au-Prince, 1975?- . weekly.

Known for its anti-Duvalier stand, *Le petit samedi soir* was shut down by the government in 1980 and resumed publication in 1986. Edited by Dieudonné Fardin, the paper has a circulation of over 10,000.

883 **Le Progressiste haïtien.**
Port-au-Prince, 1988- . daily.

A government newspaper.

884 **La Relève.**
Port-au-Prince: Impr. de l'Etat, 1932-1939. (Reprinted, Nendeln, Liechtenstein: Kraus Reprint, 1970). vols. 1-8.

An important avant-garde periodical founded by Jacques Carmeleau Antoine, Jean Fouchard and Alix Mathon.

885 **Revue de la Société Haïtienne d'Histoire et de Géographie.** (Review of the Haitian Society of History and Geography.)
Port-au-Prince, 1926- . quarterly.
Now in its sixty-eighth year, Haiti's most prestigious scholarly journal enjoys an international reputation for its historical studies. The publication was originally entitled *Revue de la Société d'Histoire et de Géographie d'Haïti.*

886 **La Revue Indigène.**
Port-au-Prince: 1927-1928. (Reprinted, Nendeln, Liechtenstein: Kraus Reprint, 1971). 1 vol. nos 1-6 (July 1927-Feb. 1928).
Although short-lived, *La Revue Indigène* was a landmark in Haitian literature. It was founded by Jacques Roumain along with Normil Sylvain, Antonio Vieux, Carl Brouard, Philippe Thoby-Marcelin and Daniel Heurtelou to publish the work of the *groupe indigène*, poets who sought to free Haitian poetry from imitation and to reconcile Haitian literature with the true origins of the Haitian people.

Published outside Haiti

887 **Haiti-en-Marche.**
Miami, 1986- . weekly.
A left-orientated weekly founded by Marcus Garcia. Circulation is 12,000.

888 **Haiti-Observateur.** (Haiti-Observer.)
New York, 1971- . weekly.
The most-widely read Haitian newspaper in the United States, with a circulation of about 50,000. Politically conservative, the *Haiti-Observateur* was founded by Raymond Joseph and is owned by the Joseph family.

889 **Haiti-Progrès.** (Haiti-Progress.)
New York, 1983- . weekly.
A weekly with a leftist orientation that serves Haitian exiles in the United States. Founded by Ben Dupuy, the paper claims a circulation of 78,000.

Reference Works

890 **Biographical dictionary of Latin American and Caribbean political leaders.**
Edited by Robert J. Alexander. Westport, Connecticut: Greenwood Press, 1988. 509p.

Percy C. Hintzen has contributed biographical articles on fourteen Haitian politicians and statesmen to this reference work. Relying on information drawn from standard printed sources, he summarizes the careers of Jean-Pierre Boyer, Henry Christophe, Jean-Jacques Dessalines, François Duvalier, Jean-Claude Duvalier, Dumarsais Estimé, Fabre Nicholas Géffrard, Elie Lescot, Toussaint Louverture, Paul Eugene Magloire, Alexandre Pétion, Louis-Félicité Lysius Salomon, Faustin Soulouque, and Sténio Vincent.

891 **Caribbean business directory 1992.**
Antigua; Miami, Florida: Caribbean Publishing Co., 1990- . annual. maps.

Business information for Haiti is included in this directory of enterprises in the Caribbean area. In its companion volume, *Caribbean yellow pages 1992*, the 'Haiti' section lists current addresses, telephone, fax and telex numbers.

892 **Caribbean writers; a bio-bibliographical-critical encyclopedia.**
Edited by Donald E. Herdeck, Maurice A. Lubin, John Figueroa, Dorothy A. Figueroa, Jose Alcantara, Margaret L. Herdeck. Washington, DC: Three Continents Press, 1977. 970p.

An outstanding reference work: its triple-hyphenated subtitle sums up the scope of this literary compendium. Haitian writers and intellectuals are listed in the section on Francophone literature. Biographical information is accompanied by exhaustive bibliographies. Includes an 'Essay on the literature of Haiti', p. 263-72.

Reference Works

893 **Haiti.**
   In: *South America, Central America, and the Caribbean 1993.*
   London: Europa Publications, 1993. 4th ed. p. 359-72. bibliog.

Presents easily-accessible information on Haiti, revised from the third edition of 1991. The work is organized into three sections: a narration of Haiti's history, physical and social geography, and economy; statistical tables covering finance, industries, agriculture, trade, population, education, transport, and tourism; and a directory of useful names and addresses.

894 **Haiti.**
   In: *World of Learning*, 1993.   London: Europa Publications, 43rd ed.
   p. 662.

Lists the names and addresses of learned societies, libraries and archives, museums, and universities and colleges in Haiti. Entries lists directors, principal personnel and publications.

895 **Dictionnaire géographique et administratif universel d'Haïti; illustré, ou, Guide général en Haïti.** (Universal administrative and geographical dictionary of Haiti; illustrated, or, General guide to Haiti.)
   Semexant Rouzier, Charles Rouzier.   Paris: Imprimerie Charles Blot, 1892-94, vols. 1-2; Port-au-Prince: Imprimerie August A. Heraux, 1927-28, vols. 3-4.

An encyclopaedic treasury of information on Haitian geography, history, literature and politics.

Bibliographies

Current

896 **Caribbean Studies.**
Rio Piedras, Puerto Rico: Institute of Caribbean Studies, University of
Puerto Rico, 1961- . quarterly.

This multi-disciplinary scholarly journal provides an accessible bibliography of Haitian
book production. The section 'Current bibliography', compiled at the University of
Puerto Rico's Institute of Caribbean Studies with the aid of regional consultants, is a
'selected compilation of current books, periodical literature and certain documentary
material of interest to Caribbeanists'.

897 **Handbook of Latin American Studies.**
Edited by Dolores Moyano Martin (et al.).   Cambridge,
Massachusetts: Harvard University Press, 1936-51. Gainesville, Florida:
University of Florida Press, 1952-79. Austin, Texas; London:
University of Texas Press, 1980- . annual.

HLAS, the basic bibliography of Latin American scholarship, includes citations to
material on Haiti and the West Indies. Since 1965, the work has been split into two
volumes published in alternate years, one for the field of humanities and the other for
the social sciences. (In 1991, volume 50 covered the humanities; in 1992, volume 51
covered the social sciences.) Every student of the Caribbean should become familiar
with the categories and indexing of *HLAS*. Entries are annotated and scholarship in all
major languages is included. A cumulative author index to the first thirty years of the
publication, compiled by Francisco José and Maria Elena Cardona *(Author index to
Handbook of Latin American studies, nos. 1-28, 1936-1966*, Gainesville, Florida:
University of Florida, 1968), facilitates retrospective searching.

Conjonction: Revue Franco-Haïtienne.
See item no. 871.

Retrospective

898 **Theses on Caribbean topics 1778-1968.**
Compiled by Enid M. Baa. San Juan, Puerto Rico: Institute of
Caribbean Studies and the University of Puerto Rico Press, 1970. 146p.
bibliog. (Caribbean Bibliographic Series, no. 1).
This reference source for doctoral dissertations and masters theses on the Caribbean
region written between 1778 and 1968 includes fifty-two citations of work on Haiti.
The main listing is alphabetical by author, with four indexes providing access by
university, date, subject and country. Coverage is most complete for theses submitted
to academic institutions in the United States, France and Great Britian.

899 **Haitian publications: an acquisitions guide and bibliography.**
Lygia Maria F. C. Ballantyne. Madison, Wisconsin: Secretariat,
Seminar on the Acquisition of Latin American Library Materials,
Memorial Library, University of Wisconsin, 1980. 52p.
A guide to the acquisition of the publications of the Haitian book industry. Ballantyne
first surveys Haiti's book trade, non-commercial publishers, and libraries and
documentation centres, then supplies a directory of Haitian trade and institutional
publishers and of bookdealers who can fill foreign orders. A very useful section of the
guide is 'Haitian serials: an annotated list of current titles', in which Ballantyne lists
sixty-eight serial items current as of 1978.

900 **Latin American and the Caribbean: a bibliographical guide to works in
English.**
S. A. Bayitch. Coral Gables, Florida: University of Miami Press;
Dobbs Ferry, New York: Oceana, 1967. 943p. (University of Miami
School of Law: Interamerican Legal Studies, vol. 10).
This expanded version of Bayitch's *Latin American; a bibliographical guide to
economy, history, law, politics, and society* includes a section on Haiti (p. 568-81), that
is most useful for locating legal materials, particularly English translations of Haiti's
constitutions.

901 **Dictionnaire de bibliographie Haïtienne.** (Dictionary of Haitian
bibliography.)
Max Bissainthe. Washington, DC: Scarecrow Press, 1951. 1,052p.
The bibliographical cornerstone of all library collections of Haitian materials,
Bissainthe's monumental work is the complete retrospective record of Haitian book
production, 1804-1949, and is also an important source for the history of Haitian
journalism. The volume is organized in four sections: works by Haitians, 1804-1949;
works about Saint-Domingue and Haiti by non-Haitians, 1492-1949; periodical
publications, 1764-1949; and a list of the journalists of Saint-Domingue and Haiti.

902 **Dictionnaire de bibliographie Haïtienne. Premier supplement.**
(Dictionary of Haitian bibliography. First supplement.)
Max Bissainthe. Metuchen, New Jersey: Scarecrow Press, 1973. 269p.
Covers Haitian book production, 1950-70, with an appendix of works published before 1950 that did not appear in Bissainthe's main volume.

903 **Bibliographie haïtienne, 1957-1967.** (Haitian bibliography, 1957-1967.)
Paul Blanchet, with the collaboration of Gérald Dorval, Jacquelin Dolcé, Jean-Miotel Casthely. Port-au-Prince: Editions Panorama, 1982. 321p.
Presents a lists of ten years of Haitian book production, including both books published in Haiti and books published abroad by Haitians. An author list, with bibliographical details, followed by a descriptive annotation is also provided. Most of the volumes listed are French.

904 **The memorias of the republics of Central America and of the Antilles.**
James B. Childs. Washington, DC: US Government Printing Office, 1932. 170p.
A bibliography, compiled by the Chief of the Catalog Division, Library of Congress, listing government reports. In the Haiti section (p. 96-108), various executive and administrative documents issued by both Haitian and American officials are cited, among them the 'Exposé général' of the President of Haiti, 1863-1927; Customs receivership reports, 1916/17-28/29; Garde d'Haiti annual reports, 1927-29; and US High Commissioner's reports, 1922-29. Items not located in the Library of Congress are marked with an asterisk.

905 **Bibliographie générale et méthodique d'Haïti.**
Ulrick Duvivier. Port-au-Prince: Impr. de l'Etat, 1941. 2 vols.
Presents a bibliographical list by subject categories, with occasional annotations.

906 **The complete Haitiana: a bibliographic guide to the scholarly literature, 1900-1980.**
Michel S. Laguerre. Millwood, New York: Kraus International Publications, 1982. 2 vols.
A massive compilation of more than 10,000 citations to monographs, dissertations, theses, essays, periodical and newspaper articles, documents, pamphlets, and conference proceedings in sixty-five subject categories. Organized in accordance with the pattern of Lambros Comitas's *Complete Caribbeana*, entries are extensively cross-listed, that same item appearing once under its main topic and then under other rubrics. A major contribution to Haitian studies, Laguerre's work makes it possible for scholars to locate many elusive bibliographical items.

907 **Bibliography on Haiti.**
Compiled by Robert Lawless. Gainesville, Florida: Center for Latin American Studies, University of Florida, 1985. 146p. (Paper no. 6).
A bibliography of Haitian Creole and English language books, articles and dissertations on Haiti, classified in twenty-three subject categories covering agriculture,

art, bibliographies, demography, economics, education, family, fiction, health, history, humanities, independence, languages, literature, migration, occupation, politics, popular works, relations with the United States, religion, society and culture, urbanism and general works. The entries are unannotated, but an occasional brief comment may be added to an entry. Items listed in the volume are located in the University of Florida libraries.

908 **Haiti: a research handbook.**
Robert Lawless, with contributions by Ilona Maria Lawless, Florence Etienne Sergile, Charles A. Woods.   New York: Garland, 1990. 354p. (Garland Reference Library of Social Science, vol. 546).

Expands on Lawless's *Bibliography on Haiti* (q.v.). The handbook is organized into thirty-one subject chapters, each having an introductory section followed by an unannotated listing of bibliographical citations. The introductory section provides selective and sometimes critical details on the books, articles and theses listed. Both English and Haitian Creole items are included in the bibliography, but publications in French and other foreign languages have been largely omitted. The author states that this book is aimed at both scholars and the lay public.

909 **Haitiana 1971-1975: bibliographie haïtienne.** (Haitiana 1971-1975: Haitian bibliography.)
Max Manigat.   La Salle, Quebec, Canada: Collectif Paroles, 1980. 83p.

Lists works written by Haitian authors or by foreigners writing about Haiti (including Saint-Domingue). The classification is first by year, then alphabetical by author. In an appendix, Manigat lists books published before 1971 but not included in either the main volume or the supplementary volume of Max Bissainthe's *Dictionnaire de bibliographie Haïtienne* (q.v.). A second appendix analyses the contents of a number of published collections of essays about Haiti.

910 **The third world: Haiti, Dominican Republic and Jamaica: a bibliography.**
E. Willard Miller, Ruby M. Miller.   Monticello, Illinois: Vance Bibliographies, 1990. 24p. (Public Administration Series Bibliography, P2919).

Includes bibliographical citations to material on twentieth-century Haiti.

911 **A selective social science bibliography of the Republic of Haiti.**
Sidney W. Mintz, Vern Carrol.   *Revista Interamericana de Ciencias Sociales*, vol. 2, no. 3 (1963), 405-19.

A bibliography of major books and articles published between 1940 and 1963 dealing with geography, demography, sociology, anthropology, economy and political structure in Haiti. The authors have omitted works on religion, particularly Voodoo, 'popular' and travel books, material on the Creole language, and historical items, and have not attempted to cover completely the publications of the Pan American Union, legal codes, official US or Haitian government documents, or UN publications. Most of the citations are to publications in English or French, with a few items in German or

Spanish also listed. Short English annotations are appended to roughly one half of the listings.

912 **Haiti: guide to the periodical literature in English, 1800-1900.**
Compiled and edited by Frantz Pratt, foreword by Lambros Comitas. New York, London: Greenwood Press, 1991. 310p. (Bibliographies and Indexes in Latin American and Caribbean Studies, no. 1).

A valuable reference tool that adds substantially to the bibliography of Haiti, listing not only periodical articles but also book reviews and entries in *Dissertation Abstracts*. The work comprises 5,045 unannotated citations, arranged chronologically in chapters under nine broad topics: the physical setting; the human element; the cultural environment; the economic factor; the geopolitical influence; the historical background; description and commentaries; bibliographies; and philately. Three indexes allow access under subject, periodical source and author.

913 **A guide to the official publications of the other American republics.**
US Library of Congress. J. B. Childs, general editor. Washington, DC: Government Printing Office, 1945-1949. 19 vols. (Reprinted, New York: Johnson Reprint Corp., 1965. 19 vols. in 2).

Volume 12 of this set is *Haiti* (25p.), a guide to Haitian government publications, 1804-1946, that may prove useful for historical research. Listed under name of government agency are *rapports*, serials, and monographs held by the Library of Congress. Details of year of commencement, frequency and title changes are supplied for serials.

Maps and charts of North American and the West Indies 1750-1789: a guide to the collections in the Library of Congress.
See item no. 29.

The Alfred Nemours collection of Haitian history: a catalogue.
See item no. 146.

Bibliography of Saint-Domingue: especially for the period of 1700-1804.
See item no. 178.

The United States Marines in the Dominican Republic, Haiti, and Nicaragua: a bibliography of published works and magazine articles.
See item no. 282.

A bibliography of Caribbean migration and Caribbean immigrant communities.
See item no. 328.

The new American immigration: evolving patterns of legal and illegal emigration: a bibliography of selected references.
See item no. 348.

Haitian migrants and Haitian Americans: from invisibility into the spotlight.
See item no. 357.

The new Haitian immigration: a preliminary bibliography.
See item no. 361.

Bibliographies. Retrospective

Etudes sur le vodou haïtien: bibliographie analytique.
See item no. 454.

Economic problems of the Black Republic: a critical bibliography.
See item no. 651.

An annotated bibliography of agricultural development in Haiti.
See item no. 693.

Land tenure in Haiti and its policy implications: a survey of the literature.
See item no. 694. .

Toward a bibliography of works dealing with the Creole languages of the Caribbean area, Louisiana, and the Guianas.
See item no. 715.

A bibliography of Caribbean Creole languages.
See item no. 720.

Bibliography of women writers from the Caribbean (1831-1986)
See item no. 741.

Writers of the Caribbean and Central America: a bibliography.
See item no. 749.

A bibliography of Haitian literature, 1900-1972.
See item no. 761.

Bibliographic guide to Caribbean mass communication.
See item no. 860.

Caribbean writers: a bio-bibliographical-critical encyclopedia.
See item no. 892.

Indexes

There follow three separate indexes: authors (including editors, compilers, contributors, translators and illustrators); titles of publications; and subjects. Title entries are italicized and refer either to the main titles or to other works cited in the annotations. The introductory definite or indefinite article is omitted. The numbers refer to bibliographical entries, rather than page numbers. Individual index entries are arranged in alphabetical sequence.

Index of Authors

Flieger, W. 310
Fombrun, O. R. 10
Foner, L. 158
Foner, N. 368
Fontaine, P.-M. 351
Fontas, M. 352 ·
Forbes Commission 280
Forbes, W. C. 280
Ford, G. 409
Fordham, M. 619
Fortune, D. 10
Foster, C. R. 5
Foster, D. W. 758
Foster, J. G. 810
Fouchard, J. 105, 159, 416, 845
Fougere, W. 571
Fouron, G. 366-67
Fowler, C. 768
Fowlie, W.
Fragomen, A. T. 354
France. Archives nationales 135
Franck, H. A. 46, 257
Franco, J. L. 195
François, A. 6
François, G. J. 10
Frankétienne, 783
Franklin, B. A. 810
Franklin, J. 223
Franklyn, I. R. 284
Franz, R. 87
Fraser, P. D. 320, 698
Frate, D. A. 532
Friedman, J. R. P. 656
Frost, M. O. 284
Fuller, A. 603

G

Gaddy, G. D. 270
Gaillard, R. 258
Galatioto, R. 353
Gali, F. 88
Galloway, P. 196
Garcia Valdes, P. 114
Garcia Zamor, J.-C. 607, 654
Garret, N. M. 751
Garrity, M. P. 664-65
Gates, H. L. Jr. 452
Gaume, M. 841

Geggus, D. 160-61, 196-99, 855
Gerace, D. T. 112, 123
Gindine, Y. 752, 769
Gingras, J. P. O. 293
Girault, C. A. 666
Gisler, A. 162
Gladwin, H. 350
Glazier, S. D. 438
Gleijeses, E. M. 234
Glissant, E. 819
Goetz-Girey, R. 662
Gold, H. 6, 47, 287, 531
Goldberg, A. 667-68
Gomez, E. A. 506
Goodwin, P. B. Jr. 594
Gosse, P. 167
Goveia, E. V. 163
Goyal, M. R. 684
Goyer, D. S. 306
Graham, S. 379
Gray, J. 448
Green, P. 444
Greene, G. 291, 811
Greene, J. P. 164
Grieb, K. J. 849
Griggs, E. L. 235
Grimard, L. 785, 803
Gruening, E. H. 259
Grunwald, J. 669
Guilbaud, T. 803
Guthrie, G. M. 544
Guyard, M.-F. 814

H

Habitant d'Haïti 865
Hackett, P. 698
Haggerty, R. A. 4
Haines, D. W. 347
Haiti. (Republic) 307-09, 601
Hall, G. M. 164-65
Hall, R. A. 717
Hall, R. B. 685
Hallewell, L. 857
Halsey, N. A. 568-69
Hamilton, J. 385
Hammond, H. D. 98
Hamshere, C. E. 236
Hanmer, T. J. 7
Hanna, S. W. 229

Hanton, Mrs A. 252
Haring, C. L. 166
Harris, L. 104
Hart, F. A. 269
Harshberger, J. W. 67
Harvey, W. W. 237
Harwood, A. 356
Hassal, M. 200
Haverstock, N. A. 848
Hayes, H. R. 782
Hazard, S. 136
Healy, D. F. 620
Heinl, N. G. 137
Heinl, R. D. Jr. 137
Helton, A. C. 352
Henige, D. 321
Henriquez, E. 410
Herdeck, D. E. 892
Herdeck, M. L. 892
Herskovits, M. J. 476, 510, 535, 653, 679
Heuer, R. 670
Heuman, G. 161
Heusch, L. de 449
Hicks, G. L. 365
Higuera-Gundy, A. 102
Hilaire, J. 750
Hill, K. 304
Hill, L. P. 812
Hill, R. R. 850-51
Hintzen, P. 890
Hippolyte, D. 803
Hippolyte-Manigat, M. 614
Hoefte, R. 328
Hoffmann, L.-F. 753-56, 777
Holcomb, R. C. 553
Holdridge, L. R. 68
Holly, A. C. 450
Holly, M. A. 686
Holt, E. 568-69
Honigmann, I. 539
Honorat, J.-J. 10, 296
Honorat, M. L. 418
Hooper, M. 602
Horowitz, M. M. 488, 533
Howards, T. P. 201
Howes, B. 784
Hubert, G. A. 642
Hughes, L. 785, 794, 806
Hugo, V. 813
Hunt, A. N. 621
Hunter, B. 699

239

240

Simon, N. 72
Simpson, G. E. 406-08, 420-21, 462-63, 488-93, 514, 537, 652-53
Slesin, S. 841
Smith, R 430
Smith, W. J.
Smucker, G. R. 654
Social Security Administration 546
Sonesson, B. 623
Spector, R. M. 277-78
Spencer, I. D. 171
Stafford, S. B. 368
Stebich, U. 820
Steele, C. 857
Stehl, F. G. 30
Stein, R. 179-80
Stephen, J. 218
Stephens, J. 317
Stepick, A. 357, 363, 369-71
Stern, R. M. 544
Stevens-Arroyo, A. M. 115-16
Steward, J. H. 114
Steward, T. G. 219, 377, 382
Stewart, J. 843
Stirling, W. 184
Stoddard, T. L. 220
Stovall, J. 415
Stowe, H. B. 380
Stycos, J. M. 538
Survival Service Commission of the IUCN 72
Swales, B. H. 78
Swartz, D. F. 371
Sylvain, G. 721, 803
Sylvain, N. 252, 785, 803
Szulc, T. 583

T

Taft, E. 56
Taillemite, E. 172
Tardieu, C. 313
Tardif, L. S. 362
Tarry, E. 383
Tata, R. J. 15
Tax, S. 535, 679

Tee-Van, J. 83-84, 86
Thacker, S. B. 547
Thoby-Marcelin, E. 409, 799
Thoby-Marcelin, P. 409, 784-85, 799-803
Thomas, L. 279, 367, 802
Thompson, B. 372
Thompson, P. M. 714
Thompson, R. F. 494, 820
Thomson, I. 57
Tinker, E. L. 801, 865
Tomasek, R. D. 297, 637
Tomasi, S. M. 354
Toth, J. 146
Toussaint Louverture 216
Toussaint-L'Ouverture, I. 785, 789, 803
Travis, C. 857
Trembley, W. A. 146, 436
Treudley, M. 631-32
Trouillot, E. 145
Trouillot, M.-R. 595
Trouillot, H. 849
Tuden, A. 168
Tyson, G. F. Jr. 221

U

Underhill, E. B. 248
Underwood, E. W. 539, 803
Underwood, F. W. 653
UN Mission of Technical Assistance to Haiti 660
US Commission for Study and Review of Conditions in Haiti 280
US Congress, Senate Select Committee on Haiti and Santo Domingo 281
US Department of Health, Education and Welfare 564
US Library of Congress 4, 913
US Marine Corps 282
US State Department 605
University of Florida Libraries 859
Usselmann, P. 24

Ussher, T. N. 227

V

Vaissière, P. de 181
Valdman, A. 5, 710, 722-23, 725
Van den Bold, W. A. 37
Van Ee, P. M. 29
Vandercook, J. W. 249, 816
Vastey, P. V. de 222
Vaval, D. 782, 785, 795, 803
Veras, R. A. 342
Verdet, P. 373
Verdoorn, F. 64, 68
Verger, P. 9
Verne, M. 765
Verstraete, A. 544
Vesey, D. I. 51
Vezina, E. 280
Vielot, K. 706
Vieux, D. 803
Vieux, S. 609
Vilaire, E. 803
Vilaire, J.-J. 803
Vincent, J. 72
Vinogradov, A. 223
Vogt, P. R. 31
Voltaire, K. 669, 674

W

Walsh, B. O. 353
Ward, L. 58
Warner, K. Q. 614
Watson, Mrs. J. H. 252
Watts, A. F. 159
Waugh, A. 58
Webb, A. 298
Webb, R. E. 301
Weber, B. C. 205
Weinstein, B. 596
Werleigh, C. 785, 803
Wernstedt, F. L. 18
West, R. C. 16
Wetmore, A. 61-62, 77-79, 91
White, W. A. 280
Wiese, H. J. C. 573

242

Index of Titles

A

Actes du colloque sur
l'enfant Haïtien en
Amérique du Nord:
santé, scolarité,
adaptation sociale: 23,
24, 25 octobre 1981 362
La administracion publica
en Haiti 607
Les Affiches Américaines
161
Africa in Latin America;
essays on history,
culture, and socialization
509
African civilisations in the
New World 444
African religious groups
and beliefs: papers in
honor of William R.
Bascom 469
Les Afro-américains 480
After the crossing:
immigrants and
minorities in Caribbean
Creole societies 320
Agricultural development
in Haiti; an assessment of
sector problems, policies,
and prospects under
conditions of severe soil
erosion 695
Agriculture in Haiti, with
special reference to rural
economy and agricultural
education 686
Aiding migration: the
impact of international
development assistance
on Haiti 330
AIDS and accusation: Haiti
and the geography of
blame 567
Ainsi parla l'oncle: essais

d'ethnographie 393-94,
726, 728, 733, 737
Alfred Nemours collection
of Haitian history: a
catalogue 146
L'alimentation et la
nutrition en Haiti 571
American odyssey 355, 357
Analyse schematique 767
Ann pale Kreyòl: an
introductory course in
Haitian Creole 722
Annotated bibliography of
agricultural development
in Haiti 693
Anthologie du folklore
Haïtien 388
Anthology of contemporary
Latin-American poetry
782
Antigone en créole 719
Area handbook for the
Dominican Republic 4
Area handbook for Haiti 4
Armée et politique en Haiti
580
Art of Haiti 817
Arztin auf Haiti 563
Arte Taino 108-09
Àshe, traditional religion
and healing in sub-
Saharan Africa and the
diaspora; a classified
international
bibliography 448
Assistance sociale en Haiti,
1804-1972 545
Atlantic port cities;
economy, culture, and
society in the Atlantic
world, 1650-1850 160
Atlas d'Haiti 24
Atlas of Central America
and the Caribbean 27
Author index to the
Handbook of Latin

American studies, nos.
1-28, 1936-1966 897

B

Banana wars; a history of
United States military
intervention in Latin
America from the
Spanish-American War
to the invasion of
Panama 273
La Banque Nationale: son
histoire, ses problèmes
661
Basic course in Haitian
Creole 723
Beast of the Haitian hills
800
Becoming black American:
Haitians and American
institutions in Evanston,
Illinois 374
Beneath tropic seas; a
record of diving among
the coral reefs of Haiti 82
Best nightmare on earth: a
life in Haiti 47
Le bête du musseau 800
Beyond all this: thirty years
with the mountain
peasants of Haiti 437
Beyond the myths of
culture; essays in cultural
materialism 691
Beyond nationalism: the
social thought of Emily
Greene Balch 251
Bibliographic guide to
Caribbean mass
communication 860
Bibliographie générale et
methodique d'Haïti 905
Bibliographie haïtienne,
1957–1967 903
Bibliography of Caribbean
migration and Caribbean

245

Index of Subjects

Voodoo *contd.*
high priest 465-66
houngans 489-90, 501,
505, 507-08
human sacrifice 54,
458-59
iconography 821, 823
in the United States 445
Lemba-Petro 483
literary influence 744
magic 477
mangé loa ceremony 485
musical instruments 414,
486
narrative material 469
origins 444, 447, 459
Petro cult 449, 473, 476,
483
poetry 781
political influence 455,
581
prayers 576
Rada cult 449
relations with the
Catholic Church 290,
435, 457, 474
relations with Protestant
Churches 290, 441, 457
rites and ceremonies
411, 464, 467, 481-82,
485-86, 489, 491
Roman Catholic
elements 474-75, 480
Saint John celebrations
492

service 481, 488, 493
songs 411, 452, 456
spirit possession 12,
496-502, 846
therapeutics 503, 505,
507-08, 550, 554
tourist performances
467, 667-68
vèvès 470, 484, 494
Zombie literature 430
Zombies 424
Voyages 125, 173, 183, 190

W

Wakefield, A.J. 658
Water supply 543, 547
West Indians
immigrants 320
West Indies
emigration to 320
WHO–UNICEF–Yaws
Eradication Campaign
658 *see also* Yaws
Wimpffen, François
Alexandre Stanislas
182-83
Wingspread Conference 5
Wirkus, Faustin 283
Women 1, 10, 329, 353,
533, 537, 541, 647
AIDS 566, 568 *see also*
Children; AIDS
emigrants 329, 353

fertility control 311 *see
also* Birth control,
Family planning
fertility rates 303
health care 573
mental illness 562
poetry 792
writers 741
Women's International
League for Peace and
Freedom 252
World Fertility Survey
313-14

Y

Yaws 557
Yaws Eradication
Cam-
paign–WHO–UNICEF
658
Yellow fever 199

Z

Zagouti
see Solenodon paradoxus
Zombies 424-29
ethnobiology 425-26, 429
literature 430, 759, 783,
809
Zoological expeditions
60-61, 75, 77, 82-86,
94-95

Map of Haiti

This map shows the more important towns and other features.

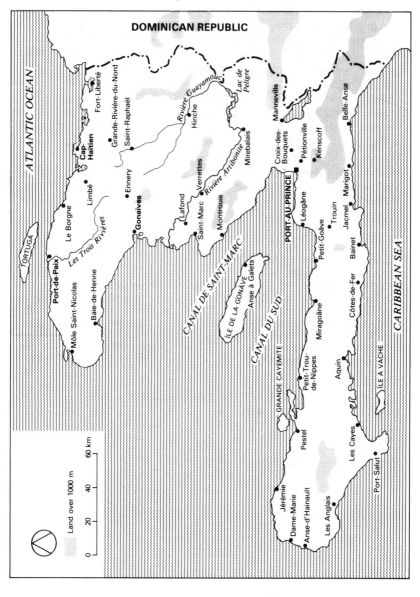

ALSO FROM CLIO PRESS

INTERNATIONAL ORGANIZATIONS SERIES

Each volume in the International Organizations Series is either devoted to one specific organization, or to a number of different organizations operating in a particular region, or engaged in a specific field of activity. The scope of the series is wide-ranging and includes intergovernmental organizations, international non-governmental organizations, and national bodies dealing with international issues. The series is aimed mainly at the English-speaker and each volume provides a selective, annotated, critical bibliography of the organization, or organizations, concerned. The bibliographies cover books, articles, pamphlets, directories, databases and theses and, wherever possible, attention is focused on material *about* the organizations rather than on the organizations' own publications. Notwithstanding this, the most important official publications, and guides to those publications, will be included. The views expressed in individual volumes, however, are not necessarily those of the publishers.

VOLUMES IN THE SERIES

1 *European Communities*, John Paxton
2 *Arab Regional Organizations*, Frank A. Clements
3 *Comecon: The Rise and Fall of an International Socialist Organization*, Jenny Brine
4 *International Monetary Fund*, Anne C. M. Salda

5 *The Commonwealth*, Patricia M. Larby and Harry Hannam
6 *The French Secret Services*, Martyn Cornick and Peter Morris
7 *Organization of African Unity*, Gordon Harris
8 *North Atlantic Treaty Organization*, Phil Williams

TITLES IN PREPARATION

British Secret Services, Philip H. J. Davies
Israeli Secret Services, Frank A. Clements
Organization of American States, David Sheinin

United Nations System, Joseph P. Baratta
World Bank, Anne C. M. Salda